KAPLAN

Other Kaplan Books Relating to Law School Admissions:

The Insider's Book of Law School Lists

LSAT

Two Real LSATs Explained

Scholarships

KAPLAN

Newsweek

Law School Admissions Adviser 1999

SELECTION • ADMISSIONS • FINANCIAL AID

by Ruth Lammert-Reeves
and a nationwide team of law school admissions advisers

Simon & Schuster

Kaplan Books
Published by Kaplan Educational Centers and Simon & Schuster
1230 Avenue of the Americas
New York, NY 10020

Copyright © 1998 by Kaplan Educational Centers

All rights reserved. No part of this book may be reproduced or transmitted in any form or by any means, electronic or mechanical, including photocopying, recording, or by any information storage and retrieval system, without the written permission of the Publisher, except where permitted by law.

Kaplan® is a registered trademark of Kaplan Educational Centers.

For bulk sales to schools, colleges, and universities, please contact Renee Memi, Simon & Schuster Special Markets, 1633 Broadway, 8th Floor, New York, NY 10019.

Copyright notices:
GRE is a registered trademark of the Educational Testing Service, which is not affiliated with this book.
GMAT is a registered trademark of the Graduate Management Admission Council, which is not affiliated with this book.
MCAT is a registered service mark of the Association of American Medical Colleges, which is not affiliated with this book.
LSAT is a registered trademark of the Law School Admission Council, which is not affiliated with this book.

Law school data: Copyright © 1997 by Midwest Association of Prelaw Advisors (MAPLA), all rights reserved. A software (Windows™) version of this data is available from MAPLA; call Mary Schilling at (740) 587-6521 to order using MasterCard™ or Visa™. MAPLA does not endorse, support, or acknowledge the effectiveness or utility of any commercial test-preparation or advising program.

Project Editor: Donna Ratajczak
Cover Design: Cheung Tai
Interior Page Design and Production: Jobim Rose
Database Administrator: Enid Burns
Production Editor: Maude Spekes
Desktop Publishing Manager: Michael Shevlin
Managing Editor: Brent Gallenberger
Executive Editor: Del Franz
Executive Director, Pre-Graduate Programs: Trent Anderson

Special thanks to: Alison May, Kiernan McGuire, and Linda Volpano

Manufactured in the United States of America
Published simultaneously in Canada

July 1998
10 9 8 7 6 5 4 3 2 1

ISBN: 0-684-84978-X
ISSN: 1097-5403

CONTENTS

Preface xi
A Special Note for International Students xiii

Part One: THE LAW SCHOOL EXPERIENCE
Chapter 1: Is Law School Really for You? 3

Part Two: SELECTING A SCHOOL
Chapter 2: Evaluating Law Schools 15
Chapter 3: The Right School for You 31

Part Three: ADMISSIONS
Chapter 4: Your Application Timeline 45
Chapter 5: Inside the Admissions Office 55
Chapter 6: Preparing the Application Form 61
Chapter 7: The Personal Statement 69
Chapter 8: Recommendations 89
Chapter 9: Completing Your Application 101

Part Four: FINANCING YOUR LAW DEGREE
Chapter 10: Planning Your Investment 111
Chapter 11: Applying for Financial Aid 119
Chapter 12: Borrowing the Money 129
Chapter 13: Your Financial Aid Package 143

Part Five: SPECIAL CONSIDERATIONS
Chapter 14: Older Students: Three Myths 155
Chapter 15: Minority Students 159
Chapter 16: Women Students 167
Chapter 17: Gay and Lesbian Students 171
Chapter 18: Students with Disabilities 177

Part Six: EXPERIENCES FROM THE REAL WORLD
Chapter 19: What Law School Students and Grads Say 185

Part Five: LAW SCHOOLS
Directory of U.S. Law Schools 197
Academic Specialities 233
Joint Degree Programs 259
Geographic Location 267

Appendix: LSAT Sampler 273

AUTHOR

Ruth Lammert-Reeves has been a college administrator for more than 20 years. For 18 of those years she has been employed at Georgetown University Law Center, where she has been assistant dean of financial aid since 1990. Active in national financial aid organizations, she has also served as a board member of the Law School Admissions Council (LSAC). She is well known within the legal educationa community, frequently speaking on topics related to legal education and how to finance it.

CONTRIBUTORS

Janice Austin, author of chapter 17, is the assistant dean of admissions and financial aid at the University of Pennsylvania Law School. In addition to serving in various administrative roles at three different law school admissions offices since 1980, she is currently a board member of the Law School Admissions Council (LSAC). She was appointed to the LSAC Workgroup on Gay and Lesbian Issues. Dean Austin has been active in addressing the issues concerning access to legal education for people of color, gays, and lesbians.

Everett Bellamy, author of chapter 15, has been an assistant dean at Georgetown University Law Center for eighteen years, where he also teaches small-business law. Before joining the Law Center staff, he served in the Office of Student Affairs at Cleveland State University. Dean Bellamy has been an instructor for the Council of Legal Education Opportunity, chairperson of the Washington, DC chapter of the National Conference on Black Lawyers, and a member of the board of governors of the National Bar Association. Dean Bellamy received his J.D. from the Cleveland-Marshall College of Law, and his B.S. and M.S. from the University of Wisconsin.

Andrew Cornblatt, who contributed to chapter 7, has served as dean of admissions at Georgetown Law Center since 1989. He was previously employed by Georgetown as director of admissions for two years and assistant director of admissions for seven years. Dean Cornblatt is the chairman of the Student and Faculty Life Committee at Georgetown Law Center and serves on the Financial Aid and Long Range Planning Committees. Dean Cornblatt received his B.A. from Harvard and his J.D. from Boston College Law School.

Chris Rosa, author of chapter 18, is Director of the Office of Services for Students with Disabilities at Queens College, where he coordinates the provision of support services to more than 450 students with disabilities. A member of the Muscular Dystrophy Association's National Task Force on Public Awareness, Rosa has written several articles published in scholarly journals on the sociology of disability and is a recipient of the Muscular Dystrophy Association's National Personal Achievement Award. He is currently enrolled in a doctoral program in sociology at the City University of New York Graduate Center.

Shelli Soto, a contributor to chapter 7, received her undergraduate degree from the University of Texas at Austin in 1991 and her J.D., also from the University of Texas, in 1994. Dean Soto has been an admissions professional since graduating from law school. Formerly the director of admissions at the University of Texas Law School, she now serves as assistant dean of admissions. Dean Soto is responsible for reading all of the application files the University of Texas Law School receives—from three to four thousand files annually.

DEDICATION

This book is dedicated to my husband, Roger H. Reeves, without whose help and support this book would not have been completed.

I wish to thank Sally Donahue, Pat Harris, and Donna Ratajczak for their invaluable contributions to the book.

—Ruth Lammert-Reeves

Preface

For over 18 years, I've been privileged to be involved as an administrator in legal education. I know many of the law school admissions officers and have learned what issues they face when deciding whom to admit to their schools. During this time, I've also talked with many people—from interested and hopeful law school applicants to graduates who have been in practice for many years.

This book contains the advice I would like prospective students to know before they apply to law school, and what graduates have told me they wished they'd known before they embarked on this journey called the legal profession. It's what I would have liked an applicant to know before making a few poor decisions and being disappointed in the choices available to them as a result. These choices include: picking the wrong law schools to apply to because it was easier to believe the common wisdom about "the best" schools when none of them is really a good match with your credentials or interests, doing a rush job on your application and losing out because of it, or creating a difficult financial picture for yourself because you mismanaged your finances as an undergraduate.

If you read this book, and follow the guidance given, you will immeasurably increase your chances of succeeding. Your journey will be much more beneficial and pleasurable as a result.

Best of luck to you!

Ruth Lammert-Reeves

A Special Note for International Students

In recent years, U.S. law schools have experienced an increase in inquiries from non-U.S. citizens, some of whom are already practicing lawyers in their own countries. This surge of interest in the U.S. legal system has been attributed to the spread of the global economy. When businesspeople from outside the United States do business with Americans, they often find themselves doing business under the American legal system.

Law schools are responding to this new international interest in the U.S. legal system. Many law schools have even developed special programs to accommodate the needs of lawyers and students from outside the United States.

> **Oh, Canada**
>
> For our Canadian readers who want more info on law schools, check out the Canadian edition of the *LSAT/LDAS Registration and Information Book*. It's available at law schools or from LSAC by calling (215) 968-1001.

If you are not from the United States, but are considering attending a U.S. law school, here's what you need to get started.

- If English is not your first language, you'll probably need to take the TOEFL (Test of English as a Foreign Language), or provide some other evidence that you are proficient in English. Most law schools require a minimum TOEFL score of 600 or better.
- Depending on the program to which you are applying, you may also need to take the LSAT (Law School Admissions Test). All law schools in the United States requires the LSAT for their J.D. programs. LL.M. programs usually do not require the LSAT.

A SPECIAL NOTE FOR INTERNATIONAL STUDENTS

- Since admission to law school is quite competitive, you may also want to select three or four programs and complete applications for each school.
- You should begin the process of applying to law schools or special legal studies programs at least eighteen months before the fall of the year you plan to start your studies. Most programs will have only September start dates.
- Finally, you will need to obtain an I-20 Certificate of Eligibility in order to obtain an F-1 Student Visa to study in the United States.

If you need more help with the complex process of law admissions and information about the variety of programs available, you may be interested in Kaplan's Access America® program.

Kaplan's Access America Program

Kaplan created Access America® to assist students and professionals from outside the United States who want to enter the U.S. university system. The program was designed for students who have received the bulk of their primary and secondary education outside the United States in a language other than English. Access America also has programs for obtaining professional certification in the United States. Here's a brief description of some of the help available through Access America.

The Access English Course

At the heart of the Access America program is the intensive Access English program. This comprehensive academic English course prepares students to achieve a high level of proficiency in English in order to successfully complete an academic degree. The course covers all skills necessary to gain admission to and succeed in a university program—reading, writing, conversation, and TOEFL test-taking strategies. Personalized instruction is combined with guided self-study to help students gain proficiency in a short period of time. Certificates of Achievement in English are awarded to certify your level of proficiency.

Law School Admissions Test (LSAT) Preparation

If you plan to enter a law school in the United States, Kaplan will help you determine whether you need to take the LSAT, while helping you to choose an appropriate law program. If you must take the LSAT, Kaplan can help you prepare for it.

Business Accounting/Certified Public Accounting (CPA)

If you are an accountant who would like to be certified to do business in the United States, Kaplan can help you prepare for the CPA exam and will assist you in understanding the differences in accounting procedures in the United States.

A SPECIAL NOTE FOR INTERNATIONAL STUDENTS

Applying to Access America

To get more information, or to apply for admission to any of Kaplan's programs for students or professionals outside the United States, you can write to us at:

Kaplan Educational Centers
International Admissions Department
888 Seventh Avenue
New York, NY 10106

Or you can call us at 1-800-527-8378 from within the United States, or at 01-212-262-4980 outside the United States. Our fax number is 01-212-957-1654. Our E-mail address is world@kaplan.com. You can also get more information or even apply through the Internet at http://www.kaplan.com/intl.

PART ONE

The Law School Experience

CHAPTER 1

Is Law School Really for You?

Before getting into the specifics of the application process, let's take a look at the whole idea of becoming a lawyer. You may have read recently that there are more lawyers being produced annually than there are legal jobs available. It is clear that the legal boom of the eighties is behind us, and that with the downsizing and the dissolution of a number of law firms nationwide over the past five or six years, the job market is increasingly competitive. You want to be sure that getting a law degree is something that you want to do, and not simply something you think you ought to want to do. Let's start with a brief discussion of just what's entailed in a legal education.

> **Joining the Ranks**
>
> During the fall 1996 academic year, there were 134,949 students in attendance at ABA-approved law schools; 39,920 professional degrees were conferred from those schools, including J.D. or LL.B. degrees.
>
> Source: American Bar Association, *ABA-Approved Law Schools*, 1998

What Does "J.D." Stand for, Anyhow?

The Juris Doctor degree is traditionally a three-year, full-time program of study designed to train you in a way of thinking about legal problems. Roughly 45 percent of the national law schools offer part-time programs that allow students to progress at a slower rate while carrying jobs, raising families, or whatever.

THE LAW SCHOOL EXPERIENCE

Traditional First-Year Curriculum
Almost all law schools design their first-year curriculum to include courses in:

- Civil procedure
- Contracts
- Criminal law
- Torts
- Property

Most include a course in legal writing and research, and many offer training in negotiation, advocacy, and counseling as well.

Nontraditional First-Year Curriculum
A few schools offer a different kind of curriculum to students. For example, Georgetown Law Center offers a program called Curriculum B, emphasizing the source of law in history, philosophy, political theory, and economics. Other schools with curriculums that offer an "atypical" first-year approach include: University of Montana, William and Mary, and the Chicago-Kent College of Law at the Illinois Institute of Technology (IIT), among others. Each school's offerings are unique. For example, the University of Montana and William and Mary organize their first-year students into law firms where students tackle lawyering problems in a simulated format. Chicago-Kent focuses on cultivating legal writing skills, drawing extensively on the use of computers in this effort. These are just a few examples. Many other schools offer special programs. Contact the schools for details on their offerings.

Second- and Third-Year Curriculum
Your second and third years in law school usually offer greater flexibility in course choice, often in more specialized areas of the law, and sometimes with a clinical component. Different law schools offer different special programs and specific requirements for graduation, but the J.D. degree is generalist in nature, and prepares you to solve current legal problems and anticipate ones of the future.

Standards of Quality

In the early 1970s, the Section of Legal Education and Admissions to the Bar of the American Bar Association (ABA) first published its Standards and Rules of Procedure for the Approval of Law Schools, which has since been revised from time to time, and which recommends a certain common standard of quality programs for all 180 ABA-approved law schools. Furthermore, most ABA-approved law schools are also members of the American Association of Law Schools (AALS), which controls for further standards of quality such as the school's admissions requirements, faculty size and quality, equality of opportunity for both students and faculty, and the quality of the school's library and its other physical facilities. When choosing a law school, it's helpful to know that these standards exist, and that they are reviewed regularly, along with each school's compliance with the most recent version.

Good Reasons for Going to Law School

So you still think that law school is the right choice for you? Good. Now let's make sure that your reasons are solid and weatherproof: The first year of law school is not for fair-weather enthusiasts. There will be plenty of opportunities for you to feel overwhelmed and thoroughly drenched in self-doubt. With an increasingly competitive job market, even 1Ls (first-year law students) aren't immune from the pressure of the placement process. And at many schools there is often the "case method" of teaching that could be another strain. In case method classes, the professor's role is to provoke students into a higher level of thinking. You will certainly be challenged on a number of levels, so let's "test drive" your reasons for choosing the law profession. We'll start on the positive side with a few sample "good" reasons.

Versatility

It is true, a law degree is perhaps the most versatile professional degree. Law might well be the field for you if you:

- Are not entirely sure of your career dream
- Feel more than half-certain that you will change "careers" at some point in the future
- Enjoy thinking analytically
- Enjoy coming up with creative solutions to complex problems
- Are inspired by intellectual challenges

Lawyers can function in the business world, whereas M.B.A.'s cannot function in a legal position. And although lawyers cannot be doctors, neither are they as closely held to their "field" as are M.D.'s.

A law degree gives you almost unparalleled mobility in your career—lawyers run movie studios, manage baseball teams, hold political office, serve in the foreign service, run Fortune 500 companies, and head a wide range of legal service organizations.

Basic Skills of Lawyering

- Analysis
- Synthesis
- Advocacy
- Negotiation
- Writing
- Counseling
- Speaking

Are You Computer Literate?

A person entering law school has to know how to use a computer. To do legal research, you'll need to search computer databases for information on court decisions and current law. You'll also need word processing skills for all the writing you'll do. At the very least, you should know how to type before entering law school. Take an introductory computer class at a local community college.

THE LAW SCHOOL EXPERIENCE

> **Think for Yourself**
>
> The case method is based on the critical analysis of a number of related judicial opinions and other documents connected with a case. The professor will ask you questions rather than give you answers. You'll be required to participate in the discussion—and to defend your reasoning.

Excitement

Although the life of an attorney is not really like that portrayed in the television series *Ally McBeal*, there are aspects of lawyering that can be a great deal of fun. Tasks such as preparing for a trial, defending a client, prosecuting an accused criminal, or putting together a business deal can give you a rush of adrenaline. The interpretation of existing law can be both intellectually challenging and exciting in itself as you participate in the continuing evolution of our legal system.

Empowerment

Many law school applicants who are already established in careers as news reporters, businesspeople, or even doctors, have found that they need a law degree in order to be more effective or influential in their field. Doctors worry about malpractice matters or become intrigued with the legal implications of prolonging life. Reporters develop urges to become part of the solution to the widespread social problems they have been chronicling for years. Businesspeople feel that a background in law will enable them to negotiate the deals they encounter in their jobs more effectively.

Job Security

Although there are very few jobs that remain secure in today's economy, the fundamental role that legal systems play in our increasingly global working world is striking. Certainly a law degree has become a necessary prerequisite for a great many jobs that could have been done without legal expertise 20 years ago. However, don't assume that attorneys stay with one firm for an entire career. The definition of job loyalty has changed in many professions and industries, including the law. Your training and skills can allow you to stay employed and prepare you for a variety of situations.

Personal Experience

You may have other, personal reasons for choosing law school. Often, people have experienced first hand the power of a training in law through involvement in lawsuits, divorces, adoption procedures, or the settlement of an estate. Whatever your particular reasons for wanting to obtain a law degree, be sure you're clear about why you want to travel down this road, and don't lose sight of your personal investment in the process.

Sound exciting so far? If you enjoy thinking, writing, solving problems, negotiating compromises, and advocating on behalf of people or causes, then law school will be a good fit for you. If you'd rather have someone else tell you how to solve a problem or how to think about a dilemma, then you might find that law is not the profession for you. Think seriously about the "fit"; be honest with yourself as you contemplate your future career. Be sure that you have chosen the right destination before you begin planning your trip.

Bad Reasons for Going to Law School

Before moving on to a more specific discussion of how to choose the right law school for you, let's dismiss some bad, but all-too-common reasons for wanting to go to law school.

1. **"I've got nothing better to do with my history, English, or political science degree."** This is a very bad reason to go to law school. There are better career moves than spending three very hard years in grad school, going heavily into debt, and then emerging with a degree in a field in which you have very little interest. Moreover, several law schools have surveyed attitudes of entering law students and later compared the responses to the same students' grades. The studies showed that those who had the least desire to be in law school in the first place usually performed rather poorly. These students, in turn, had the most problems getting jobs because of their mediocre performance.

> ### *Cash and Carry*
> Recently, Kaplan surveyed 479 LSAT students nationwide about their salary expectations. Eighty-one percent of the respondents thought they would be earning under $65,000 during their first year out of law school, and 13 percent thought they would be making $65,000–80,000. In three years, 50 percent of these respondents still expected to make under $65,000, 25 percent of these respondents expected to be making $65,000–80,000, and 25 percent expected to earn more than $80,000.

2. **"I'm good at arguing. Ever since I began to argue my points forcefully at the dinner table at the age of eight, everyone in my family has said that I'd make a great attorney."** Unfortunately for you, oral argument is a very small part of law school life and, for the vast majority of lawyers, it's a fairly small part of their practice. Additionally, a legal oral argument is quite different from the average debate with your housemate over who gets to choose the video to watch.

3. **"I'll be making six figures before I hit 30."** Just as job security and a lucrative profession can be good reasons for wanting to go to law school, the financial lure can also be a trap. Many attorneys do make six-figure incomes, especially in large, urban firms. But don't be deceived; they earn every cent. Seventy- to eighty-hour weeks, mounting pressure to bill more hours, and a lot of boring research work (at least for the first five or six years) are usually part of the deal. Even if you decide that you're willing to accept the challenge, there's no guarantee that you'll be able to get a high-paying job. Large firms see hundreds of résumés a month. Every year they have their pick of the top students at the top schools. To make matters worse, many firms are now cutting back instead of hiring. If you think you want to be a lawyer because all lawyers are well paid, think again. Even if you decide you're willing to do the hard work, the opportunities to make the big bucks are not always there.

4. **"My family always wanted me to be a lawyer."** If you really don't want to practice law, three years of study plus the span of a career is a long time to fulfill someone else's expectations. If your parents are so

THE LAW SCHOOL EXPERIENCE

gung-ho on the idea, maybe they should go to law school themselves! Age is no limitation on the feasibility of practicing law.

> ### Nontraditional Jobs for Law Grads
>
> About ten percent of law school graduates from the class of 1996 found jobs outside the legal profession.
>
> Source: *Class of 1996 Employment Report and Salary Survey*, National Association for Law Placement.

A Personal Decision

The decision to become a lawyer is a highly personal one, based on a number of factors that each applicant must weigh for herself. It's not a step to be taken just because you can think of nothing better to do, or it's what all your friends are doing. Keep this thought in mind when you're weighing the factors: Although surveys and polls do show that a significant minority of attorneys are unhappy with their career choice, most attorneys are happy with their career decision and think that they're helping society. That's what we learned when we interviewed practicing lawyers, including recent grads (their comments are quoted in chapter 19).

Keep in mind also that having a law degree no longer automatically means having to be a lawyer. There are a wealth of opportunities for people with law degrees in all kinds of professions. The truth of the matter is that, despite all the jokes, a law degree will always be an attractive commodity in the job market. Take a few minutes to jot down your personal reasons for wanting to go to law school, and try ranking them in order of importance. This exercise will help you sharpen your focus as we move through the application process.

Being able to articulate why you want to go to law school will not only help to ensure your happiness as an attorney, but will also help you to gain admission to a top law school. The top schools are looking for people who know why they want to go to law school and have focus and direction in their lives.

> ### Recent J.D. Grad Salary Survey
>
> According to a report published by the National Association for Law Placement, the national median full-time salary paid to graduates of the class of 1996 was $40,000. The mean salary was $46,499.
>
> Source: *Class of 1996 Employment Report and Salary Survey*, National Association for Law Placement.

Kaplan Asks: Why Law School?

To better understand students' concerns, not just about the LSAT, but also about their future study and practice in law, Kaplan conducted a survey of its LSAT students recently. Nationwide, 479 students responded to questions about their interest in law, their salary expectations, and other issues. Here's how these prospective law students reported their own interests in the law:

Is Law School Really For You?

Chose by Default	Prestige	Job Security	Financial Rewards	Family Influence	Enhance Non-legal Career	Intellectual Appeal	Long-Term Interest
3%	5%	3%	5%	5%	10%	28%	41%

Compare these results with why respondents thought others were interested in the law:

Chose by Default	Prestige	Job Security	Financial Rewards	Family Influence	Enhance Non-legal Career	Intellectual Appeal	Long-Term Interest
4%	14%	3%	59%	5%	1%	5%	9%

When it comes to attending law school, most students suspect others of less altruistic motives than they characterize themselves as having. How honest have you been in your analysis of your own motivations to pursue a legal education?

THE LAW SCHOOL EXPERIENCE

A Law School Trend to Use to Your Advantage

Pssst—Want to know a secret? Today is a great time to be applying to law schools!

While admission to law school is still highly competitive, the volume of applications has been falling after peak years in the early '90s. In 1990–91, some 94,000 people applied for admission to U.S. law schools. For the 1996–97 year, applications to law school were down to around 70,000. The trend is not uniform; some parts of the country had a smaller drop than others. For example, the largest percentage drop was in the Northwest (Washington and Oregon) with a drop of almost fifteen percent in applications. The West (specifically, California) experienced less of a fall-off in applications with approximately 13 percent fewer applications than the year before as reported by the Law School Admissions Council. The region of the country showing the least amount of decrease was the Southeast (Florida, Alabama, Georgia, South Carolina, and Mississippi) with a four-percent drop in applications.

What does this mean to the average applicant? Don't hesitate to apply to your "reach" school—it may just work out that you'll get accepted, especially if you plan to apply in the area where schools are receiving fewer applications.

The downturn in applicants has also led some law schools to reduce the size of their entering classes. Depending upon how the law school handles its finances, a student could benefit from smaller classes with no diminishment in quality or services. However, if a law school has had difficulty filling its classes even when applications were at record numbers nationally, a smaller class is probably a survival strategy and may indicate financial problems that could affect the quality of your academic experience.

Trends to Be Aware or to Beware Of

Law firms today are much less likely to provide training during those crucial first years after law school graduation. Although the legal profession has no formal tradition of postgraduate training equivalent to a residency in the medical profession, law graduates generally expected to be trained to the practice of law in the early years. Law firms calculated that the cost of this training would be recouped over time because lawyers tended to stay with one firm throughout their working lives.

For many reasons, the situation has changed completely. It is more likely that lawyers, like the rest of U.S. society, will have multiple employers. In law as in most other fields, a lifetime employer is a thing of the past. And since law firms no longer expect that employees will be with them for life, they are less willing to ease new hires into legal practice while paying them sizable salaries.

Traditional law firms use a rough guideline to determine whether a firm attorney is worth his or her salary. The person must work enough hours to bill clients the equivalent of two and a half times that person's salary each year, sometimes more, depending upon the region of the country. For example, if a person is offered a salary of $60,000 per year, the expectation is that the attorney must have billable hours of $150,000 or more. Depending on how much the firm charges clients for a new attorney (generally $75–150 per hour), the type of practice, and the region of the country, the new hire might be expected to bill eighty hours per week to meet the billable hour expectation. Keep in mind that not every hour an attorney works can be billed. For a novice lawyer, the number of hours actually worked might exceed the billable hours by ten to thirty percent. No longer will a firm pay a high salary to a person with a lot of education but little practical work experience, allowing the equivalent of an apprenticeship to take place over a period of several years before the employee becomes a "producer."

Many law firms do not intend to let employees move from the associate track to become a partner of the firm. (Instead of simply drawing a salary, the partner has a salary and shares in the firm's annual profits.) They want their employees to put in the time to earn their salaries, and all but a few are expected to move to other firms or other types of legal employment in three to five years.

Another trend in the legal profession is the tendency for law students to emphasize one area of the law, eschewing the broad survey courses except the minimum needed to pass the bar. This practice may be successful for those students who have a definite interest and are "following their hearts" in determining what area of law to emphasize. However, if a person picks an area because it is "hot," they are likely to be disappointed. For example, someone who emphasized classes in mergers and acquisitions subjects could be viewed as out of touch when that kind of business dries up, as it did in the early 1990s.

PART TWO

Selecting A School

CHAPTER 2

Evaluating Law Schools

As you research all 180 ABA-approved law schools, you're likely to become overwhelmed by your options. Planning for law school is similar to planning a vacation in some ways. If you were thinking about planning a vacation, you probably wouldn't browse aimlessly through a world atlas. Don't just aimlessly browse for law schools! Think back to the personal reasons you outlined in chapter 1. Stay flexible about them as you research program offerings, but maintain your focus, for you want to remember where you want to land at the end of your program. As you build your research and craft your school list, keep consulting your original goals; shift them when appropriate, but be wary of totally ignoring them. To return to our geographic metaphor, you wouldn't want to let some convincing recruiter lure you to a school smack dab in the middle of the mountains when you've always preferred the city.

> **Review this Resource**
>
> Available for $19.95 plus $2 for shipping, *ABA-Approved Law Schools* contains valuable information about ABA-accredited law schools. Contact:
>
> Service Center
> American Bar Association
> 750 North Lake Shore Drive
> Chicago, IL 60611
> Phone: (800) 285-2221
> Web site:
> www.abanet.org/legaled

Sources of Information

Now the research begins. Soon you'll appreciate having committed your reasons for wanting to go to law school to paper, because there is a wealth of information about all 180 ABA-approved law schools out there. (In addition, there are a number of law schools that are not ABA-approved, which might be fine for you, depending on what your goals are.)

KAPLAN 15

SELECTING A SCHOOL

The Official Guide to U.S. Law Schools

If you haven't already consulted *The Official Guide*, which is produced annually by the Law School Admission Council and Law School Admission Services (the producers of the LSAT), this should be one of your first reading assignments. Each year, all ABA-approved law schools submit a wealth of factual and statistical information about their programs, their applicant pools, their rate of admission, their yield, and the statistical profile of their successful candidates. In this publication you will find also the addresses and phone numbers of schools, along with useful basic information describing the application process, preparation for the LSAT, minority applicant opportunities, organizations you should know about, and a geographic guide to law schools in the United States by region.

ABA Approved Law Schools

Another useful resource, which you can obtain by calling or writing the American Bar Association (ABA), is the annually updated *ABA-Approved Law Schools*. This publication contains statistical information about every ABA-accredited law school and includes information on the size of the student body, the number of men and women, the percentage of minorities enrolled, the number and gender of faculty and administrators, the size of the library collection, the cost of tuition, and the availability of part-time and graduate programs.

In addition to *The Official Guide* and the ABA review, there are a number of other resources you should tap in your search for information about law schools.

> **Wise Reading**
>
> Read *Public Interest Career Resources Guide* (1997–98). This publication is an annotated listing of resources to law students seeking public interest employment. To order, send a check or money order for $33 (includes shipping and handling) to:
>
> National Association
> for Public Interest Law
> 1118 22nd Street N.W.
> Third Floor
> Washington, DC 20037

Your Career Services Office

If you're currently in college, or live near the school you attended, you should definitely visit your career resource center or placement office. Not only will you find *The Official Guide* on file there, but you will in all likelihood locate a number of other books which discuss choosing a career, focusing within the legal profession, and assessing the relative strengths of various law schools. If your school traditionally has a lot of students interested in attending law school, admissions officers from law schools may make special trips to your college. Find out the schedule for these visits and attend as many as you can to familiarize yourself with the types of programs each school offers and accumulate some additional knowledge about legal education. You should also visit the prelaw advisor as well. Part of this person's job is to help you assess whether law school is right for you, as well as assist you in determining which schools to apply to. By all means, make an appointment to speak with your school's prelaw advisor early on in your investigation of legal education.

Evaluating Law Schools

Law School Forums

You will no doubt receive information about these forums as you register to take the LSAT, for they are sponsored by the Law School Admission Service. Each fall at the beginning of the admissions season, LSAS sponsors six forums that are held in New York City, Boston, Atlanta, Chicago, Houston, and Los Angeles, spanning September through early November. A seventh LSAS forum is in July in Washington, D.C. A large number of ABA-approved law schools send admissions representatives and often alumni to the LSAS forums to distribute material and to meet with prospective applicants in the exhibit hall of a centrally located hotel. In addition to providing you with an opportunity to collect a wealth of application materials and descriptive brochures, you will also have the opportunity to speak with admissions representatives. LSAS provides a program with various speakers and panels on topics such as:

- How to apply
- What career options you should consider
- How to finance a legal education

The forums are free to prospective applicants, but you're expected to pay your own travel expenses.

If you can't attend one of the LSAS Law School Forums, you might be able to find a forum closer to home. For example, a law forum sponsored by area colleges is held at George Washington University's Smith Student Center in Washington, D.C. every fall, usually during the first week of October. Free to interested applicants, this forum is well attended by many of the law schools from across the United States.

If you can, you should attend the forum held nearest to you. The information you obtain in one afternoon can significantly speed up your school selection process.

Law Forums

Law School Forums dates and locations for 1998:

- Washington, D.C.: July 18
- Atlanta: October 2–3
- N.Y.C.: September 18–19
- Dallas: October 10
- Chicago: November 13–14
- Boston: October 30–31
- Los Angeles: November 6–7

Go Surfin'

Use the Web to explore law school opportunities. Most U.S. law schools now have Web sites on the Internet. Browse through their information to see what schools have to offer. Look for their addresses in the Law Schools section.

Real-World Contact

Although you might not yet be ready to make a special trip to visit a school, you certainly ought to visit your local law school to get an understanding of the general environment. While there, wander over to the bookstore and ask the salespeople to let you browse the texts used in the standard first-year

SELECTING A SCHOOL

> ### *Key School-Selection Factors*
> - Part time versus full time
> - Geographic considerations
> - School reputation
> - Placement
> - Financial aid
> - School size
> - Joint-degree programs
> - Student body
> - Faculty and staff
> - Library and facilities
> - Clinical programs
> - Student services
> - Student organizations
> - Academic rigor
> - Personal factors

curriculum. Are these subjects you would have the discipline to immerse yourself in for an entire academic year? (Most first-year courses in law school are yearlong). This is known as "the gut test"—do you find yourself absorbed in the information, or does your stomach tense up when you look at the material? If it does, think a little harder about whether law school is for you.

Most law schools will permit you to visit a class or two, if you make arrangements ahead of time, usually through the admissions office. (Remember that you are a guest sitting in the class—it's very impolite to talk while the class is going on, or get up in the middle and leave. You're not in a movie theater!) If you can, you should also sit in on an upper division course or two. This will give you a feel for how classes are conducted when students select the class themselves, and give you the flavor of what life as an upperclassmen might be like. During this process, you should become more familiar with law school life and begin to understand a little bit more about the process called "a legal education." Ask students questions:

- How did they decide which school to attend?
- What different decisions did they make?
- What kind of environment do they need in order to thrive?

Talk to Current Lawyers

If you're looking at law as a career because many of your family members have become lawyers, try speaking to someone outside your family to get a different perspective. If you've never known a lawyer, try to work through your undergraduate career services or alumni office to locate an alum who has been practicing for awhile. If possible, see if you can find an alum who has a practice in an area you think you might be interested in, or one who lives where you might like to reside after you finish law school. Many schools have programs where they will actually match seniors with graduates in chosen professions for a week or a day, so students have the opportunity to shadow that professional and learn more about a chosen career.

Of course, getting a job in a law office is one of the best ways to find out about the legal profession, and it's also a good way to meet lawyers and talk to them about various schools and applications of the law.

Key Selection Factors

Although specific factors to consider in choosing the right schools will vary by individual, there are some common sorting factors that will ease your process considerably. Certainly you don't want to read *The*

Evaluating Law Schools

Official Guide to U.S. Law Schools from cover to cover without some fairly effective sorting mechanism in place!

As you read through the following discussion of factors, consider each one in terms of its importance to you. You might want to jot down some notes on a separate piece of paper to remind yourself why or how the particular factor is connected to your reasons for going to law school, the reasons you've already thought about in chapter 1. Jot down any other points you need to consider for each of the factors. Add any other factors that are important to you that aren't on the list.

Part Time Versus Full Time

This is a fairly basic distinction that is likely to be an integral part of your planning from the start. You might not even be able to consider going to law school without the option of doing it in the evenings or on a part-time schedule. On the other hand, you might never consider anything different from the full-time traditional route. A number of law schools offer evening or flexible programs that can allow you to maintain your job as you work toward your J.D. at a slightly slower pace than the traditional three-year program. Usually these programs are filled predominantly with older students who may either be seeking a law degree for career enhancement (possibly financed by their employer) or who cannot forego the steady income of a job because of previous financial commitments (like a family). There are certainly pros and cons to each schedule.

Flexibility

For schools offering part-time programs, check the Law Schools section at the back of this book.

It's generally agreed that you should attend law school full time if possible. Full-time study is preferable because it gives you the opportunity for a more total immersion into legal training, which probably means that you'll learn more quickly and fully to think like a lawyer. However, the sense of balance that can accompany a part-time schedule has its own advantages. Added to this is the opportunity to establish job contacts on a more regular basis. Whatever your preference, this is one of the first factors to consider because it may quickly sort out the rest of your options.

Geographic Considerations

Where Do You Want to Practice Law?

Statistically speaking, most lawyers practice law within fairly close proximity to their school. Why? There are many reasons, but the most important are probably recruitment and academic focus.

At many law schools, most on-campus recruiting is conducted by local employers. It's also easier to conduct your own job search locally. So, there is a good chance that your summer internships and your first permanent position will be in the same geographic region as your school.

SELECTING A SCHOOL

Also, most law schools teach some of the substantive law of the state in which they are located. Thus, it is more likely that you will take the bar exam in the state in which you went to school and will be better prepared to practice law in that state. This is not to say that relocation is impossible. Still, there's at least some chance that in choosing a school, you may also be increasing your chances of practicing law in that general area.

Certainly for older students who are applying to law school in order to increase their effectiveness in a particular field (e.g., negotiating business deals), a local law school makes a great deal of sense. On the other hand, an older student who is looking for advanced training in order to shift careers may benefit from a totally new location replete with new possibilities. Looking at the financial implications, though, keep in mind that some schools charge state residents significantly less for tuition. Check the Law Schools section in the back of the book for in-state and out-of-state tuitions for 180 U.S. law schools.

> **Close to Home**
>
> The majority of law graduates accept jobs in the same geographic area as their law schools. Statistics for the graduating class of 1995 show that, on a national basis, 77 percent of jobs were accepted by graduates who had attended law school in the same region.
>
> Source: *Class of 1995 Employment Report and Salary Survey*, National Association for Law Placement.

Urban Versus Rural

As you mull over the various issues connected with geographic location, don't forget to consider your personal preference for an urban versus a rural location. Although professional factors may sometimes outweigh this kind of personal preference, it is important at this stage of self-reflection to acknowledge the impact that your likes and dislikes can have on your choice of school. There is no one "right" school for everyone; rather there are over 180 law schools that will prepare you for a career as a lawyer, and they each feature unique programs, locations, connections, environments, advantages, and disadvantages.

It is of vital importance as you plan your application process that you remember that only you can choose the right group of schools for you. Remember that the final choice is yours, and that this discussion is aimed at expanding your consideration to include factors that you had not perhaps considered "valid" or applicable to your choice of school. Law school is full of challenges, and may stretch you further than you have ever stretched before. You will need to be able to unwind and find some way to relieve the inevitable stress that comes from experiencing new limits and challenges. If you despise cities, you are likely to have a tough time finding ways to unwind in New York City. On the other hand, if you are someone who thrives in urban environments, the rural calm and chirping wildlife in rural West Virginia is likely to drive you to distraction.

Climate

Finally, you really should pay attention to your personal choice of climate. If you're someone who's miserable in the heat, you might look at schools in the northeast, whereas if you cannot physically tolerate cold weather, you'll probably be unhappy shivering through three long winters in upstate New York or Boston.

School Reputation

Before moving onto the more substantive discussion of academic and extracurricular program distinctions between schools, let's pause for a moment on reputation. This often exerts a major influence on applicants' views of various schools. However, the American Bar Association does not stand behind any law school rating system beyond the simple statement of a school's accreditation status. Why? The ABA realizes that every prospective law student needs to choose a school based on his or her own criteria.

Despite the fact that the various annually published ratings of law schools are intrinsically flawed in their very assumption that there would be one ranking valid for everyone, the general location of a school in the top 50 or bottom 50 can be moderately useful information for you as you compile your list of chosen schools. Broadly applied, reputation may translate into more or less successful placement rates, professional contacts, or even personal recognition. (Although clearly a better way to compare your placement potential out of various schools is to compare placement rates and location of jobs for graduates from different law schools.)

Beyond referencing the various annual rankings of law schools, perhaps the best way to research the reputation of a school is to ask lawyers or law students. Another method is to look through law school catalogs to see which schools the professors attended. And you should also decide whether local, national, or international reputation is most important to you.

Placement

If you're one of the roughly 75 percent of all law school candidates nationally who will need some form of financial assistance to pay for law school, you'll probably find that at most private law schools you'll likely have to borrow at least $60,000 over three years. This means that after graduation you'll be repaying your loans at a rate of

---

Deer Crossing

These law schools offer peaceful, rural environs:

- Cornell University (NY)
- U.N.C.—Chapel Hill
- William and Mary (VA)
- Ohio Northern University
- Southern Illinois University
- Washington and Lee University (VA)

Rate Your School

Annual rankings for law schools are published by *U.S. News & World Report* and *The Gourman Report*, among others.

SELECTING A SCHOOL

> ### Toast of the Town
>
> Here are 12 schools located in major U.S. cities:
> - Boston University (MA)
> - Columbia University (NY)
> - Detroit College of Law (MI)
> - Emory University (GA)
> - George Washington University (DC)
> - Hamline University (MN)
> - Northwestern University (IL)
> - Oklahoma City University (OK)
> - Tulane University (LA)
> - University of Houston (TX)
> - U.C.L.A. (CA)
> - University of Washington (WA)

roughly $9,500 annually. Although we have devoted an entire section of this book to the financing of a law degree, it's worth mentioning briefly here as one of the reasons you should be concerned about the placement resources that a school has to offer. Furthermore, virtually all accredited schools processing federal financial aid for students are required by law to disclose basic information to entering students about their placement rates, average cumulative educational loan debt, and average starting salary.

As you research the right school for you, be sure to spend some time familiarizing yourself with each school's placement rates, the location of job placements, the on-campus recruitment programs, and law school personnel devoted to helping you find the right job within the legal profession. In addition to these materials from an admissions or placement office, you should also ask for the names of recent graduates who might be willing to speak with you about their own experiences. When you visit schools, make it a point to ask current students about their impressions of a school's placement resources. Particular questions to ask include the following.

Summer Employment

How helpful (and successful) is the placement office in assisting students in their search for summer employment—particularly between their second and third years of law school? Employment in the summer has enormous influence on possible job offers for post graduation.

Job Search Skills Support

Are there support services offered by the school for students to refine their interviewing and résumé-writing skills? How extensive are these services?

Job Placement Survey

Do some research into the specific facts behind the school's placement rate:

- What was the response rate to the job placement survey that produced the school's placement rate?
- At what point was the survey done? Before graduation? six months out?
- How long did it take students on average to find their jobs?
- What were the locations of the jobs for the graduating class, and what types of jobs did they get? Public interest? Government? Judicial clerking? Law firms?

Financial Aid

Although this is mentioned with reference to the placement process, and although it's addressed in depth in a later section, financial aid will be a serious consideration for most students in choosing the right school. Rate this consideration now, but be sure to refer to the discussion in part 4 before making any final decision on its level of impact on your search for the right school. Financing law school involves a very different process than financing a college education, largely because of your access to loans and your potential earning power after graduation.

School Size

Although size is perhaps less a factor in law school than it might be for some people in college, this is one easily sortable feature of law schools. Before you choose your preference, remember that the potentially smaller classes and more intimate environment of a smaller school is balanced by the advantage that a larger school usually has in the greater size and diversity of both its faculty and students. Larger schools also potentially offer a broader selection of upper-division courses. Beyond the immediate consideration of the size of the law school, think also about the relative desirability of the law school being part of a wider university setting. Check the Law Schools section in the back of the book for statistics on class size.

Joint-Degree Programs

Given the proven advantage of advanced degrees in the job market, joint-degree programs are becoming increasingly popular. These programs are often offered within larger universities with a good selection of graduate and professional programs, and usually allow you to earn two degrees in a shorter time than it would take to earn each degree separately, saving a year's tuition. Some schools also offer joint-degree programs with other graduate schools within the same area. The J.D./M.B.A. joint degree is perhaps the most widely desired example of this feature, but there also exist possibilities for joint degrees in the Foreign Service, Divinity and Law, or Ph.D. in Philosophy/J.D., Masters in Public Policy/J.D., and so on. Attending a law school within a larger university also provides you with the opportunity to cross register in other, nonlaw courses either

Lawyer Beware!

If you really must consider an unaccredited law school—either because of location or cost—be careful. Generally a grad of an unaccredited law school can take the bar exam only in the state where the school is located. And the quality of these schools varies widely. Two advantages: The schools are usually cheaper than accredited law schools, and they often schedule their classes to accommodate students with full-time jobs.

Very Big

Some programs with a total student body over 800:

- Boston College
- Columbia University
- Fordham University
- Georgetown University
- Harvard University
- U.C.L.A.
- University of Michigan
- University of Pennsylvania
- University of Texas—Austin

SELECTING A SCHOOL

> ### *Odd Couples*
>
> Here are some interesting joint degrees to consider:
>
> **Brooklyn Law**
> J.D./M.U.P. Urban Planning
>
> **Case Western Reserve University**
> J.D./M.N.O. Nonprofit Management
>
> **Georgetown University**
> J.D./M.S.F.S. Foreign Service
>
> **Indiana University at Bloomington**
> J.D./M.L.S. Library Science
>
> **Samford University**
> J.D./M. Divinity
>
> **SUNY at Buffalo**
> J.D./M.D.
>
> **Suffolk University**
> J.D./M.S.I.E. International Economics
>
> **University of Denver**
> J.D./M.A. Mineral Economics

> ### *Double Up*
>
> See Law Schools section at the back of this book for more information on joint-degree offerings.

for variety or perhaps to learn or continue training in another language. If these are features that appeal to you, include them in your law school search.

Thinking It Over

You should enter a joint-degree program only if you know how the experience is going to further your career goals and interests. Did your statement of reasons for going to law school provide a clear linkage to a joint-degree program? Another approach: What courses do I really want to take in the business school, philosophy department, or school of public health? Can I cross register for them and get credit for the classes towards my law school degree? Most law schools that are affiliated with a university allow their students to take graduate-level classes in other parts of the university. This can be another way of getting the knowledge you think you'll need without the extra year or more and the extra expense.

Student Body

In law school you'll spend a great deal of your time interacting with your classmates. In a fundamental way, they will determine the level of intellectual challenge you face. Depending on the mix of ethnic, racial, socioeconomic, and other distinguishing features represented in the student body of any school, your personal experiences stand to be broadened considerably. Use the data in the Law Schools section of this book, or the academic qualification grids in *The Official Guide* not just to gauge where you might get in, but also to determine at which schools you might expect to fall in the top percentile points in terms of measurable academic qualifications, and at which schools you will be stretched. Be honest with yourself—if you prefer to be at the top of the heap and want to be certain you'll make it into the law review, don't choose to attend a school that admits students who on average have higher academic credentials than yours.

On the other hand, if you respond to intellectual challenge and want to be stretched, but do not care that much about being in the top ten percent of your class, then select your "right" schools accordingly. Larger schools generally have more diverse student populations, although this is not always the case. Also consider the geographical mix of students, and if it matters to you, ask about the average age of a school's students and the ratio of men to women. Remember, the student body will become your future business associates, and are likely to be the people with whom you remain in contact for the length of your law career.

Faculty and Staff

You should know that ABA standards for law schools suggest that there should be one faculty member to 20 full-time students. Although not all schools will meet this standard, one faculty member to 30 full-time students is considered the outside limit of acceptability. Certainly this ratio should be taken into consideration as you are assessing the comparative desirability of schools. Beyond this basic ratio, however, you might also want to assess the following characteristics of a school's faculty:

- Educational background (for breadth and depth, as well as quality of school)
- Professional experience beyond the classroom
- Ethnic, academic, gender, and racial diversity
- Accessibility (Is teaching a priority?)
- Reputation (Are they considered experts in their field?)
- Continued professional activity

We mentioned that your fellow students will play a big role in setting the level of academic challenge you will encounter. Certainly the faculty has an equally profound impact on the level of intellectual stimulation you will receive. Talk to current students, read faculty evaluations, ask graduates, and consult the Association of American Law School's *Directory of Law Teachers* for more specific faculty credentials.

> ### Women and the Law
>
> Most law schools have an enrollment that is at least 40 percent women. For some law schools, the ratio is closer to 50-50. However, women have not yet come close to parity on the faculty. If role models are important to you, look closely at this number. Some law schools do much better than others.

Library and Facilities

You will surely spend a great deal of your time in law school in the library. Spend some time assessing the research facilities and resources available at each of the schools you are considering. ABA standards require that schools maintain adequate libraries to support their programs, and that there be sufficient study space available to accommodate 50 percent of their students at one time if it's a day school. Library hours should be adequate to service your needs. With the recent explosion of online legal research services such as LEXIS or WESTLAW, you should ask what services schools support, and what your access is to those services.

> ### Faculty Counts
>
> The ABA recommends a full-time student-to-faculty ratio of 20:1; a 30:1 ratio is considered the outside limit of acceptability.

SELECTING A SCHOOL

Be sure to ask about the nature of a school's library collection beyond the factual listing of numbers of volumes—frequently used books should be available in multiple copies, and rarely used manuscripts in abundance will only be of interest to a small number of scholars. However, if you are one of those scholars, an extensive collection in your area of interest may be the deciding factor in your choice of school. Other questions include:

- How current is the school's cataloging system?
- How many terminals for legal research are available?
- How knowledgeable is the staff of professional librarians?
- How adequate is the library staff?

Clinical Programs

Clinics allow law students to try out their legal skills representing clients in a variety of settings. Over the course of the past decade, the popularity of clinical programs in law schools has increased dramatically. The introduction of the client into the law school experience vastly alters the nature of the education. Not only are you learning how to think about, analyze, and research legal issues, but you are also required to respond to clients and explain the legal issues to them and perhaps serve as their advocate. In a clinical experience, the legal skills of negotiation, interviewing, and investigation also become honed. Students often cite their clinical experiences as the most challenging and satisfying components of their education. However, not all clinical programs are of the same quality. Again, ask current students about their clinical experiences. The most useful programs generally include a combination of the following characteristics:

- Close faculty or clinical instructor supervision
- Involvement of the clinical experience into the classroom material
- Genuine commitment on the part of the school to its clinical programs in terms of placement, staffing, and student-to-supervising lawyer ratio

All clinical programs are not alike. Law schools offer many different settings. Find out whether the clinical experience is a simulated or a real-world experience, and decide which you would prefer. Also, make sure the kinds of topics the clinics deal with are interesting to you. If you would like to represent children in cases

---

Four-Footed Clients

The Animal Rights Clinic at Rutgers is a very popular offering. The clinic once helped a canine on death row for injuring a little girl. But this unique clinic often fails, since U.S. laws treat animals as property.

A Clinical Pioneer

Dickinson School of Law of Penn State University was one of the first U.S. law schools to offer clinical programs. Clinics include: a Family Law Clinic, a Disability Law Clinic, the Mediation Center, Students in the Prison Clinic, and the Art, Sports, and Entertainment Law Clinic—one of the few of its kind in the United States.

of neglect, but the school offers only clinics on legal services to the elderly, this may diminish the appeal of the clinic experience for you.

Externships

Like clinical programs, externships provide law students with real-world work experience. Externship programs allow students to work for course credit. Students may be placed in government agencies, the judiciary, nonprofit organizations, or private firms. Externships are usually reserved for upper-level students.

Student Services

Beyond the placement facilities, library resources, and clinical programs, there are other administrative offices at each school that will have an impact on the quality of student life at institutions. If the registration process is a nightmare, and you are unable to get into the courses you select, this certainly will affect your experience. What if you do not qualify for as much financial aid as you need in order to attend a school, and the financial aid office refuses to speak with you about alternative loan programs or other means of financing your education? Or, what if you find that the stress of law school is beyond your ability to handle, and you need counseling services, but none are available within the school? Perhaps you are one of 49 million people in the United States with a disability. You may need specific accessibility information and arrangements, assistive technologies, attendant care, support groups, and advocacy help within the administration.

Service needs like these can have a dramatic impact on your whole school experience and, correspondingly, on your ability to concentrate on your academics, which will in turn affect your ability to find a job. Talk to current students, read school literature on these various services, and call the offices yourself to judge how responsive you think the staff will be to your situation as a potential student. Other student services generally include the following offices:

- Registrar
- Financial Aid
- Dean of Students

Hands-on Credit

American University's externship program places students in federal government agencies in Washington, D.C.

In John Marshall's Clinical Law Externship Program, Chicago becomes the classroom. Students work with judges, government agencies, and law firms around the Windy City.

Franklin Pierce offers externships in intellectual and industrial property law, a specialty at New Hampshire's lone law school. Externs can get a headstart on practicing patent law.

Pen Pals

If you want law schools to contact you, sign up for the Candidate Referral Service (CRS) when you register for the LSAT or LSDAS service. Law schools can use this service to recruit potential applicants on the basis of specific characteristics such as LSAT score, GPA, age, ethnic or socioeconomic background, age, or citizenship. You may be contacted by schools that you would not otherwise consider as possible choices.

SELECTING A SCHOOL

> ### Call AHEAD!
>
> The Association for Higher Education and Disability (AHEAD) provides key information on issues concerning students with disabilities. And AHEAD members can access a job bank, or post resumes through the organization.
>
> AHEAD
> P.O. Box 21192
> Columbus OH 43221-0192
> Voice/TTY: (614) 488-4972

> ### Law for All
>
> For info on reasonable accommodations, contact HEATH, a U.S. government–funded clearinghouse about post secondary education for individuals with disabilities. Free information is available in print, disk, and audiocassette formats. Contact:
>
> HEATH Resource Center
> 1 Dupont Circle, Suite 800
> Washington, DC 20036-1193
> Fax: (202) 833-4760
> E-mail: HEATH@ace.nche.edu
> Voice: (800) 544-3284
> TTY: (202) 939-9320

Student Organizations

In addition to the administrative services mentioned above, much of your law school experience will be flavored by your involvement in a number of extracurricular activities. Law schools usually have a range of student journals that you can join, with some being more competitive and prestigious than others. Schools will usually provide you with a list of student organizations on request or even in their catalogs, and you can tell a lot about a school by the nature of its student organizations. Check to see if there might be something there for you. Remember that you will need a release from the academic stress and a way to nurture your other interests.

Is there a place for you to feel at home while attending law school? Student organizations give you a sense of whether people of similar interests and backgrounds attend the school. The admissions application should provide a list of student groups and their purposes. Look at this information carefully to get a sense of what the interests of other students are. Are there potential places for you to feel connected? Most law schools have organizations representing a wide range of ethnic, religious, cultural, and social concerns. Try to verify that your interests will be represented. The ABA publication *ABA-Approved Law Schools* gives data on minorities and women for the student body, faculty, and administration. To order, call (800) 285-2221.

Academic Rigor

Although we mentioned this briefly in terms of the nature of the student body, it's important that you assess how vital it is for you to go to an academically competitive school. Most law school applicants will aspire to the most academically competitive schools within their range of possibility based on LSAT scores and GPAs. While this makes a lot of sense in a number of ways, it is not the best strategy for all people. Think carefully about what your reaction to landing at the bottom of your class might be. Are you someone to whom it is important to be in that top ten percent, top third, top half? Rank this factor honestly for yourself before you begin the process of sorting through the various applicant grids in *The Official Guide to Law Schools*.

Personal Factors

You may also have other personal factors that will play a big role in your choice of law school. If you have a disability or if you use English as a second language, you will want to ask schools directly about their accommodations for your distinguishing characteristics. Don't make the mistake of waiting until well into your planning to ask this vital question of schools, for you can waste a lot of time and energy focusing on the wrong schools.

Remember that this is a search for the school that is right for you, and not simply for the schools that will accept you. If a school is not responsive to your inquiry about a particular kind of support service, then chances are you would be miserable there even if it is a "big name" school. Remember to include any personal factors you may have and rank them as you have the other factors.

For example, what kinds of academic support services does the law school offer? Suppose you need some one-on-one assistance to progress in a class that you find difficult. How easy is it for you to obtain assistance, and what will it cost? If available, these services should be described in the admission application booklet.

For more in-depth discussions of a number of personal factors that might affect your choice of a law school, see the Special Considerations section of this book.

CHAPTER 3

The Right School for You

Most law school applicants seem to begin their search by figuring out where they might expect to be accepted, and then looking at what those schools have to offer. We're suggesting you reverse this order. Try evaluating the other important characteristics of a school, as we did in chapter 2. Then think about your chances of admission.

Your Academic Profile

Law school is an academic program. The most important determination admissions committees will make about you is whether you have the necessary intellectual firepower to succeed in such an environment. This is why law schools rely so heavily on your GPA and LSAT score. These are perhaps the two most important pieces of information about you that admissions committees will consider.

Your undergraduate GPA is probably set in stone, or is nearly so. Therefore, your last best chance to improve your odds of admission is to improve your LSAT score. And your LSAT score is important regardless of your GPA. If you have an impressive GPA, the test can be a liability; a poor performance can call your academic record into question. If you have a poor GPA, the test is an opportunity; it can overcome doubts raised by your transcript. The Admissions section of this book includes information on getting a head start on your LSAT preparation.

GPA and LSAT aren't everything, but most schools will begin their evaluation process by somehow sorting their applicant pools by academic profiles. It's fairly easy to plot your academic chances of getting into most schools, although this becomes increasingly difficult with the more selective schools, some of which don't even publish the numerical statistics (LSAT and GPA) of their entering class.

SELECTING A SCHOOL

> **Academic Profile**
>
> Use this space to record your:
>
> Highest LSAT _____
>
> Average LSAT _____
>
> Cumulative GPA _____

Note your highest LSAT, along with your cumulative GPA. Keep these numbers in mind as you peruse school listings, for it makes no sense to compose a list of schools that match your other characteristics when your chances of admission are highly unlikely based on these "performance" factors. Beyond the numbers, you should know also that schools will scrutinize your transcript for academic rigor and course content. Admissions committee members will be interested in your academic trend. Did your GPA rise or fall over the four years of college? If you had a rocky start, did you recover, and if so, how long did this recovery take you? (How to address these and other potential negatives are discussed in chapter 9.) All of these considerations combine to form your academic profile. Use your profile to help you sort through the great number of schools that will otherwise look like a great fit for you.

Academics and Applications

Common application strategies suggest that you apply to three categories of schools. Allow yourself to dream a little with "reach" schools and select two or three schools whose academic statistics suggest that you have only a ten to 20 percent chance of being accepted. Next, include a strong base of "50-50" schools whose numbers suggest that you have an even chance of making it. Finally, include in your chosen schools a few "safety" selections where it seems clear that you'll be an attractive candidate based on your LSAT and your GPA.

> **How Many?**
>
> Apply to a minimum of six law schools:
>
> - Two "reach" schools at which you have a 10–20 percent chance of getting in
> - Two (or three) "50-50" schools at which you have an even chance of getting in
> - At least two "safety" schools at which you're likely to get in based on your LSAT scores and GPA

It might help to consider for a minute how many applications you actually want to file. Although the cost of filing multiple applications might be a strong consideration for you, most schools will consider requests for application fee waivers in cases of extreme financial hardship. (Fees range from about $20–75 per school.) It's well worth applying to a comprehensive and tailored list of schools, given the fundamental impact that your eventual choice of law school will have on your future.

Be honest with yourself about your academic credentials. When choosing the schools to which you'll apply, be certain to be honest with yourself about where your credentials will take you. If nothing else, think of your poor roommate or coworkers who will have to deal with your moods when the flood of rejection letters come in because you've applied to schools that accept only one out of ten applicants with your qualifications. You hope the fact that other family members graduated from this law school will make up for the ten-point spread between you and the school median LSAT. It won't. Save yourself a lot of grief, money, and effort, and spare those around you by honestly evaluating your chances of admission when selecting law schools.

Law School Grids

Each year, the Law School Admission Council (LSAC) publishes the *Official Guide to U.S. Law Schools*. This guide includes a wealth of information on all ABA-accredited law schools. The schools themselves provide most of the information for the book, including the LSAT scores and GPAs of the most recently admitted class. These are generally presented in grid form, such as the grid below, and are a valuable tool in determining your chances of being accepted at any particular law school. Below is a hypothetical grid, similar to the ones found in the guide.

Applicant Group for the 199X-9X Academic Year

GPA	120–139	140–149	150–154	155–159	160–164	170–174	175–180
4–3.75	11/1	21/3	29/5	41/12	62/33	68/55	48/47
3.74–3.5	16/0	14/0	8/2	38/16	84/38	115/64	102/81
3.49–3.25	18/0	9/1	12/0	24/8	73/28	96/38	76/48
3.24–3.0	13/0	13/0	22/2	25/6	55/15	71/28	53/27
2.99–2.75	3/0	5/0	8/0	19/2	38/6	49/10	31/9
2.74–2.5	1/0	0/0	3/1	18/3	41/2	32/4	11/5
2.5	1/0	1/0	3/0	9/1	9/0	6/2	3/1

(LSAT Score across top)

First, find the line where your GPA fits in. Then read across until you find the score category of your existing or anticipated LSAT score. There you'll find two numbers, divided by a slash. The first number indicates the number of people in that range of LSAT scores and GPAs who applied to the school. The second number is the number accepted.

Although the grid system is a helpful tool, it does have its problems. Each category in a grid covers a fairly wide range of numbers. Don't be fooled into thinking a 3.51 and 160 falls into the same category as a 3.74 and 165, even though they might fall in the same place on a grid. There are significant gaps in every category.

Some law schools do not provide LSAC with grids. However, these schools generally will tell you the average GPA and LSAT score for the previous year's entering class. If you want to get a picture of your chances at these schools, try determining which other schools are similar in reputation. Then determine which of these other schools most closely matches the original school in application volume, and use that grid. This is not a precise measurement, but it will give you some idea of the applicant pool.

SELECTING A SCHOOL

Your preliminary list of possible choices might include 12 to 15 schools. Here's how to narrow down your choices.

- Search for schools meeting your priorities and academic profile in the Law Schools section at the back of this book, or in *The Official Guide*.
- Keep comparing your list of priorities to the information about schools to find the programs that combine offerings in a way that seems best suited to your tastes.

After listing your school options, chart your chances of being admitted based on the statistical data, and focus on the five or six schools that span the "reach" to "safety" categories.

> **Major Majors**
>
> The three most common undergrad majors for law students are history, political science, and English.

Are the Schools You're Considering Up to Par?

Is the curriculum offered by the law schools you're considering going to give you the training you need to succeed? Law school curriculums have changed over the years, but change has been slow. Because law firms are no longer providing the apprenticeship training they once did, more emphasis is being placed on skills training in law schools. While not every law student expects to be a courtroom litigator, training in trial advocacy and related writing skills are important experiences that should be widely available at the schools you're considering.

Another aspect of law school curriculum that is gaining wider acceptance is clinical training. Law school clinics give students the opportunity to represent clients in a specific subject area. For many students who are tired of a passive learning process, clinical experiences offer the opportunity for the integration of the classroom and real life. Look closely at the clinical options available to make certain there are several whose focus is of interest to you. Clinical experiences are usually offered to a small number of students, typically fifteen to twenty per term. Be certain you identify more than one clinic that you are interested in so that you have alternatives if you don't get your first choice.

Getting a Social Life in Law School

Many law students, at least in the first year, ask, "How can I have a social life if I don't even have a life?" This is an exaggeration, but it contains more than a grain of truth. Certainly, law students cannot socialize in the way they might have as undergraduates without doing serious harm to their academic performance. Of course, your partying ways might make you very popular with your classmates. They'd appreciate you for your social contributions, of course, but they'd really love you for helping to pull down the grading curve!

The Right School for You

Law students usually create a social life from the people in their first-year section, or within the numerous clubs found at most law schools. At Georgetown, there are over 60 student organizations, ranging from the Gilbert and Sullivan Society ("the only musical club with a law school attached") which puts on a play and a musical each year starring law students, to the Society of Law, Health, and Bioethics. Law school Web sites are excellent places to find out what kinds of clubs and activities each school offers. Try to make sure the schools you apply to have groups with activities you might like to be involved in. You'll probably have little time to locate extracurricular activities outside school unless you're going to law school in a place where you already have ties.

Apply Yourself!

Let's take a look at several simulated examples of matching your academic profile, personal priorities, and school selection factors with real-world law school choices.

Urban and Urbane

Let's say you're a big-city person. You thrive on a fast-paced schedule and intense competition, and really want to begin practicing in a big law firm as soon as possible. You expect to spend your legal career negotiating major business deals. You want a major city law school that offers a joint-degree opportunity, one that makes it possible to carry a term-time job in a law firm, working up to the ABA limit of 20 hours a week. You probably want to aim high in terms of academic rigor, and clearly want a school with a top-notch placement office.

Post-J.D. Degree

After your J.D. degree, you may want to pursue a Master of Law or LL.M. degree. LL.M. programs allow you to specialize in a field such as taxation or comparative law.

Some Big City Law Programs Offering Joint J.D.–M.B.A.

School	Location	Median LSAT	Median GPA
Columbia U.	New York City	169	3.60
Georgetown U.	Washington, D.C.	166	3.50
N.Y.U.	New York City	168	3.67
U.C.L.A.	Los Angeles	162	3.59
U. of Chicago	Chicago	169	3.67
U. of Pennsylvania	Philadelphia	165	3.58
U.S.C.	Los Angeles	164	3.50
U. of Washington	Seattle	162	3.56

SELECTING A SCHOOL

Nature Lover

Let's say that you're someone who wants to have a wide selection of environmental law courses in your second and third years of law school. Working with the Environmental Protection Agency has been your dream for years. Beyond this, you love to backpack and hike in your spare time, and find that you best learn things when forced to dive right in. School size may not be a big factor for you, but expense will be.

Search through the Law Schools section at the back of this book and *The Official Guide* for programs that self-identify with strong environmental law programs, and consider those that are located close to some mountains in a primarily rural setting.

Some Law Schools with Environmental Programs

School	Entering Class Size	Tuition	Median Academics	Setting
Boston College, Newton, MA	289	$22,300	LSAT 161 GPA 3.50	suburban
U. of Denver, Denver, CO	333	$18,569	LSAT 154 GPA 3.14	city
Lewis & Clark College, Portland, OR	220	$17,395	LSAT 160 GPA 3.23	rural
U. of North Carolina, Chapel Hill, NC	230	$2,881* $14,743**	LSAT 160 GPA 3.50	rural
Ohio Northern, Ada, OH	129	$18,980	LSAT 147 GPA 3.96	rural
University of Southern California, Los Angeles, CA	200	$23,464	LSAT 164 GPA 3.50	city
Stanford U., Stanford, CA	178	$24,166	LSAT 167 GPA 3.79	suburban
Vermont Law School, South Royalton, VT	146	$18,490	LSAT 154 GPA 3.10	rural
Washington U., St. Louis, MO	197	$21,675	LSAT 160 GPA 3.40	city
Widener U., Wilmington, DE	514	$17,770	LSAT 148 GPA 2.95	suburban

*in-state tuition   **out-of-state tuition

Newshound-Turned-Legal Eagle

Say you're 38 years old, well ensconced in your career as a reporter for an urban newspaper, but anxious to study law because, increasingly, legal considerations have been spotlighted in your articles. Furthermore, you'd like to be more a part of the solution to the multiple public policy problems you realize underlie your stories; you're weary of simply observing and reporting. You hope to encounter other older students in your law school classes, and want to have the opportunity to enroll in public policy courses. On the other hand, you don't want to spend the extra year it would take to get a joint degree in public policy.

You have your eye on schools in or near New York City or Washington, D.C., because most of your friends are settled in these two cities, and you're involved in a serious relationship with someone whose career is thriving in the Big Apple. You might consider attending a law school with an evening program, if you can find one that matches your needs.

Some Law Schools with Public Policy and Public Interest Programs

School	Part Time	LSAT	GPA
U. of Baltimore	yes	151	2.98
Brooklyn Law School	yes	157	3.33
Catholic U.	yes	155	3.10
Cornell U.	no	165	3.56
Columbia U.	no	169	3.60
Fordham U.	yes	162	3.40
Georgetown U.	yes	166	3.50
N.Y.U.	no	168	3.67

Suburbanite

You might be a little conflicted about what kind of setting you want in a law school. For you it's important to have access to the superior quality of urban cultural offerings, but you really don't like living in the city. You appreciate beautiful natural surroundings, and yet you don't want to be cloistered in a remote setting with other students who are very much like you. You might like to be a law professor eventually, so you would like to have access to graduate LL.M. courses. Although you're from the Midwest, you're willing to relocate anywhere, and are looking to broaden your horizons.

SELECTING A SCHOOL

Some Suburban Law Programs

School	Location	LSAT	GPA
Arizona State U.	Tempe, AZ	160	3.46
U. of Michigan	Ann Arbor, MI	N/A	N/A
Pepperdine U.	Malibu, CA	157	3.30
Northern Illinois U.	DeKalb, IL	156	3.00
Stanford U.	Stanford, CA	167	3.78
U. of Tulsa	Tulsa, OK	153	2.90
Widener U.	Wilmington, DE	148	2.95

Rock Solid, Yet Flexible

You're someone who learns by doing, and you're a little bit concerned about a lecture-only format for your law courses. Although you think it's important to be able to have access to a solid clinical program where you have some options, you might also want to attend a law school that offers a co-op program where you can alternate going to school for a semester, then working in a legal setting for a semester. Costs and financial aid are big considerations, and you think that with a cooperative program, you might be able to finance more of your expenses through your earnings, because you owe $25,000 in student loans for your undergraduate education. You're a practical person, and you are pretty flexible about location, size, and reputation.

Some Law Schools with Multiple Clinics

School	Tuition	LSAT	GPA
CUNY—Queens	$5,700* $8,930**	147	3.09
U.C.L.A.	$10,861* $19,255**	162	3.59
Georgetown U.	$23,000	166	3.50
Northeastern (Boston, MA)	$21,300	156	3.3
U. of New Mexico at Albuquerque	$3,284* $11,015**	156	3.24
U. of Maryland at Baltimore	$8,536* $15,602**	156	3.15

*in-state tuition   **out-of-state tuition

Author, Author!

You love to write. In college, you spent the better part of your time working on the school paper, and also served on the editorial staff of a human rights newsletter. You can see your legal career going in a number of different directions, but you know it's important to you to be involved in a student law journal. Although your school's law review would be nice, it's not overwhelmingly important to you; you simply want a school with a wide choice of student journals from which to choose. Beyond that, you know it is important to continue your work with human rights in some fashion.

Some Law Schools with Numerous Journals

School	Location	LSAT	GPA
Boston College	Newton, MA	161	3.50
U.C.L.A.	Los Angeles, CA	162	3.59
U.C. Berkeley	Berkeley, CA	166	3.76
Duke U.	Durham, NC	166	3.60
Northwestern U.	Chicago, IL	165	3.52
U. of Texas at Austin	Austin, TX	162	3.56
Tulane U.	New Orleans, LA	159	3.27
Yale U.	New Haven, CT	172	3.88

Some Law Schools with Human Rights Specialties

School	Location	LSAT	GPA
American U.	Washington, DC	156	3.27
Benjamin N. Cardozo, Yeshiva U.	New York City	157	3.30
Columbia U.	New York City	169	3.60
Howard U.	Washington, DC	151	2.98
U. of Cincinnati	Cincinnati, OH	160	3.42
U. of Miami	Coral Gables, FL	154	3.20

SELECTING A SCHOOL

Rights Fight

Human rights issues are a hot topic in legal education right now. A sample offering: the Urban Morgan Institute for Human Rights at the U. of Cincinnati. Participants may work around the world with international human rights organizations.

Road Scholar

From the time you were young, you've loved to travel. You're fascinated by different cultures and find it boring to live in one place for too long. You are particularly interested in how different cultures create their own spoken and unspoken codes of behavior, and now you want to study law in order to prepare yourself for a career as an international lawyer, perhaps with some training in business. You want to be involved in the globalization of the economy, and can see yourself settling down for brief periods in a number of different countries.

Some Law Schools with International Programs and Joint J.D.-M.B.A.

School	Location	LSAT	GPA
Cornell University	Ithaca, NY	165	3.56
Florida State U.	Tallahassee, FL	157	3.31
Georgetown U.	Washington, DC	166	3.50
University of Hawaii—Manoa	Honolulu, HI	157	3.25
U. of Iowa	Iowa City, IA	159	3.49
U. of Minnesota	Minneapolis, MN	162	3.56
U. of Pennsylvania	Philadelphia, PA	165	3.58
U. of Texas at Austin	Austin, TX	162	3.56
U. of Utah	Salt Lake City, UT	159	3.51
Vanderbilt U.	Nashville, TN	163	3.63
Wake Forest U.	Winston-Salem, NC	160	3.27
Washington U.	St. Louis, MO	161	3.40

Your First-Draft Picks

Whatever your mix of considerations, you can now list 12 to 15 schools that look promising to you. Remember to consult your original reasons for wanting to go to law school, and sort through schools using your established screening items as we discussed in the previous chapter.

Break down your list of law schools into three tiers ("Dream," "50-50," "Safety"). The number of schools on your list will depend on your individual circumstances. Indicate the dates you requested and the dates you received catalogs and other information from each school on your list.

Your list will be reduced (or perhaps expanded) in response to the information you receive from the school, and your real world research. Your real world homework should include talking to graduates of the schools, partners in law firms, or attorneys who are working in jobs that you find conducive to your interests.

Refining Your Picks

When you've gathered all your resources, reflected on your reasons for wanting to go to law school, and compiled a first-draft list of potentially good matches, it's time for further refinement of yours School Selection List. You might consider attending a second Law School Forum if you're fortunate enough to live in a location that makes this a possibility. In many ways you can get a lot more information the second time around because you will have done your research about the schools to make your discussion with admissions and alumni representatives quite a bit more specific. Keep in mind that this is your search for the right school for you. You may find as a result of this process that you want to add a school or two to your list, and you may find that you can whittle your list down to the ideal six to eight schools comprising your final list.

> **Real World**
>
> In Northeastern's co-op program, second- and third-year students alternate between three months in the classroom and three months in full-time work in legal positions. The program at CUNY—Queens is notable for its emphasis on integrating real-world experience into the academic program.

> **On Target**
>
> To refine your list of schools, do more research:
> - Attend a second Law School Forum
> - Visit the schools
> - Speak to students and alums
> - Speak to school administrators

If you're fortunate enough to live close to some of your choice schools, by all means visit them, speak to current students and administrators, and attend classes. In some cases, it might be worth your trip from a distance to "try on" a school, but the majority of applicants will save this close comparison until after they have received their offers of admission. The decision of where to go to school after receiving multiple offers of admission is an entirely different process, though one with great similarities. First, you need to think about getting into the schools of your choice, and beyond that you need to consider seriously your plans for financing law school. If you've planned well in your choice of schools, been honest with yourself about your interests and needs, and taken the time to consider the factors that will be important to you, you'll find an unexpected reward. Writing the applications will be dramatically easier than if you had not really given your selection of schools much thought. After all, you already know that these schools are a good fit—now you just need to communicate that wisdom to the admissions committees!

SELECTING A SCHOOL

Ideally you'll have time to draft a list of schools that reflect your personal interests before attending one of the Law School Forums, but you can certainly use the forums to help you refine your selection. Whichever order you choose, you'll end up with a good selection strategy and valuable information gleaned from speaking with alumni and law school representatives.

PART THREE

Admissions

CHAPTER 4

Your Application Timeline

When the number of applicants to law schools exploded in the '80s, law schools made a number of adjustments that affect how you apply for admission. The two changes that have the most effect on you and your application schedule are the lengthening of the admissions process—it now extends from October through the following spring—and the shift to rolling admissions. Both of these should affect your approach to the application process.

> **Is It Ever Too Early?**
>
> Begin planning your application and getting yourself ready financially 15–18 months before you hope to register for law school classes.

The Best Time to Apply

Generally, law schools send out application forms in August and September, begin accepting applications in October, and start sending out acceptance letters by November. Some law schools have begun to send out application brochures even earlier. One well-known law school began mailing application materials to requesters in June for enrollment 15 months later. This shift to an earlier publication date was largely in response to applicants who wanted sufficient time to prepare their applications.

While applicants who are accepted are notified beginning in November, most law schools do not mail out rejection letters until January. Application deadlines may still be in February or March, but because the schools have begun filling their classes in the fall, it is not unusual for more than 75 percent of the anticipated acceptance letters to have been sent by the spring deadline date. This is what's known as rolling admissions, which creates the alarming scenario of the uneducated applicant who proudly deliv-

ADMISSIONS

> **Look Smart**
>
> Earlier applicants look smarter. Applicants who apply earlier tend to appear to admissions officers as being better prepared, better organized, and more serious. These are all virtues to which every applicant aspires.

ers his application to the school on the deadline date only to find that he has put himself at a distinct disadvantage.

Applying early provides you with three major advantages.

1. Credentials Are Evaluated More Carefully Later in the Process.

Suppose you were an admissions officer at the beginning of the application cycle for the upcoming year. You don't know how many applications you'll receive, and you don't know how strong an applicant pool will be. At the beginning of the process, admissions officers tend to set the criteria for admission, called an index number, lower than they do later in the cycle. Law schools use an index number, which is derived from a combination of your LSAT score and GPA. We'll discuss index numbers in more detail in the next chapter.

Students whose credentials meet or exceed that number are generally automatic accepts as long as the recommendations and student essay do not raise any concerns. As the season progresses, the index changes, usually upward, as the profile of the typical application becomes clearer. It stands to reason that you want to get the benefit of the lower index number to increase your chances of becoming an automatic accept.

2. The Later You Apply, the Tougher the Competition.

It stands to reason that if schools are more lenient in the initial phase of the application cycle, more students will be accepted then, leaving fewer spaces for later applicants. Additionally, those later applicants will probably be judged under more stringent criteria than applicants accepted earlier. By February, a law school may have sent out 75 percent of the acceptance letters it plans to send. And they still have applications from some of the people who applied earlier who haven't been notified yet. These files are reviewed several more times as the applicant pool keeps shifting. Some of these earlier applicants will now get accepted. And a student who completes the application just as the deadline approaches will be vying for a smaller number of spots in a fairly substantial pool of applicants.

3. Your Application Always Looks Fresher Earlier.

One other factor that you should keep in mind is fatigue. Not yours, theirs. The admissions officers are much fresher at the beginning of the fall season than they are the following spring. Fatigue and a certain cynicism may begin to creep in when they read their three thousandth essay on the seminal experience that sparked a student's desire to persue a legal education.

Plan Ahead

Some prelaw advisors and even a few admissions officers dispute the importance of early applicants, and at a few schools, there may be no special advantage. Law schools are almost always open to exceptional applicants, and will sometimes admit someone well after the deadline if there's space in the class. There are also a few schools that routinely accept applications up until a week or two before classes start. But these are exceptions. You increase the risk of not having your application fully considered if you get it in just at the deadline.

> **Call LSAC**
>
> For LSAT registration info, call (215) 968-1001.

If you want to complete all of your applications by late November, your planning should begin five or six months before that. A schedule that you can use to organize your campaign is included later in this chapter. You'll notice that we've allowed plenty of time to devote to the application process the summer before the November target date. Since the largest number of law school applications are from students coming directly out of college, the timetable assumes you will go to school the fall after your college graduation.

The LSAT

You should register to take the June LSAT in the spring of your junior year in college. Taking the test in June allows you freedom to take the test again the following fall if you need to try to improve your score. *The LSAT/LSDAS Registration and Information Book* is available from any law school admissions office, most colleges, or at any Kaplan education center.

Here are a few LSAT tips:

Registration

Phone the Law School Admission Council (LSAC) at (215) 968-1001 for automated help, Tuesday through Thursday 6:00 A.M. to 11:00 P.M. (E.S.T.), Friday 6:00 A.M. to 8:00 P.M. (E.S.T.), Saturday through Monday 4:00 P.M. to 11:00 P.M. (E.S.T.). Live help is available at the same number, Monday through Friday, 8:30 A.M. to 8:00 P.M. (E.S.T.), from September to March, and 8:30 A.M. to 4:45 P.M. (E.S.T.), from April to August. We've heard that Mondays are the busiest days, so plan to call later in the week to save yourself a few dollars on the phone bill and reduce your aggravation level or send an e-mail to lsacinfo@lsac.org.

Online

You can register for LSAT online through the LSAC Web site at http://www.lsac.org. This site contains helpful information about the LSAT, including a complete sample test. You can also obtain a *LSAT/LSDAS Registration Book,* a *Disabilities Accommodations Request Packet,* a *Fee Waiver Packet,* and other free LSAC publications online.

ADMISSIONS

Testing Fee

The LSAT fee is about $86. (Fees increase a little every few years.)

Registration Tip

Register early to secure a seat at a popular testing site. There is limited seating at many of the most popular sites.

Fee Waivers

Eligibility is more stringent than for other financial aid processes, and LSAC states that only those with extreme need should apply. You may request a fee waiver through LSAC or any participating LSAC-member law school. To obtain a waiver form from LSAC, call the phone number above or write to Office of Minority Affairs, LSAC, Box 2000, Newtown, PA 18940-0998. You can also obtain the form from LSAC's Website. Apply early if you wish to obtain a fee waiver for a particular test administration. If you're approved for a waiver, you must submit the waiver with your test registration form by the regularly scheduled registration deadlines.

> **50 Shopping Days 'Till . . .**
>
> If you apply to law schools before Thanksgiving, you'll be among the early entries. If your application is received after the holidays, though, you may be one of the last 30 percent to apply.

Late Registration

Registering late will cost you about an extra $52. Phone registration is available only during the late registration period. You may use Visa™, MasterCard™, Discover™, or American Express™ to pay your fees whether registering on time by mail or late by phone. Walk-in registration the day of the test is not permitted.

LSDAS

The registration booklet gives detailed information about the LSAT and also the LSDAS (Law School Data Assembly Service). The LSDAS is the administrative service that will be sending your LSAT scores and transcripts to the law schools you apply to (more on LSDAS later). LSAC recommends setting up your LSDAS file in September after the June test. You may want to set an earlier deadline for yourself, say early August, to be certain your file is handled in a timely fashion. The LSDAS service costs about $85. The fee for sending your information to additional schools is about $10 per school.

Early Applications

Having established the importance of early applications, the next question is: What constitutes an early application? A pre–Labor Day application is definitely overdoing it. When that fall's class is just

Your Application Timeline

enrolling, you run the risk of your application being caught up in admissions materials filed for the entering class. Pre-Thanksgiving is the preferable choice and assures that you'll be among the early entries. Shortly before Christmas is not as desirable, but should still hold you in good stead. After Christmas and the holidays, however, you're on the downside and may well find yourself among the last 30 percent of all applications received. And if you go with a post–Valentine's Day application—well, you'd just better have strong numbers.

Remember that this discussion applies to the date on which your application is complete, not just the date on which the school receives the application forms from you. Applications are not considered complete without the LSAT score, LSDAS reports, transcripts, and all recommendations. Even though other people are sending these things, it's your responsibility to see that they arrive at the law school promptly. This does not mean calling the law school three times a week to see if they've arrived. It means prodding your recommenders or your college to send in the necessary documentation. This can be done without antagonizing them by explaining the importance of early applications. Most people aren't aware of the importance of early application, and are more than willing to cooperate if you explain why.

Check It Out

Make a master schedule. Use the checklists we give you at the end of this chapter to keep yourself on track. Check them often to make sure you're not letting an important deadline pass.

Make a Schedule

If you want to have a complete application at the law schools by, say, late November, you can't start planning just a few weeks in advance. Your campaign for admission should begin five or six months before that deadline, i.e., 18 months before your first day as a law student. We've included a schedule that you can use to organize your campaign. What should become clear as you examine it is that you should plan to devote plenty of time to your applications the summer before they're due.

> **Kap Call**
>
> Before taking the June LSAT, of course, you'll want to prepare thoroughly. Kaplan offers a variety of test-preparation options. Call 1-800-KAP-TEST for more info.

Applying to law school and arranging the financing is a time-consuming process that tests your organizational skills and your attention to detail. Students who believe that they can simply plot out four hours on a weekend to complete this ordeal are kidding themselves. Law schools like to see applications that are carefully thought out and well organized. After all, good organizational skills and attention to detail are traits that all lawyers need. It makes no sense to spend a great deal of time improving your GPA and studying for the LSAT and then blow off the application itself. Plan to set aside some big blocks of time well in advance to work intensively on this important step in achieving your admissions goals.

Don't worry if the following schedule doesn't exactly meet your needs. Keep in mind, though, that a few dates are written in stone. You should find out what they are as early as possible and incorporate them

ADMISSIONS

into your own personal application schedule. This "personal" schedule is organized to help you understand how to proceed through the admissions process. Within each section, you have plenty of room to move things around.

Summer

After getting the LSAT behind you, you'll want to focus on your applications. Start thinking about a "theme" for your application, which can serve as a way to stand out from the crowd, and as an organizing principle for personal statements, recommendations, and everything else in your file. Think about how you'd like to be identified. As the environmentalist who plays oboe recitals for the local recycling center? As the gymnast who volunteers with children in the Special Olympics and who's concerned about health care issues? Of course, you don't have to have an elaborate theme, but any kind of "high concept" will help your application stick in the minds of admissions officers.

You should also be assembling your list of schools at this point. Visit as many schools as you can. Send away for catalogs and applications.

> **Score Big**
>
> Try to "get it right" the first time. Do a thorough job of LSAT test preparation, because retaking the test does not assure that you'll get a higher score the second or third time around. The *LSAT/LSDAS Registration and Information Book* charts out the results of test takers who sit for additional test administrations and how they did—getting a better score is not a sure thing.

Of course, if your performance on the June LSAT doesn't live up to your hopes, you should use the summer to really prep this time. Don't just skim the test-preparation materials (as you probably did the first time, right?).

If you're planning to apply for financial aid to help you pay for your trip to law school, you need to do some serious thinking about your long-term expenses and how you'll meet them. At this point, it would be wise to obtain a copy of your credit history from one of the three national credit bureaus to find out if any of those late or missed payments on your credit cards is reflected on your report, or if there is any incorrect information.

If you haven't already done so, now is the time to buy the publication *ABA-Approved Law Schools*. If you can't find it in your local bookstore, you can order it from the American Bar Association at www.abanet.org/legaled, or by calling (800) 285-2221.

Early Fall

Here's where the action really starts. Applications will start arriving. In filling them out, follow the procedures outlined in the next chapter. Line up your recommenders. Make sure they have everything they need to write you a great recommendation. Take the October LSAT, if you've decided to do so.

Revise your personal statement. Revise it again. And again . . . .

Late Fall

Finish and send in your applications. Mail your matching forms to LSDAS, so they know where to send your scores and transcripts. Prod your recommenders, so that your applications are complete before Thanksgiving (remember, no application is complete until all recommendations, scores, and transcripts have been sent to the law schools).

Review the admissions booklet from the various law schools for information on how each school determines its financial aid awards. Obtain the necessary financial aid applications and begin completing them. Some forms may be due in December, others should not be completed until January 1 or later.

Winter

Wait as patiently as you can. Make sure that your financial aid applications are complete. A crucial error students make is waiting to see where they've been admitted before applying for financial aid. Remember that your application may be one that is put in the "review again" pile, and you may not be admitted until late spring. You can't wait until then to apply for aid, because you'll be six weeks, at a minimum, waiting for the results. Since funds are limited, your aid file needs to be ready to be looked at as soon as possible after your acceptance. Once you've spent all this time and effort applying and getting admitted to a law school, don't omit the crucial step of arranging how you're going to be able to pay for it!

ADMISSIONS

Law School Application Checklist

Your campaign for law school admission should start up to 18 months before you step into your first law classroom. Here's a checklist/schedule of what you should be doing during each season.

Spring

- ❏ Get *The Official Guide to U.S. Law Schools* from LSAC and the *ABA Guide to Approved Law Schools* from ABA.
- ❏ Register for the June LSAT (you can retake it in October if your score needs improvement).
- ❏ Register for a Kaplan LSAT class to fully prepare for the LSAT.
- ❏ Obtain a copy of your credit report from one of the three national credit bureaus for a nominal charge.

Summer

- ❏ Take the June LSAT.
- ❏ Start drafting your personal statement.
- ❏ Think about whom you'll be asking for recommendations.
- ❏ Make a list of schools you'll be applying to, using the grids from *The Official Guide* as an aid.
- ❏ Send away for applications, and start visiting as many schools as you can.
- ❏ Register for the October LSAT if you're not satisfied with your June score.
- ❏ Contact any creditors with whom you have problem accounts and make arrangements to begin mutually agreed upon monthly payments to satisfy your debts.

Early Fall

- ❏ Familiarize yourself with the applications as they roll in.
- ❏ Use the LSAC Web site at http://www.lsac.org to obtain information and admissions applications from schools offering Web-based applications.
- ❏ Make a checklist and schedule for each application, and photocopy all forms.
- ❏ Subscribe to LSDAS, if you haven't already done so (they take care of sending your transcript and LSAT scores to each school you apply to).
- ❏ Attend a Law School Forum if you are able to do so.
- ❏ Send transcript request forms to all undergraduate and graduate schools you've attended.
- ❏ Line up your recommenders. Give them the specific info they need to write an outstanding recommendation for you.
- ❏ Revise your personal statement. Tailor it to specific essay topics, if any, on individual applications.
- ❏ Make sure your credit card payments are on track. Avoid encumbering yourself with any additional debt.

Your Application Timeline

Mid Fall

- ❏ Finalize your personal statements.
- ❏ Transfer application information from the photocopies to the actual application forms, or put the finishing touches on your Web-based application, if you're going that route.
- ❏ Make sure your recommenders are on board.
- ❏ Take the October LSAT (if you need to).
- ❏ Send in your applications. Make sure you don't mix up the mailings!
- ❏ Request financial aid application materials from the schools and make sure you read the instructions for financial aid applications carefully.

Late Fall

- ❏ Remind your recommenders to send in recommendations ASAP.
- ❏ Get the Master Law School Report from LSDAS, summarizing transcripts, etcetera.
- ❏ Submit any financial aid applications due early to schools that request them.

Winter, Spring, Summer

- ❏ Receive monthly updates from LSDAS.
- ❏ Cross your fingers while you wait for the acceptances to roll in.
- ❏ Complete all applications for financial aid several weeks before the due dates.
- ❏ Review financial aid notices from the law schools and project your resources and costs.
- ❏ Decide which law school offer to accept.
- ❏ Send in acceptance of admission and financial aid.
- ❏ Complete your student loan applications.
- ❏ Review your finances at the start of the summer to be certain you'll have sufficient resources to meet your law school expenses.

The Following Fall

- ❏ Start the semester at the law school of your choice.
- ❏ Implement your financial management plan and review it periodically to make sure your financial plan is on track.

ADMISSIONS

LSAT/LSDAS Checklist

Use this checklist to track your progress in taking the LSAT and subscribing to LSDAS.

- ❑ Order/Receive *LSAT/LSDAS Registration and Information Book*.
- ❑ Subscribe to LSDAS by completing the registration form in the Information and Registration Booklet. (Parts A, C, and D apply to LSDAS).
- ❑ You can subscribe to LSDAS on the same form you use to register for the LSAT, although this is not required.
- ❑ Don't forget to sign the form and send payment!
- ❑ Request official academic transcripts from all undergraduate and graduate institutions that you've attended.
- ❑ Direct all transcripts to LSDAS.
- ❑ Order one set for yourself and review it. Make sure the information is correct.
- ❑ Receive LSDAS Subscription Confirmation.
- ❑ Receive Master Law School Report, summarizing your academic information. (The report is sent shortly after LSDAS receives your academic transcripts). Check the report carefully and report any inaccuracies to LSAC.
- ❑ Review monthly reports from LSDAS. If you find discrepancies, report them to LSDAS: (215) 968-1001
- ❑ If you've decided to apply to more schools than you originally planned, order extra reports from LSDAS and pay an additional fee.

CHAPTER 5

Inside the Admissions Office

The decision-making process in law school admissions varies from school to school. At some schools an admissions committee makes the majority of decisions. At others the dean of admissions is the chief decision maker, and at still others the power rests with individual admissions officers. But for the most part, schools rely on all three to play a role in the process. The best way to show you how this works is to take a typical application from a borderline candidate and demonstrate how it is likely to be treated, step by step.

Step 1: Creation of the File

When your application form arrives at the law school, a staffer will first create a file for you. The file will likely include a checklist of all the forms and information required for the file to be complete. As each piece arrives, it will be checked off the list.

Normally, a school will notify you if some important piece of your application is missing, but given the advantages of completing your application at the earliest possible date, you'll definitely want to make sure that the law schools receive everything they need in a timely fashion.

> **Keep Track**
>
> A school will usually notify you if some part of your application is missing—but do try not to forget anything. It's your responsibility to track your app.

> **By the Numbers**
>
> If you don't do a good job on your personal statement and your letters of recommendation, schools will rely on numbers: your GPA and LSAT score.

ADMISSIONS

> **What's Your Number?**
>
> Many students are obsessed with the index number and how it's derived at a particular school. The exact formula, however, isn't all that important. Most people know roughly how good their index numbers are—once they know how good their GPA and LSAT scores are.

Step 2: LSDAS Formalities

After creating your file, the law school will request your record from the Law School Data Assembly Service (LSDAS). The LSDAS organizes and categorizes a variety of statistical information on law school applicants on a standardized form, so that the data can be easily compared to that of other applicants. You'll already have registered with the LSDAS and provided them with the necessary information. They in turn will have put the information into a report, ready to send back to each law school you apply to. The report includes, among other things, your most recent and previous LSAT scores, copies of all college transcripts that you have provided them, an index number (which we'll discuss below), and a copy of your writing sample from the LSAT. The services of the LSDAS are not optional.

Once the LSDAS receives a request for information from the law school, they check to see that their file is complete and that all fees are paid. They will then send the law school a report on you. The report will include an index number. Although applicants are often curious about the index number, there is nothing very mysterious about it. It's simply an easy way for the school to combine an applicant's LSAT score and GPA into a single weighted number, in order to compare it with that of other applicants. Each law school can tell the LSDAS the formula they want to use to determine the index number, carefully specifying whether they want the GPA or the LSAT score to be more heavily weighted. Or the law school can just use the standard LSDAS formula, which weighs the two numbers equally.

A typical index-number formula multiplies the applicant's GPA by some constant, multiplies the LSAT score by a second constant, and then adds them together. This number is then added to a third constant. The formula looks like this:

$$(GPA \times A) + (LSAT \times B) + C = \text{Index Number}$$

Although the LSDAS sends you monthly updates on which schools they've sent your records to, they don't tell you what your index number is at these schools. However, they do send you a printed form that lists all formulas in use by the different schools. Thus, you can compute your own index number if you wish. Doing the math won't help you much, because law schools rarely tell you how high your index number needs to be for a competitive advantage.

Once the law school has your LSDAS report back, it waits until the rest of the file is complete and then sends you the self-addressed postcard, letting you know that the application is ready for consideration. See the LSDAS checklist at the end of chapter 4 to help you track these steps.

Step 3: Preliminary Screening

At most schools, an admissions officer will have a look at your numbers. One of three things will happen:

If the index number is above the automatic acceptance level, she will take a quick glance through the file to make sure you can write clearly and have good recommendations and, if so, will send out an acceptance letter.

If the index number is below the automatic rejection level, she will take a quick glance through the file to see if there is anything exceptional about your application and, if not, send out a rejection letter.

If the index number is within the acceptable range (i.e., either high enough for automatic admission nor low enough for summary rejection), the admissions officer will make notations on the file or perhaps even rank you in some manner before putting you in the borderline pool.

Because our hypothetical example places you as a borderline case at this school, the borderline pool is where your application would go. And if truth be told, that's where the majority of applications go. For most students, acceptance will not be "just a numbers game."

> ### Your App Will Move You
>
> Your law school application—beyond your GPA and LSAT scores—determines how you'll move between categories.

Step 4: Second Screening

The application will next receive a second reading by one of three sources: a senior admissions official, the dean of admission, or an admissions committee, which is usually made up of several professors. Not all files are read by every faculty member. If the admissions pool is really large, the faculty may be divided up into teams, which each read a certain number of applications. Third-year students may also participate in the admissions reading process. (They can be tougher to win over than the faculty.) Whoever receives the application for its second reading now faces some tough decisions. Because of a lack of space, many good applicants will have to be rejected. The second screening therefore consists almost entirely of narrowing the borderline candidates into an even smaller pool of applicants. This pool may be anywhere from 50 to 500 applicants that are so closely matched it is very hard to differentiate among them.

It's at this point that almost all schools turn these final decisions over to an admissions committee. If you were a borderline applicant in this final pool, every part of your application would be carefully scrutinized by anywhere from two to seven people, all of whom will be looking for a little edge or deficiency in the application upon which to base a decision.

> ### Details, Details
>
> At a certain point during the second screening, admissions officers will be looking for excuses not to accept you. That's why it's crucial that every detail of your application be exactly right.

ADMISSIONS

> ### Aid Yourself
>
> Apply for aid sooner rather than later. If you are on the waiting list, follow through on completing the forms that the school requires to apply for financial aid. The cost is very small, especially relative to the missed opportunity if you get admitted just before registration day and can't enroll because you don't have the money and the school won't permit you to enroll without either payment or a complete financial aid file. Don't give the excuse, "I didn't apply because I didn't think I'd get in." It doesn't wash.

Step 5: Decision

Based on the strength or weakness of the details of your application (a stellar recommendation, an inept or obnoxious personal statement, an LSAT writing sample that sings or falls flat), a decision is made. Suppose your hypothetical application—ever the borderline case—wasn't quite good enough to merit acceptance straight out, but you were strong enough to be considered desirable as a potential member of the class. In that case, the committee might decide to wait-list you.

Wait-listing is a kind of law school purgatory, the school's way of saying that they can't take you right now, but if they don't fill their class by August, they'll let you in just before school starts. The prestigious schools can get away with this because there are always students willing to wait it out in the hope of getting in. But a word of warning: Schools won't tell you how many other people are on the wait list, or how many from the wait list ultimately got in the previous year. Being put on a wait list may be better than an outright rejection, but don't put too much faith in your chances. The vast majority of students on a wait list never get in. But you never know. You could be the exception.

Law School Purgatory

If Elite University Law School puts you on their wait list, congratulations! That's an indication that they regarded you as a highly qualified candidate. But before you go out and buy an entire wardrobe of clothes emblazoned with the Elite U logo, remember this: Most wait-listed applicants are ultimately rejected.

> ### Puzzled?
>
> If you have a question about law school admissions procedures, feel free to give the school a call. Don't worry, the people in the admissions office won't hold your curiosity against you. They realize that you deserve to know how they pass judgment on you.

One other possibility should be mentioned: Some schools, particularly those with a large number of applicants, have trouble making decisions on early applicants. These schools want to get a better idea of what the entire pool of serious applicants will look like, so they create a "hold" category. A school will notify you that you are a serious candidate but that it's not yet able to make a decision on your application. They'll put your application on hold, therefore, until all applications have been received, and then will notify you of the decision shortly thereafter. This has the effect of thwarting your efforts to get in an early application, but at least you know you are being seriously considered.

Inside the Admissions Office

This chapter gave you a general picture of how the decision to accept or reject is made. Obviously the central decision-making procedure at any law school depends upon the personalities involved and the past success the school has had with the system. If you're curious about how a particular law school handles the decision-making process, don't be afraid to ask. Most schools are very open about their procedure and are willing to answer questions about it.

In the next chapter we'll give you specific strategies for handling law school application forms.

CHAPTER 6

Preparing the Application Form

After you've made the decision to apply to law school and have decided where and when to apply, your first move is to order the application forms from the various schools you've chosen. This can be done by sending a postcard to each school. But if you don't want to wait, you can call the admissions offices in late June and be put on their mailing lists. You can also browse through the online offerings of many law schools by using the Internet.

However you obtain your applications, once they begin arriving you'll notice that no two are exactly alike. Some require one recommendation, others two or three. Some ask you to write one essay or personal statement, while others may ask for two or even three. Some have very detailed forms requiring extensive background information; others are satisfied with your name and address and very little else.

> **Online Info**
>
> If you have Internet access, you can connect to law school homepages via the World Wide Web. Many law schools have detailed information about their schools on the Internet, and many can facilitate your application info request online. See the Law Schools section at the back of the book for URL's for many schools.

Despite these differences, most applications follow a general pattern with variations on the same kinds of questions. So read this chapter with the understanding that, although not all of it is relevant to all parts of every application, these guidelines will be valuable for just about any law school application you'll encounter.

ADMISSIONS

> **Like Snowflakes**
>
> No two law school applications are exactly alike, but most ask for the same kind of information and look for the same qualities in the applicant. You won't be writing ten different applications so much as ten variations on a single application form.

> **Theme It**
>
> Start thinking early about what theme you want your application to convey. Decide what your real purpose is in applying to law school, and make sure that this sense of purpose comes through in all aspects of your application.

> **Take Control**
>
> You control the way in which you are perceived by the admissions committees—through your application. Don't miss this opportunity to make yourself seem desirable as a law student.

The Application as Marketing Tool

Probably the most important thing to keep in mind about your law school application is that it is, above all else, a sales pitch. The application is your single best opportunity to sell yourself—to convince a group of strangers that it would be a huge mistake if you were not in their school's first-year class next fall. Remember, every person who applies will have strengths and weaknesses. It's how you present those strengths and weaknesses that count. You are in control of what that admissions committee sees on your application and how they see it. Always keep in mind that you are, in effect, selling yourself to them.

So what's the best way to sell yourself? We all know that some people are natural-born sellers in person, but the application process is written, not spoken. The key here is not natural talent but rather organization—carefully planning a coherent presentation from beginning to end and paying attention to every detail in between. Ask any public-relations specialist and they'll tell you that to sell a celebrity or a politician successfully, it takes a carefully orchestrated campaign that concentrates on detail while at the same time conveying an overall theme.

But be careful not to focus so much on the overall theme that you neglect the details. Let's draw an analogy from the world of U.S. politics. During presidential elections, both major parties go to great lengths to choreograph every moment of their conventions to make sure that their candidate comes across in the best possible light. No detail is too small, because the experts realize that the convention is the only part of the campaign in which they have complete control over what is seen and heard. The clothes must be right, signs the exact color, backdrops perfect, and even the balloons must fall at precisely the right moment.

The law school application is your political convention. It's the one part of the admissions process over which you have complete control. Many of the individual things discussed below may seem like small points, but lots of small points together add up to a complete package. It is this package that you're selling.

Preparing the Application Form

Getting Organized

The first step in organizing your campaign for admission is to put together a checklist of the forms that each of your chosen schools requires, double-checking to make sure you don't overlook anything. Some schools may require you to fill out residency forms or financial aid forms in addition to the regular application forms. Don't ignore these and put them off until last. Often the schools may require proof of residency or income verifications that might not be readily available.

The next step is to make photocopies of all forms to be filled out unless you use the application software option. (If you're applying using law school application software, the cumbersome photocopying step can be eliminated.) Admittedly, this is time-consuming, but the photocopies are what you'll work on. Changes and corrections will have to be made no matter how careful you are. These changes should not be made on the original form, which will go to the school. Neatness is a big factor for both admissions and financial aid applications. The feeling is that if the application is sloppily prepared, the student is not very serious about attending that law school. Make photocopies for every form and write on the copies until you are sure you are ready to transfer items to the original application.

Once you've gotten yourself organized, you're ready to start your campaign for real. Most applications provide you with many opportunities to show yourself in a good light. Let's see how you can do so starting with the application form itself. (In the next two chapters we'll discuss the other two main parts of your application, the personal statement and recommendations.)

The Application Form

For the most part, filling out the application form requires simply putting down factual information. But even in something so apparently mindless, you can still make sure you present yourself as a thorough, organized person who can follow directions. The key to filling out the application form can be summed up in a single sentence: Don't make the admission officers do more work than they have to. Make sure that they have all of the information they need at their fingertips. If they have to hunt up your statistics, if your application is full of unexplained blanks, if they can't read what you've written—all of these things will just serve to annoy the very people you want to impress.

Neatness Counts

A sloppy application says more about you than you may think. Law schools want people who display organization and care in all of their endeavors. So put in the extra time to make sure your application is neat and typo free.

Don't Annoy

Admissions officers are human beings. They're overworked. They've got piles of applications on their desks. Many of them will be looking for any little excuse to reject yours and get on to the next one. Don't give them that excuse. Make sure that nothing about your application is annoying to them.

ADMISSIONS

Pitfalls to Avoid

One key to not annoying the admissions people is to make sure you answer all of the questions asked on the application form. If some questions don't seem to apply to you, type in "not applicable"; never leave the question blank. If the admissions officers see blank spaces, they don't know whether you found the question not applicable, just didn't want to answer it, or overlooked it. Many schools will return the application if even a single question is left blank. This can be a real problem, because it may be a month or more before the application is looked at and returned and then filled in and looked at again. That kind of delay can easily turn an early application into a late one.

Along these same lines, don't answer questions by saying "see above" or "see line 22." Most applications will ask you for things like your address or phone number more than once. Go ahead and fill them in again. Remember that law schools are flooded with documentation and may separate parts of the application. They don't appreciate having to find what you wrote on line 22 if they've asked you for that information again on line 55. Again, keeping admissions officers happy is a big part of your job.

> **Follow Directions**
>
> Admissions officers are amazed at how many applicants simply refuse to follow directions. Don't think that you're an exception to any rules. If the application asks for X, give them X, not Y!

As long as we're talking about practices that annoy the decision makers, another one that officers refer to frequently is the failure to follow directions on the forms. If the form says, "Don't write below this line," then don't write below the line. You are not an exception to this rule. If they ask for an explanation in 150 words or fewer, then don't give them 300. One admissions officer told me that the comment, "He couldn't even follow directions," is heard several times a year in committee meetings.

Addendums

An important part of the application form will not be in the package sent from the law school. These are your addendums. Addendums (or addenda, if you want to be fancy) are the additional page or pages that you staple onto the forms when the space they give you to answer a question is too small. For example, the application may ask you to list awards or honors received in college and then give you four lines to do so. This is a problem if you've received more than four and you need to explain one or two of them.

This is where an addendum comes in. Simply write "continued on addendum" on the application form after you've used their space up, and then clearly mark at the top of the addendum what you are listing. Staple this addendum on the back, and you've solved a tricky problem. Law schools appreciate addendums because they're much neater than attempts to cram things into a limited space—and they show careful organization. But don't overdo it. One or two addendums should be sufficient for any application. More than that is overkill. Once again, don't do anything that might annoy admissions officers.

Preparing the Application Form

What should addendums be used for? Primarily, they should be used to preserve neatness when the application blanks are of insufficient length. But they can also be helpful if an answer requires further explanation. For example, if you were the recipient of the Evergreen House Scholarship, it's not enough just to list it. You need to explain what it is, what it's given for, and possibly how many others were competing for it or how prestigious it is. Another example would be a job you've mentioned on the form that is not self-explanatory. (You were lead ride manager at Outdoor Adventure every summer during college?) In short, any answer you've given on the application that may need explaining—or for which a more detailed answer will enhance your application—is acceptable. This kind of elaboration is simply another way of selling yourself.

> **Early Bird**
>
> A few law schools now encourage applicants to submit their applications early—by October 1, usually, and promise to respond around Thanksgiving. Some schools offering this option are Columbia, NYU, Boston College, and Georgetown.

Addendums are discussed in more detail in chapter 9, Completing your Application.

Honesty

One final topic about the application form that needs to be discussed is honesty. If you think you can get by with a lie or two on your application—well, you may be right. Law schools as a rule don't have the resources to verify all aspects of every application. But before you go overboard and decide to put down that you were once the Prince of Wales, you should realize that are taking a big chance.

Many schools are beginning to devote more time to checking up on applicants' claims. The Law School Admission Council (LSAC) devotes a large amount of time to following up on misconduct or irregularities in the law school admissions process. Types of misconduct, as described by LSAC, include obvious no-nos like falsifying an academic transcript or recommendation or submitting false or misleading statements. The LSAC method of investigating a charge of misrepresentation is to forward the case to a panel gathered for this purpose. If the panel determines that there is significant evidence of misconduct, a report with this information is forwarded to all the schools to which the applicant has applied, or subsequently applies to. The record is maintained for an indefinite period of time. The individual law schools decide how to respond to this information, in accordance with the law schools' own procedures for matters of this type. It may result in recision of admission or other penalties. Don't get yourself into this sort of mess!

Even if you fool the law school, get in, and graduate with honors, you'll find that any state in which you apply to take the bar exam will do a much more extensive background check than that done by the law school; this check very well might include looking for contradictions in your law school application. Lying on a law school application, in fact, is considered grounds for refusing admittance to a state bar.

ADMISSIONS

> **Prioritize**
>
> Always list your most significant scholastic accomplishments before other honors or awards.

These reasons should point out the danger of being dishonest on your application. What about the moral implications of lying on your application? If you're going to cheat your way into law school in the first place, you'll probably give in to stronger temptations down the line when you become a lawyer. Don't put yourself through three years of law school, thousands of dollars of debt, and the pressures of taking the bar exam only to find yourself disbarred. No law school is worth that.

Additional Application Tips

Here are a few more things to take note of when filling out the application form:

1. Be Sure to Type the Application from Start to Finish.

A surprising number of applicants still handwrite the application. This is something that could cost you dearly.

2. Don't Use Application Forms from Previous Years.

Most applications change from year to year, often substantially. Also, don't use another school's forms because you lost the form of the school you're applying. (Yes, people have done it, believe it or not).

3. No Cross Outs or XXXs.

You're applying for admission to a professional school, not for a summer job at the local swimming pool. When you're an attorney, you won't submit a brief with words crossed out.

4. Staple Extra Sheets to the Forms.

Do not use paper clips unless you are told to do so. Paper clips—and the pages they attach—tend to get lost in the shuffle.

5. Always Double- and Triple-Check Your Application for Spelling Errors.

You lose a certain amount of credibility if you write that you were a "cum lade graduate."

6. Check for Accidental Contradictions.

Make sure that your application doesn't say you worked for a law firm in 1993 when your financial aid forms say you were driving a cab that year.

Preparing the Application Form

7. Prioritize All Lists.
When a question asks you to list your honors or awards, don't begin with fraternity social chairman and end with Phi Beta Kappa. Always list your significant scholastic accomplishments first.

8. Don't Overdo Extracurricular Activities.
Don't list every event or every activity you ever participated in. Select the most significant and, if necessary, explain them. Admissions officers become suspicious of people who list 25 extracurricular activities and yet still manage to attend college. Remember that no amount of extracurricular activities will make up for a GPA that is significantly below the average for students entering a particular law school.

9. Don't Mention High School Activities or Honors.
Unless there's something very unusual or spectacular about your high school background, don't mention it. Yes, this means not taking note of the fact that you were senior class president.

10. Clear Up Any Ambiguities.
On questions concerning employment, for instance, make sure to specify whether you held a job during the school year or only during the summer. Many applications ask about this, and it may be an important point to the admissions officer.

The "Self-Completing" Application
No, this isn't a form that fills itself out; it's an application procedure used by some law schools. "Self-completing" means that various parts of the application are returned to the applicant, who mails all the materials together in the same envelope. The advantage of the self-completing format is that the candidate knows when his application form and recommendations are complete. For some schools, this is an option; for other schools, it's a requirement. When the self-completing format is used, recommendations are returned to the applicant in a sealed envelope (the recommender has signed the back of the envelope so that any alteration of it will quickly be noted). That's all there is to it.

Be Compulsive!

When juggling several law school applications at once, it's easy to make careless mistakes. Double-check yourself at every step.

Applications on CD

Law Services now offers LSA*CD*, a CD-ROM that includes applications for all ABA-approved law schools. Call (215) 968-1001 to order by phone or you can order online through lsacinfo@lsac.org. The cost is $49.95. Note that you should still contact the law schools directly for admissions information including recommendation forms.

CHAPTER 7

The Personal Statement

There are about as many theories on what constitutes a winning personal statement as there are viewpoints of the O.J. Simpson trial—and, unfortunately, many of them have about the same validity. To begin with, how can you tell 85,000 annual applicants with 85,000 different personalities and backgrounds that there is one correct way to write a personal statement? You can't. Even if a small percentage of those applicants read and come to believe that a certain way is the correct way, it automatically becomes incorrect, because law schools despise getting personal statements that sound all too familiar—that are, in other words, impersonal.

In this chapter, we'll look at the procedure of putting together a personal statement. Then we'll look at a list of DOs and DON'Ts that admission officers most frequently mention. Then we'll show you some sample personal statements. But keep one thing in mind. Because this is a personal statement, it cannot be modeled on something you see in a book. This section provides guidelines to follow, but the essay itself has to come from the individual.

**Pressed for Time?
Have Questions?**

Kaplan Admissions Consulting provides personal, one-to-one admissions advice. We help you:

- Select appropriate schools and programs
- Develop polished applications
- Brainstorm and create winning essays
- Master the art of interviewing
- Deal with special circumstances

For more information about Admissions Consulting, call 1-800-KAP-TEST or e-mail us at admissions@kaplan.com.

ADMISSIONS

> **Primary Purpose**
>
> The personal statement is where you can best establish a theme for your entire application. A theme also will help keep your statement focused.

Next to your LSAT score and GPA, the personal statement is probably the most important part of your application. If your numbers are excellent or very poor it may get only a cursory glance. But if your numbers place you on the borderline at a school, then the essay may very well make the difference between acceptance and rejection. Personal statements are especially important at the top schools, because the number of qualified candidates makes it harder to choose. So many of the applicants to top schools have impressive GPAs and LSAT scores that admissions officers have to look at other factors, particularly the personal statement.

Essay Types

The personal statement is exactly what its name implies—a statement by you that is meant to show something about your personality and character. But don't be confused by this. It's not meant to be a lengthy essay detailing every aspect of your life since birth, and it's not intended to be a psychological profile describing all of your character attributes and flaws. Law school admissions officers can learn a lot about a person's character and personality from a simple story or even from the tone of the essay. In some instances the best essays are often only remotely related to the applicant. The personal statement may just be an essay concerning a book the applicant recently read, or something she observed on television. The point is that you need not write an in-depth personality profile baring your innermost soul. Admissions officers are adept at learning what they want to know about you from your essay, even if it doesn't contain the words "me," "myself," and "I" in every sentence.

One exception, however, should be noted. Although most schools still provide wide latitude in their directions about what the personal statement should be about, some schools are becoming more specific. For example, some schools now ask that you write about a specific achievement that you feel has been of personal significance to you; others ask you to describe any unique qualities you have that relate to your aptitude to study law. The problem with specific requirements like these is that you may well have to write a separate essay for that school alone. Be sure to check the instructions carefully and follow them closely. If a law school asks for a specific type of essay and you provide them with a more general one, they'll likely feel that you're not very interested in attending their school.

> **Give It Time**
>
> Start drafting your personal statement now, so that you'll be able to put it aside for a few weeks or even months. You'll be amazed at how different it will look when you go back to it.

But take heart. Most schools provide few restrictions on what you can write about, so unless you're very unlucky, you should be able to limit the number of essays you must write to two or three.

Essay Length

How long should the personal statement be? Some schools place a word limit on the essay; others specify one or two typed pages. Always follow the specific directions, but you should be in good shape with virtually all schools if your essay is one and a half to two pages in length. Any shorter than this makes it more difficult for the reader to evaluate your personality. Any longer and your reader may go from interested to bored by the end. Obviously, an essay that runs a little longer than two pages is okay. But beware the three-, four-, or five-page essay. Unless your experiences and/or style justify the extra length, you may find yourself dismissed as long-winded and boring. Better to keep your essay to around two pages.

> **Line 'Em Up**
>
> Try to line up as many people as possible to read and comment on your personal statement. But don't be swayed by everything that every person says. Listen to all comments, but only take them to heart if you really think they're valid.

Essay Writing

The personal statement shouldn't be done overnight. Quite the contrary: A strong personal statement may take shape over the course of months and require several different drafts. One practice that we've found particularly effective is to write a draft and then let it sit for four to six weeks. Time adds an interesting perspective on something you've written. If you leave it alone for a significant period of time, you may find (to your astonishment) that your first instincts were good ones; on the other hand, you may shudder at how you could ever have considered submitting such a piece of garbage. Either way, time lends a valuable perspective.

Try to start the essay sometime during the summer before you apply. Allow at least three months to write it, and don't be afraid to take it through numerous drafts or overhaul it completely if you're not satisfied. Get several different perspectives. Ask close friends or relatives to scrutinize it to see if it really captures what you want to convey. Be sure to ask them about their initial reaction as well as their feelings after studying it more carefully. Once you've achieved a draft that you feel comfortable with, try to have it read by some people who barely know you or who don't know you at all. Such people may include prelaw advisors at your school, professors not familiar with your work, friends of friends, or even professional services who charge a fee for reading and advising on essays. Strangers or semistrangers often provide interesting perspectives on your work. Since they haven't heard the story before and don't know the characters, they're often better able to tell you when something is missing or confusing.

Bottom line: Let a reasonable number of people read the essay and make suggestions. If certain criticisms are consistently made, then they're probably legitimate. But don't be carried away by every suggestion every reader makes. Stick to your basic instincts because, after all, this is your personal statement, no one else's.

ADMISSIONS

Proofreading is of critical importance. Again, don't be afraid to enlist the aid of others. If possible, let an English teacher review the essay solely for word choice and grammar mistakes. Law schools receive numerous complaints from practicing attorneys about law students who don't possess even basic English skills and writing ability. As a result, the schools are keeping a close eye on writing basics. And every time you revise your essay, be certain you use the spell check feature on your word processor.

Brainstorming Exercises

Deciding what to write about for a personal statement can be as difficult as actually writing it! Here are some tips for beginning this important process.

If you're having a difficult time deciding on a topic, think of stories first.

Most people have stories about themselves that they repeat to more than one person. Granted, many of these aren't appropriate personal statement material—but if you keep guidelines in mind, you may find an appropriate anecdote that ties into what you want to say. Asking friends and family for suggestions may also help.

Try focused freewriting.

Freewriting is a technique often used by writers to get at what might evade them in a more polished draft. In freewriting, you set a time (say, 15 minutes) and a topic (maybe, why you decided to go through the madness-inducing law school admissions process). When the clock starts ticking, you begin writing whatever comes into your head.

The following topics are good places to start for focused freewriting. Do even more of it, if you can. Freewriting turns off the "mental editor" and allows you to get at different ideas and directions in an indirect, and perhaps more creative, way.

1. What are your three most significant accomplishment, and why does each one make this list?

2. Jot down two funny stories—preferably self-deprecating ones—that happened to you during the last five years.

3. You are going on a cross-country automobile trip and your radio is broken. With the prospect of endless stretches of lonely highway ahead of you, name three traveling companions—real or fictional—you'd want to take along, and explain why you chose them.

4. List one significant event that has had a dramatic impact on your thinking and describe that impact.

5. What makes you unique? Write at least 100 words.

6. What are two things about which you feel strongly—that get you motivated or fired up?

7. Name one major failure you have had, or mistake you have made, and describe what you learned from it. (If you can give two examples, do so.)

8. You are 80 years old, looking back on your life. In what ways do you consider yourself to have been a success?

9. If you had college to do over again, what would you do differently, and why?

10. Where do you see yourself five years from now?

11. Where do you see yourself ten years from now?

12. Choose one law school in which you are interested, and write down at least two detailed and specific reasons for your interest.

Keep in mind that brainstorming is best done over time. Put away your responses to the brainstorming exercises for a day or two. Then reread them, and write whatever comes to mind as a result.

> **I've Always Dreamed . . .**
>
> . . . . of becoming a lawyer. The first impulse of most people when writing the personal statement is to talk about their reasons for wanting to go to law school. That's a good reason why you shouldn't. Admissions officers read a hundred such essays a day. So, unless the application specifically asks for that topic, you should consider writing about something else.

Making Essay Content Great

We now move to the content of the personal statement. As stated earlier, there's no one correct way to write an essay, but admissions officers do provide some helpful tips about what they like and don't like to see in a personal statement. Let's begin with a list of the things that officers most often mentioned they disliked seeing.

Essay DON'Ts

Avoid the Résumé Approach

This is the personal statement that begins at birth and simply recites every major (and sometimes minor) event of the person's life. Most of this information is repetitive since it's included on other parts of the application. But worse than that, it probably doesn't answer the question being posed. Bland list making is a common mistake made by applicants in their personal statements, and typically results in a very cursory read by the admissions officer. Unless your numbers are outstanding for a particular school, don't use this approach.

ADMISSIONS

Avoid the "Why I Want To Go to Law School" Essay
Although this can be a part of any law school essay, too many people make it the entire focus of their statement. The problem is that there are not many new variations on this theme, and the admissions officers have likely heard them all before, probably many times. You really don't need to convince them of your earnest desire to go to law school. What person in their right mind would go through this hassle if they didn't really want to go?

Avoid the "I Want to Save the World" Essay
Most applicants feel that they can accomplish some good by getting a law degree; very few are strictly mercenary. Admissions officers understand this and don't need to be convinced of your good intentions. Furthermore, overly idealistic essays can be very damaging if your record shows no previous commitment to public service. This kind of discrepancy can make the essay seem insincere. This doesn't mean, however, that if you do have a genuine, specific public-service goal in mind—and you've shown interest in it before law school—that you shouldn't discuss it and why it is important to you. Just remember that you're playing to a fairly skeptical audience.

Avoid Talking About Your Negatives
In a later chapter, you'll learn to handle potential negatives by the use of addendums. The personal statement is not the place to call attention to your flaws. Don't forget that you're selling yourself, and the personal statement is your most prominent sales tool.

Don't Be Too Personal
Stories of abuse or trauma are often very moving and can be particularly effective if tied into a person's reason for wanting to practice law. Several admissions officers, however, have noted a trend toward describing such problems in graphic detail in personal statements. This kind of confessional essay can easily cross the line and become too personal. If you do decide to go this route, just remember that graphic details are not important; what's important is to show how the trauma affected you and your future plans.

> **Not Another Albert Schweitzer!**
>
> Admissions officers hear about a lot of noble intentions in personal statements. Naturally, they're skeptical of such claims, especially if the rest of your application demonstrates no such selfless impulse. So be careful with protestations of high ideals. If you can't back them up with hard evidence, they're bound to come off sounding empty and insincere.

> **Save It for Geraldo**
>
> Confessional essays can easily cross the line and become too personal. Use this personal statement approach with caution.

Watch the Use of Fancy Vocabulary

Don't try to impress the law school with your command of the English language. First of all, the trend in law these days is toward simpler, more easily understood language, with less "legalese." Moreover, misusing a 20-dollar word can be very embarrassing and costly.

> **Eschew Lexical Profligacy**
>
> Don't try to impress your reader with lots of difficult words. It won't work. Take our word for it.

Don't Discuss Legal Concepts

Along those same lines, don't try to engage the reader in a deep legal discussion to show how much you already know about the law. The school assumes that they can teach you what you need to know, regardless of what level at which you start. By discussing a legal concept, you also run the risk of showing a certain amount of ignorance about the subject, while at the same time appearing arrogant enough to have tried to discuss it.

Avoid Immature Subjects

Most applicants are at least in their early twenties and should be mature adults. Therefore, a story discussing how drunk you got last summer, or the time you went to the local strip joint, is not appropriate. Law school officials are certainly aware of youthful excesses, but they're not particularly impressed if you consider yours important enough to discuss in your essay.

Don't Put Down Lawyers or the Legal Profession

Although it may seem that spewing cynicism about the legal profession is a clever device, trust us when we tell you that it isn't! The legal profession's attitude toward its members is similar to that of the fraternity member in the movie Animal House who, after seeing one of their pledges disgraced, said, "Nobody can do that to our pledges. Only we can do that to our pledges." Once you become a member of the legal profession, you can make as many lawyer jokes as you want. Until then, watch your step.

> **No Laughing Matter!**
>
> You may think it'll come across as refreshing when you put down lawyers and the law profession in your personal statement. It won't. Your reader won't be amused.

Shy Away from the Bizarre

It's true that law schools claim to value creativity, but some applicants confuse being creative with being outlandish. Shock value doesn't work. Although you do want to stand out from the crowd, imitating David Lynch is not the way to do it.

ADMISSIONS

Don't Try to Cover Too Many Subjects

Focus on one or two areas you really want to talk about. One of the worse mistakes applicants make is that their essays ramble from one subject to another and back again. Fight the desire to talk about every highlight of your life.

Now that you've got a sense of what not to do in your personal statement, let's turn to a list of suggestions for things that you should do.

Essay DOs

Tell Stories

Readers respond much better to a concrete story or illustrative anecdote than to an abstract list of your attributes. Instead of just writing how determined you are, for instance, tell a story that demonstrates it. Courtroom attorneys always emphasize the importance of creating a story for the jury rather than just relating the facts. Why? Because stories stick in people's memories. The same holds true when you're trying to make sure the admissions officers remember you.

Winning Essay Excerpt

> *Competitive gymnastics training grew harder and harder as I became older. When I was sixteen years old I tore the rotator cuff in my left shoulder. Due to my age, my doctors did not want to operate. Instead, I went to physical therapy four times a week for five months. One year later, I fractured a vertebra and stopped training for several months due to intense pain. After each setback, I returned to the gym with a burning desire to compete and to qualify for the Junior National Championships. I never gave up . . . .*

Make it Interesting

Before you decide what to write about, try to picture yourself as an admissions officer who reads hundreds—perhaps thousands—of essays in a six-month period. In the middle of the afternoon, having already read ten essays on how the applicant has wanted to be a lawyer since the age of four, imagine how great it is to come across an essay that grabs your interest for a few minutes. In moments of candor, admissions officers admit that these essays are few and far between, but are very welcome when they do appear. As mentioned earlier, many of the most interesting essays are only peripherally about the applicant; instead they may talk about a book or some current event or even some funny story the applicant heard. This is one reason it's so important to let others read your essay. Get an honest opinion from them on whether or not the essay truly interested them and held their attention.

Winning Essay Excerpt

> *While sitting outside my apartment complex waiting for my father to arrive, I was asked if I had a green card. The police officer questioned me, a 14-year-old Puerto Rican, about my immigration status and my involvement, if any, in a prior night's criminal activity. Incidents such as these have increased my desire to learn the law and use my knowledge to benefit my community . . . .*

Be Funny—If You Can Pull It Off

Humor, particularly self-deprecating humor, is a very effective device. Law applicants tend to be life-and-death serious, so admissions officers appreciate occasional flashes of irony. However, be careful in your use of humor. Check with others to make sure that any attempted humor works. Don't overdo it: A couple of funny lines or a funny story can be great, but include too many jokes and you start to sound flippant. Finally, think about using self-deprecating humor. Law schools often complain about the lack of humility among students and appreciate those who show some.

Winning Essay Excerpt

> *I went to my local bookstore the other day and noticed that Black's Law Dictionary was shelved next to Teach Yourself Sanskrit! The possibility that this placement was deliberate has not deterred me from wanting to study law . . . .*

Be "Unique"

The term *unique* has been overused. Even some applications now ask you to describe what is "unique" about you. Applicants rack their brains trying to figure out how they're different from the other 5,000 people applying to that law school. Or worse, some interpret unique to mean "disadvantaged," and rack their brains trying to think how they have suffered more than others. But what the admissions officers want to know is what qualities or experiences in your life would make you a particularly valuable member of a law school class. A major part of the learning process in law

She's So Unusual

Admissions officers try to assemble a law school class that includes a rich variety of perspectives. Let them know what you could contribute to the diverse intellectual atmosphere they're trying to achieve.

ADMISSIONS

school is interacting with your classmates. Let them know what you would bring to that class, i.e., what interesting perspectives and strengths, not necessarily what makes you different.

Winning Essay Excerpt

> *While I sought the advice of professional counsel for this acquisition, I also enjoyed doing my own due diligence in an effort to minimize costs and further educate myself on how businesses are bought and sold. I researched tax implications as a result of the possible transfer of ownership to an outside third party and the necessity of competition restrictions. In the course of my business experience, I have greatly improved my mediation ability and learned to listen to others before addressing their concerns.*

Start with a Great Lead

In private moments, admissions officers will often admit that they don't read every essay carefully. They may just glance at an essay to get a general impression. That's why it's important to grab them from the beginning. Let them see that this is not the run-of-the-mill personal statement. Start with a joke or story. Tell the ending of a story first and make them want to read on, to see how it all started. Begin with an interesting question that they'll want to see your answer to. Remember that your essay should not be more than one and a half to two pages and won't take them more than a few minutes to read. Make them want to take the time to read it carefully by grabbing them from the beginning.

Have a General Theme

The main point here is not to ramble. A general theme helps avoid that kind of drift, and also creates at least the appearance of a well-organized essay. A theme can also give you a good way to begin and end the essay. Don't feel that you have to stick rigidly to your theme in every paragraph, but instead use it as a kind of organizing idea for your essay.

Don't Be Afraid to Express Opinions

Applicants tend to shy away from stating political views or opinions. They worry that the reader will hold the opposite view and reject them automatically. But the opposite is usually true. Law schools are looking for people with a lot of different ideas, from all parts of the political spectrum, in order to create an exciting intellectual atmosphere. Don't be afraid to express your views. But, again, don't overdo it; you don't want to offend anyone.

Tailor Your Statement to a Particular Law School

If you're especially interested in a law school because they offer a particular program or professor, be sure to talk about that in your personal statement. Let the admissions officers know that their school is number one on your list, and make sure you explain why. Schools will appreciate that you took the time to research their strengths or specialties. This kind of specific enthusiasm also lets them know that you'll probably accept any offer of admission they may care to extend you.

Winning Essay Excerpt

> *Given my interest in international law, I am particularly excited about the prospect of attending Dickinson and participating in one of your many summer abroad programs.*

Open Up a Little

No, you don't have to bare your soul to these strangers, but don't be afraid to let them know a little about yourself. A bit of emotion or excitement or even embarrassment is not bad for them to see. Granted, two pages isn't a lot of space to show your innermost feelings, but neither should you completely hold back for fear of appearing wimpy.

Winning Essay Excerpt

> *Last year, I spent a semester studying abroad in Paris, France. While I had traveled away from home before, that was the first time that I felt the full burden of responsibility for my life and for my actions. Handling my problems no longer involved just a short drive up Interstate 95 from Washington, D.C. to my parents' home in New Jersey. When I arrived in Paris, I became acutely aware of how out of place I was, and realized that I had no one to turn to except myself....*

Sample Personal Statements Reviewed by Experts

The following sample personal statements were actually submitted by real law school applicants. Each sample statement is followed by feedback from admissions officials from the University of Texas Law School and Georgetown Law Center. Looking at sample statements and the accompanying critiques will give you a sense of what worked and what didn't work for other students. This might help you make some decisions about your own work. But keep in mind that the personal statement that will work best for you is the one that is uniquely your own.

> **Be Personal**
>
> These samples will give you an idea of what an effective personal statement is like. But your personal statement has to come from *you*.

ADMISSIONS

Sample Statement A

George behind the counter thinks I'm nuts. In a booth in the back of the diner, I sit from 5:30 A.M. until the library opens at 9:00 A.M., typing away on my laptop and drinking coffee, black. This is not the first time I've sat in this particular booth, and every time I do, George pours the refills and asks me the same question: "What are you doing awake at this hour?"

The reason is simple. When the opportunity to participate in the betterment of the public interest presents itself to me, I invariably give my all without reservation. Perhaps this is what you get when you combine the altruism of my mother (an art teacher and unapologetic liberal) with the drive of my father (a Naval Academy graduate and straight commission salesman). I find that when working or teaching in the pursuit of the public interest, the only thing which exceeds my devotion is my endurance.

After graduating college with a degree in psychology, I found myself employed at a local mental health center. My duties included managing a caseload of 10–15 patients, each diagnosed with a major mental illness. One particular case involved a 43 year old who, affected by schizophrenia, had ordered 25 subscriptions from various magazines and $500 worth of food from The Swiss Colony. She was unable to pay these (and other) debts, and her meager income from disability would never provide her with the means to do so. For weeks, I spent every morning at the diner, writing letters to her various debtors. I tried to explain that their repeated and unrealistic demands for payment were only exacerbating her already extreme paranoia. After several months, I was referred by a colleague to the Mental Health Law Project, a nonprofit group of lawyers who devote themselves to protecting the interests of the mentally ill in New Jersey. An attorney from the group was able to accomplish more in 15 minutes than I had with my weeks of worry and dozens of letters. This experience planted a seed in my mind. A seed which sprouted the application you are now examining.

I now believe there are two places in this society where one can effectively enact lasting social change: the classroom and the courtroom. One year ago, I set my sights on beginning a relationship with both. Toward that end, I set three goals for myself. The first was to use my speaking and writing skills as an advocate for the public interest. Within the past year, I have served on the faculty of New York University and Ramapo College, have been published in Et Cetera: The Journal of General Semantics, and have debated one of my research interests on the national PBS program "World.Com." My second goal was to pursue further insight through my own graduate education at New York University. In addition to maintaining a GPA of 3.97, I was selected as research assistant by internationally renowned author Dr. *** for his newest book. My third and final goal is to bring the success I have found in an academic research setting to the courtroom, where theory combines with action to serve the public interest and render lasting social change.

Thus, you are holding in your hand my application to *** University School of Law. You are clearly a school dedicated to producing the finest in public interest lawyers, a dedication embodied in your *** Center. From my volunteer work with the terminally ill, to my work at the mental health center, I have been at my best when pursuing the public interest. I am confident that my dedication to public service, combined with the outstanding experience of a *** legal education, will arm me with the resources to make a positive social impact through the American judicial system.

In the past, I've tried to explain to George why I've been awake at 5:30 A.M. in the back of his diner. Perhaps even he will understand the importance of the answer which I now ask you to provide.

"I'm studying law at ***."

Critiques of Sample Statement A

Admissions Official #1

Many applicants have adopted the method of opening with an anecdote and returning to it to wrap up the statement. This applicant uses the diner anecdote effectively, but not exceptionally.

Essay A, without the context of the entire application, would reveal someone committed to public service—a dedicated individual. However, the reviewer will likely seek out additional evidence that applicant A's commitment to service is truly unique from that of other applicants. In some applications, that evidence will be found in a resume or list of public service/community activities; in others, it may be found in letters of recommendation or additional statements. Since the goal of this essay is to persuade the law school that the applicant is unique because of his commitment to public service, the reader will want to determine if the claim is truly valid. The fact that he is employed by a mental health center and that he works so many extra hours to help his patients is strong evidence that his commitment is real.

> **An Important Note**
>
> It is important to mention at the outset that different law schools may prefer different kinds of personal statements. Thus, my opinions may not express the views of other schools to which you are applying. Please read each institution's information carefully to determine what would be most persuasive for each application. It is likely that you will need to create more than one version of your personal statement.
>
> —Admissions Official #1

This essay unnecessarily spends the first paragraph of the second page covering information that the reader will see in other parts of the application—the résumé and transcripts. Such a waste of limited space should be avoided.

This applicant's essay provides strong evidence of public service and, when looked at in combination with the other pieces of the application, might present a compelling argument that public interest law will remain his focus. Most applicants should not express plans to practice in a particular area of the law, because those plans so often change. Law schools are more interested in learning about the experiences have made you the person that you are today. Applicants should also avoid the temptation to express

ADMISSIONS

the desire to become a lawyer so that they can "change the world." Applicant A is reasonable in his goals: using the system to make "positive social impact."

I'd like to make an important point here. The personal statement for law school is not the time for applicants to take literary license. Sentence structure, punctuation, and spelling must be flawless. Eyes that have not read a particular statement before will catch every error. Those errors can be distracting to the reader and costly to one's quest for admission.

Admissions Official #2

Really nice beginning. We read thousands of personal statements and it's really nice to be drawn into a story that opens with a different character than the applicant, and hear a different voice from the applicant's. Within the first two paragraphs, I already have a sense of the applicant's theme, his goals, and his family background. Well done.

The anecdote about the patient is effective, although the seed metaphor stretches a little. Don't try too hard when writing a personal statement: Err on the side of understatement. The transition to the applicant's credentials is smooth. One small point: There is no need to get into specifics on your GPA. For one thing, I can find that information elsewhere. For another, it sounds unnecessarily defensive. This applicant does a good job in referring to the individual law school. If you are able to make your statement school-specific without seeming forced, go for it. Believe it or not, even we admissions officers love to be loved.

Nice finish. The applicant has managed to let me know him better by being himself and using language that is informal, conversational, and most importantly genuine. In addition, the applicant has made his involvement in public interest seem real by talking about a specific experience and not being heavy handed about saving the world. Really good job—this applicant has definitely helped himself.

Five Ways to Help Your Cause

Admissions Official #2 gives these tips for writing an effective personal statement.

1. Try very hard to be the writer and reader at the same time. Imagine that you're sitting in an admissions officer's chair, charged with reading thousands of these, and then evaluate your work.
2. Stay focused and to the point. Have you ever heard, "Sorry to be writing you such a long letter, but I didn't have time to write you a short one"?
3. Give your statement to a friend and ask if she knows you better than before she read it.
4. Be yourself and trust your own voice.
5. Don't explain your weaknesses in the personal statement; it inevitably sounds too defensive. Use an addendum instead.

Sample Statement B

By the time I completed my doctoral exams in the History Department at *** University, my research interests as a graduate student had led me to desire a rigorous legal education. When I began my graduate studies, I planned to focus upon the historiographical issues surrounding the rise of Islam and the earliest Islamic centuries. Due to the legal nature of the surviving sources for this early period, my interests subtly changed over time to reflect the body of material I studied. As I began to translate and analyze Islamic legal sources, I found that I had to confront theoretical issues of jurisprudence in addition to considering the historical milieu in which these documents were produced. For example, in studying fourteenth-century legal opinions (fatwas) from Morocco, I became increasingly interested in how Muslim jurists (muftis) created religious law through different authoritative sources, ranging from statements of the Prophet Muhammad and verses of the Koran, to the legal opinions of subsequent jurists. By weaving together these related sources, the muftis constructed a form of jurisprudence which not only arrived at a legal resolution to the case, but also demonstrated how religion and law could become harmonized and unified through legal discourse.

In order to augment my understanding of Islamic law and legal theory, I found it helpful to undertake a comparative approach and relate my findings to medieval European legal history and jurisprudence. For historians of Islam, the evolution of canon law offers an alternative framework in which jurists have struggled to reconcile religious law with preexisting traditions. Moreover, these comparative studies have also challenged me to consider broader theoretical issues that are relevant to all legal systems, such as the relationship between formal legal codes and actual lived experience. In a course entitled "Conflict Resolution in Medieval Europe," I read Robert Ellickson's *Order Without Law,* an analysis of how cattle ranchers in Shasta County, California, constructed their own norms of behavior independent of the formal legal system. The culture of Shasta County is, of course, substantively different from medieval Islamic society; nevertheless, Ellickson's work invites Islamic historians to address the relationship between formal law and individual decision-making when assessing the significance of fatws in the formation of Islamic civilization.

Since completing my doctoral exams in 1996, I have returned to the specific topic of my dissertation research which concerns the origins of the Islamic trust, or waaf. Although I have a containing interest in this subject, I now believe that attending law school will offer me a greater opportunity to attain my personal and career goals. If I continue a career in academia as a legal historian, attaining a law degree will significantly enhance my ability to offer a comparative approach to Islamic law. A legal education will also improve my theoretical understanding of the relationship between law and society, and the subtleties of property law. And yet, despite my academic interests in the law, I recognize that a career as an academic historian may not be well-suited to my broader life plans. Although I have attended summer programs in Jordan and Egypt, my wife and I remain uncertain whether we are prepared to endure longer periods of separation, or years of living abroad, in order for me to conduct the research necessary to continue my career as a medieval Islamic historian. In light of these concerns about pursuing an academic career, I am interested in

ADMISSIONS

exploring aspects of the legal profession, such as international law, which will allow me to combine my academic interests in the law with my knowledge of Islamic history and society.

In applying to *** Law School, I have sought a program of study that would afford me the opportunity to pursue both my academic and professional interests in the law. The scholarly nature of the law program at *** complements my own academically oriented focus towards the law, while the school's commitment to training law students in the practice of law ensures that I will leave law school prepared for whatever path I may ultimately pursue. I believe that my knowledge of Islamic and medieval European law, as well as the analytical skills I have acquired in graduate school, will allow me to contribute a unique perspective to the law school classroom.

Critiques of Sample Statement B

Admissions Official #1

> **The 6 Most Common Mistakes**
>
> Admissions Official #1 lists these as the most common mistakes appearing in personal statements.
>
> 1. Spelling and grammatical errors
> 2. Sending an essay to School B that says, "I really want to go to School A."
> 3. Putting résumé information in essay form
> 4. Focusing on the weaknesses of the application instead of submitting such explanations as separate addenda
> 5. Being too cute (e.g., submitting the statement in the form of a brief to the court)
> 6. Writing a statement that is not personal and does not reveal information about the applicant

This statement is very well written and is probably part of a strong application from an academic. However, it does not take full advantage of the opportunity presented. Applicants have a limited amount of space with which to sell themselves to admissions professionals and/or faculty. Each piece of the application should present new information to continue to add to the picture that the reader is developing, and it should be personal. We are looking for insight to who each applicant is as an individual. The discussion of Ellickson's book from the course, "Conflict Resolution in Medieval Europe," tells the reader nothing about Applicant B. I would prefer to see information about the applicant's performance in that class, and particularly about his written work for the class, in a letter of recommendation from the professor.

This essay nicely explains how the applicant's interest in law developed and how his current academic interests and research have led to legal studies. Although this applicant's motive for legal study is defined, that is certainly not always the case, and it is not a necessary part of a personal statement. Applicant B also chose to discuss his career plans following law school. I admire the fact that he is willing to admit he is unsure where a law degree will take him. However, the issue did not need to be mentioned at all. In general, law schools are not interested in or persuaded by what an applicant claims she will do with a law degree because we recognize

The Personal Statement

how often those plans change. There are occasions when an applicant's academic background or work experience show a true aptitude for and interest in an area of the law, and statements to that end can be effective, but only to the extent that the ambition seems to be consistent with the past experiences and academic background reflected throughout the entire application.

Finally, this essay is not a personal statement, but more of a topic paper which is not what law schools generally request. Some law schools may ask for an essay of this type to showcase writing ability, but the applicant should pay attention to the directions from each school. It is very important for applicants to provide each law school with the kind of information it requests. It may be appropriate to use one personal statement for School A, but not for School B.

Admissions Official #2

Applicant B's opening is lifeless and worse, it promises to be about his specific area of study rather than who he is. While this applicant may find Islamic law and history interesting, the truth is that most of us do not read these things to be educated about anything except who the applicant is.

The applicant's choice of topic and use of language make it really hard to get through this statement, especially considering how many statements we read. In writing on this topic, the applicant should have touched on the lighter aspects of its importance to him. Now that I am finished reading, I really can't say that I know the applicant better than I did before I read it. Remember: I have your application at my fingertips. I suspect that I could learn most of what the applicant has covered here from his transcript and letters of recommendation. The language is much too dense, as is the topic. I'd advise this applicant to put himself in an admission officer's place. After reading this, would he say, "This is exactly who we need at this law school"? Neither would I. In short, back to the drawing board.

Sample Statement C

My eyes burned as the wind gust sent a wave smashing into my face, forcing another mouthful of salt water down my throat. After three years of attending to crying kids with jellyfish stings and of kicking nonresidents out of the private parking lot, I finally found out what being a lifeguard really entails. Of course, these two elderly men had to pick a cold, windy day with an unusually strong current and high tide to try to swim to the rocks a half-mile off shore. They were drowning. I felt helpless as the undertow pushed me further away from them and I saw their heads slip beneath the water once again. While my arms felt like lead and my legs seemed as if they would fall off, I gasped for a deep breath and con-

Overcoming Adversity

The theme of overcoming adversity is a common one in law school personal statements. In Personal Statement C, the author describes his struggle and how it led him to want a legal career.

ADMISSIONS

tinued on, knowing two lives were depending on me and a fellow lifeguard. I was determined to reach the men before they drowned.

It is that same determination that has carried me through many challenges in my life. I squeaked into *** on a prayer and a shoestring. My SAT score was not dazzling. The school required me to start college in the summer term, a week before I graduated from high school, to prove that I could cut it academically. Nearly four years later, I will graduate in the top ten percent of my class.

I entered college determined to succeed, but without a clear focus. I spent many days meeting with advisers exploring a broad spectrum of possible areas of study, and many nights poring over the course catalogue. By the end of my sophomore year, still unable to find a conventional major that suited me, an adviser and I hammered out a unique Letters, Arts, and Sciences major with a "legal studies" theme. This allowed me the freedom and opportunity to gain a broad background in several related subjects, including History, Political Science, Speech Communication, and Labor and Industrial Relations. I have minors in Spanish and Information Systems and Statistical Analysis. This field of study has enhanced my critical thinking, reading, writing, and speaking skills, all of which will be useful in law school.

When an adviser told me last fall that I would be unable to get an internship at a law firm as an undergraduate, I grabbed the phone book and literally dialed every attorney's number listed. After several days of perseverance and rejection, I finally located the one lawyer in town who was willing to take me. The attorney and I then created our own program, and I convinced *** to give me academic credit.

On the first day of the internship, after about a half hour in the law library, I discovered why most attorneys hire law students to be legal interns. I was overwhelmed. I spent the greater part of the day just trying to decipher the legal jargon with which I was completely unfamiliar. However, after the work I had gone through to get this internship, I was not about to give up. I soon gained the respect of the partners in the firm, which became evident by the increasingly challenging tasks I was given. My Spanish minor proved to be useful in translating letters written to the attorney for whom I worked by a client in jail who did not speak English. By the end of the semester I proved to be a capable and competent legal intern, as reflected by a grade of "A," and was told by one of the lawyers that I had accomplished much more than he thought possible by an undergraduate. More importantly, I left the law firm with a reaffirmed feeling that pursuing a career in law is the right thing for me.

When I think about the obstacles I will face in law school, I know it will not be an easy road. Yet I also know that through hard work and determination to succeed, I will be able to overcome any challenges with which I am presented. I will not be satisfied with anything less.

I drove myself to push on that day last summer on Long Island Sound, as the two men kept disappearing below the water. I would not let my first and only rescue attempt end in a fatality. Somewhere deep in myself I found a second wind, and used every bit of energy left in my body to *kick harder and faster. I grasped the men by the wrists and pulled them onto a rescue board with a fellow lifeguard. As I realized they were going to make it, I was finally able to breathe a sigh of relief.*

Critiques of Sample Statement C

Admissions Official #1

This essay focuses on showing the applicant to be a determined and persevering person—a fighter. The lifeguard anecdote is very catchy and creates suspense by not disclosing whether the swimmers survive until the end. The anecdote also does a good job of introducing the theme of this statement—determination—and is followed by several other examples. Although this style may be appropriate for some law schools, it may not be the ideal style for others. There is no single correct style for a personal statement. Law schools are not looking for any particular technique or formula, but rather want simply to learn as much as possible about the applicant. Whatever story or style allows that insight is the right one for that individual. In general, it is a good idea for an applicant to get a second opinion as to whether the anecdote and the statement as a whole work and accurately portray her.

Applicant C uses his performance on standardized tests as an example of how his determination has allowed him to overcome challenges. However, in most cases, the argument that the SAT was not predictive of one's abilities in undergraduate school and that the LSAT will be equally invalid in predicting law school performance is best made in a separate addendum, not in the personal statement. Personal statements should be positive and sell the applicant. Explanations of weaknesses detract from that positive attitude. Different schools view these arguments in different ways, and some addenda are more compelling than others.

Creating one's own major shows initiative and is a somewhat unique accomplishment. However, law schools do not need the personal statement to list the types of classes taken since we examine copies of all transcripts, and certainly reviewers are aware of what skills particular classes teach.

The internship was used well in essay C. The applicant subtly demonstrates his ability to use his knowledge of a foreign language and completes the picture by explaining what he gained from the overall experience. Many times specific events in one's life or particular stories from one's past are appropriate and revealing topics for a personal statement. Law schools are interested in how those events or experiences affected the applicant or what was learned from the experience.

This applicant selected a manageable topic and attempted to focus on only a few examples from his background that he thought relevant. This is important. An applicant has only a limited amount of time and space in which to persuade a committee to admit him, and he must be sure to keep the reader's attention and pick a story or stories that can adequately be revealed in limited space.

ADMISSIONS

The 5 Most Common Mistakes

Here are the top five mistakes that have emerged from Admissions Official #2's experience of reading thousands of personal statements.

1. Too many adjectives and big words
2. Simply giving us information we have elsewhere—a paragraph form of your résumé
3. Staying too detached in writing style—this thing is called a "personal" statement, not just a statement
4. Claiming that you are the one who, if we just accept you, will in fact save the world
5. Piling a lot of information on us and assuming that we will sort out what we want. There are too many of you and not enough of us!

Admissions Official #2

The opening might have worked had the applicant not used such overheated language. It's okay to open with a story but trust your facts without feeling the need to embellish them.

The transition to the second paragraph is very awkward. The difficulty probably comes from equating the courage to save someone from drowning with the courage to improve one's LSAT score. It feels much too melodramatic. The middle parts of the statement are essentially reduced to listing things that I could find elsewhere in your resume, transcript, and letters of recommendation. Statement C contains a promising theme of the applicant's ability to persevere and work hard. However, the applicant needs to find a way to develop it without repeating what the admission officer already knows and without making it seem like life and death.

Bottom line: Now that I am done, I know more about what the applicant has done rather than who he is. The applicant should use *I*, *me* and *my* less when he reworks this. Overusing these words makes the applicant sound far too self-involved and self-important. I know that the applicant must write about himself in the personal statement, but a light touch is so much more effective.

A Final Tip

The above points are as much general advice as we can responsibly give about the personal statement. We hope that they'll provide you with some ideas or keep you from making some costly mistakes. In the end, however, it is your personal statement, and it must come from you.

CHAPTER 8

Recommendations

Over the years, law school applicants have taken various approaches in order to make their applications stand out from the crowd. From the all-too-common videotaped plea for admission to the now-famous *Penthouse* centerfold sent as part of one prospective student's application, the ploys used by applicants to make sure they're remembered have become increasingly imaginative. Too often overlooked in this mad pursuit, however, is one of the very best ways for an applicant to stand out: getting terrific, vividly written recommendations.

> **Ask Early**
>
> An important organizational step: Get recommenders their forms early rather than late.

Because most recommendations tend to be complimentary and full of the same standard phrasing (e.g., "He is a real go-getter," and "She has an exceptionally quick mind"), it may be hard to believe that recommendations are of much use to a law school. To a certain extent, the admissions officers confirm that many recommendations are indeed bland and are therefore quickly dismissed. But you should know that when recommendations do play a role in the process, it's usually a pivotal one. Because so many recommendations tend to be blasé, an outstanding recommendation that goes beyond the standard language can really make an applicant stand out. Not only does such a recommendation serve the purpose of pointing out an applicant's strengths, it also shows that the recommender thought enough of the person to put time

> **Here's Looking at You**
>
> Your recommendations probably won't matter all that much in the admissions decision—unless, of course, your recommendations are outstanding or your recommenders point out serious flaws.

ADMISSIONS

and effort into carefully writing it. Thus, if you truly want to stand out, spend some time ensuring that your recommendations are outstanding.

When it comes to recommendations there are two things that every law school applicant wants to know:

- What makes a recommendation outstanding?
- How do you make sure your recommender writes an outstanding recommendation?

Let's look at each of these questions in turn.

"I Love What's-Her-Name!"

Beware the impersonal recommendation. It's a definite red flag to the admissions officer. It's better to have a recommendation written by a TA who knows you well than one from the Nobel-winning professor who doesn't even remember your name.

What Makes An Outstanding Recommendation?

While you can't actually write the recommendations yourself, you can have a great deal of influence over how accurate and persuasive they are. But first, you need to understand what makes a recommendation great. As with outstanding personal statements, great recommendations can vary in format, but there are several qualities they all tend to have in common.

An outstanding recommendation must be personal. By far the most common mistake made by applicants is believing that the prestige or position of the recommender is more important than what that person writes. In fact, the exact opposite is the case. Admissions officers tend to treat recommendations from senators, governors, and chief executive officers with a great deal of skepticism, because very few applicants have a truly personal relationship with such people. To make matters worse, these officials tend to respond with very standard recommendations that rarely offer any real insight into the applicant's character; in a worst-case scenario, they may even be computer-generated. Imagine how effective a recommendation is when it is identical to five others sent to that law school by the same senator.

Even a particularly well-written or honest appraisal from a public official is of limited value. Admissions officers are aware that the recommendation was likely written with an eye toward the next election. Perhaps the all-time classic example of the useless public official recommendation was one written by a former vice president of the United States, which read in its entirety:

Dear Sir,

I recently met ***** during a campaign rally in Chicago. Although I do not know him well, he seemed to have a firm handshake and I'm sure would make an excellent attorney.

Sincerely,

*****

The point is to find people who truly know you and are able to make an honest assessment of your capabilities. This means that it may be better to have the teaching assistant with whom you had daily contact write the recommendation rather than the prestigious professor you spoke to once during the year. By the same token, have your immediate supervisor at work write the recommendation, rather than the president of your company (assuming she knows you only in passing). The best recommendations are those written by people who know you, regardless of how "important" they themselves are.

An Outstanding Recommendation Compares You to Others

When an admissions officer reads a recommendation, he or she often has to to put into perspective the meaning of overused phrases—such as hard-working and quick mind as they relate to the applicant. This is particularly problematic when a recommender throws around complimentary phrases that are not self-explanatory. Such a recommendation tends to be ineffective. A much better format, and one that admissions officers appreciate, is the "comparison recommendation" one that compares the applicant to other people that the recommender previously knew in the same position, or (in a best-case scenario) to people he or she has known who are alumnis of that particular law school. Here are a few examples:

- "Susie is the best student I have had in my World Literature class in the last five years."
- "John compares very favorably to Sam Smith, a former student, who I understand is a recent graduate of your law school."
- "During the last ten summers I've hired many students to work at my store, but none as hard working and responsible as Sally."

Comparisons are effective because they provide admissions officers with a frame of reference, rather than merely a list of superlatives.

An Outstanding Recommendation Tells Stories

As with the personal statement, being concrete and specific in a recommendation helps it to stand out. Rather than merely listing attributes, a good recommendation engages the reader by telling an insightful story about the applicant. A fictional example: Suppose Abraham Lincoln were applying to law school today and asked for a recommendation from the manager of the store where he worked. The store manager would most likely mention how honest Abe was and leave it at that. The admissions officer would read the recommendation and think, "Big deal, most people are honest," and move on. But imagine the store manager instead detailing a story about how young Abe, realizing that he had overcharged a customer by two cents, trudged two miles through the cold to return the money. You can bet that at the admissions committee meeting of that law school, when Abe's name was brought up, someone would say, "Oh yeah, that's the guy who walked four miles to refund two cents."

ADMISSIONS

> ### Honest!
>
> Would your choices for law school have admitted Abe Lincoln? Maybe not, if his recommendations said only that he was honest and nothing more. But if his recommenders told the famous two-cent story, the law schools probably would be more likely to consider young Abe's application more seriously.

An Outstanding Recommendation Focuses on Scholastic Abilities

Although recommendations often cover a lot of ground, from the applicant's attitudes about school to his or her personality traits, admissions officers focus on comments about a person's scholastic ability. Obviously, this means that a strong recommendation from a professor carries a great deal of weight. However, lots of people are in the position to observe a person's intellectual aptitude. Employers, friends, clergy, and workers at volunteer agencies all are usually able to discuss an applicant's scholastic abilities—and should.

An Outstanding Recommendation Ties In with the Personal Statement

It helps if a recommendation can be tied in with at least some aspect of your personal statement. For example, if your personal statement discusses your lifelong desire to be an environmental lawyer, it helps if the person writing the recommendation discusses your commitment to environmental problems or relates a story about how you started a recycling program at your local school. An obvious discrepancy between the recommendation and the personal statement, in fact, can be a serious drawback.

An Outstanding Recommendation Will Contain Some Negative Comments

In many ways, this is the trickiest area of writing a recommendation, yet it can also prove to be a vital component. A recommendation that is only laudatory, failing to mention a single negative thing about an applicant, may lose credibility. By pointing out a small character flaw or a potential weakness, the recommender gains credibility with the admissions officers and tends to make them less skeptical about the preceding positive comments.

One word of caution, though: Admissions officers universally hate "fake" negatives. Examples of fake negatives are: "If Suzy has one fault, it is that she works just too darn hard," and "Sometimes Johnnie tends to worry too much about other people's feelings." Much more appreciated are such comments as "Joe can afford to improve his attention to detail." Combined with effusive praise for the applicant's strong points, this sort of comment impresses admissions officers as being straightforward and helpful.

How to Get Outstanding Recommendations

Now that you know what makes an outstanding recommendation, all you have to do is ensure that each of your recommenders writes one. Impossible? Well, maybe. But here are some tips to help you get the best recommendations possible, short of writing them all yourself.

Choose the Right People to Recommend You

What are the qualities of a good recommender? Obviously, you should choose someone who likes you, who thinks you're good at what you do. This doesn't mean that you have to be intimate pals, but sworn enemies don't often write good recommendations. It helps if the person is a good writer, so that he or she can clearly express an opinion about you. Poor writing skills on the part of a recommender probably won't reflect badly on you, but an incoherent assessment of you won't help you much either.

> **Let's Do Lunch**
>
> Try to set up an appointment with each of your recommenders—to make sure they're up to speed on who you are and what you are all about.

Most, if not all, of your recommendations for academic programs should come from professors or other academic faculty. Understandably, admissions officers like to hear good things about you from someone who has worked with lots of students. That way, your recommender can make an accurate (and favorable) comparison of your credentials with those of other students.

In general, a thorough, meaningful recommendation from a famous, prominent person will help. But as mentioned earlier, a generic letter from a VIP will probably carry less weight than an insightful letter from someone less prominent.

If you've been out of school for a few years and haven't kept in touch with your professors, the first thing you should do is call or write the admissions offices of the schools to which you're applying. Don't assume that it's okay to send fewer letters than required or to substitute other kinds of information for recommendation letters. Most schools have specific policies on this subject and you'll feel better knowing that you're not just winging it. Most likely, schools will allow you to submit recommendations from employers or from other people who have knowledge about your background, skills, and goals.

Balance Your List of Recommenders

So you've narrowed your list of potential recommenders down to several choices, all of whom could probably write you a good letter. Play with your list a little and try different groupings. Three professors from your undergrad major department will probably have similar things to say about you. Why not include someone from another field who knows lots about your thinking and writing skills? It's not always easy to form a perfectly balanced selection of recommenders, and it's more important that each one be good than that they balance one another. It's just that three carbon copies of the same letter may make you seem a little one-sided!

Be Considerate of Your Recommenders

There are two cardinal rules to follow when asking for recommendations: Ask early and ask nicely. As soon as you decide to go to law school you should start sizing up potential recommenders and let them know that you may ask them for a letter. This will give them plenty of time to get to know you better,

ADMISSIONS

Information Packet

Providing an information packet helps recommenders write a more detailed recommendation. Your information packet can contain:

- An overview of your plans
- Why you're applying
- Why you've chosen particular schools
- Your relevant activities
- Summary of your planned personal statement
- A copy of your résumé
- Samples of your work (academic and/or professional)
- Stamped, pre-addressed envelopes
- Time line, including date you will follow up and final deadline
- Your address and telephone number
- Anything else that your recommender requests

and to think about what to say in the letter. Once they've agreed, let them know about deadlines with plenty of lead time to avoid potential scheduling conflicts. The more time they have, the better the job they will do.

So much for "early." Let's hope "nicely" will come naturally to you. All this means is that you should let the person know that you think highly of their opinion and you'd be happy and honored if they would consider writing you a letter of recommendation. You don't have to get down on one knee, just be polite.

Make Sure Your Recommenders Know What They Need to Know

Once the person has agreed to consider writing a letter for you, you should arrange an appointment to discuss your background and goals for your future. Many students don't bother with this step—probably the most crucial step to getting a great recommendation—and thus mediocre, vague letters are born.

Bring to the appointment copies of appropriate documentation such as your transcript, papers you've written, your résumé or curriculum vitae, your personal statement, and a sheet of bullet points that you plan to feature in your application and essay. These "leave-behinds" will go a long way toward making sure that your recommenders say relevant things about your good points and your background. Supply recommenders with the appropriate form or forms, as well as stamped, addressed envelopes and a copy of your home address and phone number.

Keep the appointment relatively brief—you're already taking up enough of their time. Give your recommenders a good idea of why you want to go to law school. Play up your good points, of course, but be reasonably humble. If you have a very specific "marketing" image that you're trying to project, let your recommenders in on it. They may want to focus on some of the same points you're trying to stress. It's often a good idea to explain to recommenders why you chose them, since it will give them an idea of the perspective from which you would like them to write. But don't tell your recommenders what to write! Don't even give them the impression that you're doing so! Recommenders tend to resent any attempts at manipulation, and they might even, as a consequence, refuse to write your letter.

Keep Your Recommenders on Schedule

Finally, make sure your recommenders know how important it is to complete the letters as early as possible. If they procrastinate, gently remind them that their deadline is approaching. Also, be sure to tell them to return the recommendation to you if you're applying to a school which uses the self-completing application format. Don't make a pest of yourself, of course, but don't let them forget you—or what they've promised to do for you.

Common Questions, Short Answers

Here are a few other points about recommendations that you will want to consider.

> **Be a Diplomat**
>
> Don't be (obviously) manipulative. Be diplomatic. Make sure you let your recommenders know what kind of things you'd love their recommendations to contain. But be careful not to create the impression that you're manipulating them. It could easily backfire.

How long should a recommendation be?
Like the personal statement, the recommendation should be short and concise. A one-page recommendation is usually sufficient. In any case, it should be no more than two pages.

What about schools that use a recommendation form?
The recent trend among law schools is to provide standardized recommendation forms on which the recommender simply checks or "X's" the appropriate box next to a character attribute. The best way for an applicant to handle this kind of form is to ask the recommender to fill it out but also staple it to the written recommendation that he or she has been sending to other schools. If you find it troublesome to get the recommenders to complete the form filled out by recommenders, you can always call the law school and ask if a written recommendation can be substituted for the standardized form. Most schools will agree to this.

Should I ask to look at the recommendation?
Easy answer—no! Almost all schools have a box you check to indicate whether or not you would like to be able to see the recommendation once it's provided to the school. Just say no! If the school believes that the recommender cannot be completely honest for fear of offending the applicant, the school will heavily discount what is written, no matter how laudatory.

Can I send more recommendations than the school requests?
Be careful. Law schools may request anywhere from one to four recommendations from an applicant (the recent trend is toward fewer recommendations). Invariably, the situation arises in which a student has three good recommendations, but the school only asks for two. Some schools are very specific in

ADMISSIONS

their instructions that they will not accept more than the exact number requested. Any more than that, and they will throw them in the trash. Thus, the last recommendation to come in, which may be your best, is thrown away. Other schools will accept additional recommendations, but may or may not look at all of them. Finally, some schools welcome additional recommendations (up to a point) and will read and consider them all. If the application doesn't spell out how the school handles it, call the school and ask to make sure. Remember that blitzing the law school admissions offices with recommendations will not, in most cases, allow a less-than-stellar academic record to be ignored.

What if my recommender says, "Write it up and I'll sign it"?
An absolute no-no. Explain to the recommender that beyond the strong ethical considerations, a recommendation reflects the distinctive voice, personality and point of view of the writer, things that you the applicant cannot possibly duplicate. Law school admissions officers are expert at sniffing out frauds.

What is a Dean's Certification Letter?
Most law schools require a letter from the Dean of Students or the registrar at your undergraduate college(s). The letter proves that you attended the institution and lists any disciplinary actions that were taken against you.

Sample Letters of Recommendation

Since applicants rarely get to see letters of recommendation, we've included some samples so that you can see the types of letters likely to be included in your application file. Two of the recommendations which follow were the result of much care and preparation on the part of the applicants. Note how recommenders were obviously made aware of applicants' work experience, abilities and goals.

Sample Letter 1: Well-Prepared Recommender

Sample recommendation letters 1 and 2 work because they're based on personal knowledge of the recommendee. Obviously, your recommendations should be based on your life, not on these models.

To the Admissions Committee:

How pleased I am to be able to support Jane Doe's candidacy for law school! She has worked for me as a paralegal for the past year. I can say without reservation that Jane's inquisitive mind, personal stamina, high ideals, and tenacious nature would be an asset to any law school class.

Jane was recommended to me last summer by a family friend. A recent graduate of Top Ten College, she impressed me not so much with her prestigious alma mater as with her skills. This young woman maintained a 3.8 GPA while overseeing Top Ten College's Student Campus Patrol program! When she spoke of this delicate balance and hard work with a gleam in her eye, I decided to hire her.

It has been my experience that 'creative types' emerging directly from college sometimes have difficulty as paralegals. Jane has, to put it mildly, risen splendidly to the challenge. She may keep a Snoopy Pez dispenser on her desk, but she has taken on more work in the past year than her predecessor did in two. She proposed, developed, and maintains our firm's World Wide Web site. Her thinking and writing can be playful at times, but it is also remarkably eloquent and lucid, as I'm certain you'll see for yourself in her application.

Please don't hesitate to call if I can provide any additional information. Jane Doe belongs in law school. As a 1989 alumna, I know she would shine at XYZ Law School.

Sincerely,

Ann Recommender, Esq.

ADMISSIONS

Sample Letter 2: Well-Prepared Recommender

Dear Admissions Committee,

When one of my colleagues complains that students are lazy, I like to tell this story: A couple of years ago, I had a bright young man in my senior seminar on mass spectroscopy. So bright, in fact, that I asked him to work with me on a research project with PenEast Pharmaceuticals. He readily accepted the offer. I said, "I know you work part time . . . will that limit your available time at all?" "Oh, no," he replied. "I get out of work at 8 A.M."

That young man was John Smith. He is the sort of person that one meets and does not forget. Consider this: Despite three years of "graveyard shift" employment (which paid for his entire college education), John found time to serve as president of the Chemistry Club, co-author several published papers, and graduate cum laude. He is an honest, pleasant man who happens to be an outstanding student, writer, and chemist. I have taught over 1,000 students in the past five years, and I would easily rank him in the top 2 percent.

While I am sorry that science must lose him to the legal profession, I can understand why John feels law school is his next step. As a working pharmaceutical chemist for the past year and a half, he has become fascinated by the intricacies of patent and intellectual property law. He has completed graduate level course work in pharmaceutical regulatory affairs, and feels he has found his "niche" after investigating the various other options available to an analytical chemist.

In my position as an academic and a scientist, I am well aware of the growing need for lawyers with top-notch backgrounds in technical and scientific fields. I can assure you that John Smith will more than fit the bill, and is likely to make a mark in both the legal and technical arenas.

Sincerely,

Dr. Recommender

Sample Letter 3: Less Well-Prepared Recommender

While this letter of recommendation is certainly favorable, it is not particularly memorable. Personal contact, reference materials, and courtesy can make a significant difference in the quality of the recommendations you receive.

> The Admissions Office:
>
> Student Name has my unqualified recommendation for admission. I have known Ms. Name since 1983, when I taught several seminars in which she participated. She was a conscientious, talented student who did well in all of her courses. Professors in my department were especially impressed with her willingness to work at something—whether research, writing, or editing—until it was mastered.
>
> Ms. Name has held several jobs that have provided her with an excellent background for law study. She first worked as an associate editor for the News-Times in Danbury, Connecticut. She was responsible for covering city and county government, the courts and law enforcement agencies. After leaving the newspaper, she went to work as a legal assistant to A. Person, a Hartford lawyer specializing in criminal, family and personal injury law.
>
> Ms. Name was contemplating a career in law as an undergraduate, and her work since then has compounded her interest in the profession. She would bring a great deal of experience to law school. Her background in editing and legal research is a strong foundation for law school courses and assignments. It is also an indication of her discipline.
>
> Ms. Name would be a talented, idealistic attorney at law whose work would reflect the highest standards of the profession.
>
> Sincerely,
>
>
> Professor X

CHAPTER 9

Completing Your Application

Most students assume that if they package the application form, personal statement, and recommendations together and send them in, they have done all they can. But remember that this is your sales pitch, and you may have to go a little farther and push a little harder to make the sale. Unfortunately, there's a fine line between providing helpful information and going too far. So let's take a look at what is generally acceptable to add to your application and what may be considered too much.

What to Send

The following additions to your application file may enhance your chances of admission.

College Questionnaire

Most schools will also ask you to forward a "College Questionnaire" to the dean of students of your undergraduate college. The purpose of this process is to ferret out any disciplinary or academic concerns about you that have not been reported elsewhere. Even if you never met your dean of students, this questionnaire must still be provided in order to complete your application for law school, if requested. Plan on allowing extra time for this information to be completed and forwarded to the schools where you're applying.

> **Seal It**
>
> When asked whether you want to see what your recommenders have written about you, say no! If admissions officers know that you'll be seeing your recommendations, they'll discount much of what is said in them.

ADMISSIONS

Addendums

Earlier, we mentioned that the personal statement was not the place to discuss negatives or weaknesses in your application. A better way to proceed is to address a major problem or glaring weakness in a short addendum that can be stapled to the application form. For example, if your GPA slipped substantially during one semester and it affected your overall GPA, you can explain in a brief one- or two-paragraph addendum that this was the semester you were involved in a car accident and missed a month of classes. Or if you took the LSAT twice and the second score was dramatically higher than the first, you can use the addendum to explain why.

In fact, you can even use addendums to put a spin on your weaknesses, turning them into strengths of a kind. For instance, show how being laid up for a month after that car accident gave you a different perspective on your academic goals. Have you been out of school for ten years drifting from menial job to menial job? Well, tell them how that experience gave you valuable insight into the need for legal aid and public defenders.

A cautionary note: It's not necessary to use an addendum to explain every glitch or perceived weakness in your application. It's easy for an addendum to escalate from a reasonable explanation of an unusual problem to a litany of excuse making. Admissions officers don't expect a perfect application, so you don't have to go overboard with addendums.

Résumés

Even though you're not applying for a job, consider adding a résumé to your admissions materials. Give the committee information about positions you've held and skills you've developed. Sending a résumé helps when there's not enough room on the application for everything you need to write. It also frees up the personal statement, which can then focus less on what you've done and more on who you are.

The tips below will help you put together a great law school admissions résumé.

- Your résumé should be typed and limited to one page.
- It should state your name, current address, and telephone number on the first four lines of the page.
- It should then list the most recent college or university that you have attended; give the full name of the school, its location, and the degree that you received.
- List other educational experiences in reverse chronological order.
- Honors include: dean's list, national and subject-specific honor societies, and academic honors such as Phi Beta Kappa or cum laude. Highlight any honors that you received, delineating how or why you received them.
- List your work experiences, beginning with the most recent. Summarize the experience using descriptive words and phrases. List your title, the name of the organization, and the location and dates of your employment. Imagine that the reader knows nothing about your experience. Use active and specific language to discuss how the experience affected you—and what you accomplished.

At the bottom of your résumé page, you can list some of your current interests, whether it's roller skating or involvement in political action committees.

There are many different accepted formats for résumés. It's easier to show these formats than to describe them, so take a look at the sample résumés at the end of this chapter. The sample résumés were based on actual résumés that worked for real students. Remember, your résumé has to reflect *your* experiences and achievements. These résumés are not for copying; that would be a bad idea.

Papers and Writing Samples

Schools differ about the inclusion of research papers or writing samples by the applicant. Some claim to toss them immediately, but others say they glance at them. But the truth of the matter is, it probably won't hurt you as long as the writing sample you send is brief and can easily fit in a manila folder. Bulky dissertations or even published materials almost always get overlooked because of space and time limitations. In a few rare cases an extra writing sample has made the difference.

If you've been lucky enough to have had a newspaper article written about you or some feat you've accomplished, feel free to include it. A nice puff piece about your having saved a baby from a burning building is a good way of bragging without having to do it for yourself.

Don't worry about an extra writing sample: Your LSAT essay should give the schools whatever information they need about your writing ability.

Postcards

Finally, make sure you include the self-addressed postcards that the schools provide for you in the application packet. These postcards tell you when your application is received and when it is considered complete. This can be important if there are problems with recommenders or if a school has inadvertently lost something. The postcards are the only way you'll know if a problem has arisen.

What Not to Send

This list is as long as an applicant's imagination. We'll limit our discussion to the most common unwelcome items.

Videotapes

With the rising popularity of camcorders, it was only a matter of time before law schools starting receiving videotaped appeals for acceptance. At first, this may have seemed novel; now it's overwhelming. Some schools explicitly request that you not send videotapes. The admissions officers generally don't have the time or the inclination to view them, so they usually discard them or send them back. There is

ADMISSIONS

one exception though. One law school is now asking students considered marginal to provide them with videotapes explaining why they should be accepted. Perhaps video is the wave of the admissions future. But not yet.

Photos

Photos of yourself are also frowned upon. A few schools list a photo as optional, but most don't want them, so don't send them. This rule was recently broken by the previously mentioned ex–*Penthouse* Pet who sent in her photo layout. Apparently, the pictures weren't enough to get her accepted (but one suspects that her application did stand out from the crowd).

Other Materials

Don't send any material that's bulky or just plain difficult to handle. Most law schools operate with limited space as it is; they may resent it if your application takes up half of the filing cabinet. Most of the filing work will be done by secretaries, but don't be fooled into thinking that an exasperated secretary won't have some input into the decision-making process.

You don't need to make copies of awards or achievements and include them in your application. If you list an award you've won, the school will typically believe you—unless and until there is reason to doubt your honesty. Copies of everything just clog up the system.

Also, there's no need to include a cover letter. Such letters tend not to be put with your file but instead are usually tossed in the trash can.

Final Check

After you've completed everything and are getting ready to place your application in a manila envelope and mail it, make sure you go through everything one more time and check each document. Do you have everything? Have you included the check for the application fee? Are all of the documents meant for the school you're sending them to? Law schools frequently receive documents that were intended to go to another law school. With all of this paperwork, it's easy to see how that can happen, and the law schools expect a certain amount of it. However, it can be embarrassing if you've written in your personal statement that ABC Law School is the one and only place for you—and then you accidentally send it to XYZ Law School instead.

Completing Your Application

Sample Résumé #1

This applicant has full-time work experience and an impressive list of undergraduate academic honors. She highlighted her honors by listing them as separate lines, rather than as a list.

Name
Address
City, State, Zip
Phone

EDUCATION
Iowa State University, B.B.A., Finance with honors and distinction   December 1995
   Cumulative GPA as of 12/13/94: 3.9/4.0; Class rank: 2/188
   Member, Beta Gamma Sigma, selection based on GPA and leadership qualities
   Member, Golden Key National Honor Society
   Member, Phi Kappa Phi
   Outstanding Freshman Scholarship, presented to the academic top 2%
   John Holt Duncan Memorial Scholarship, selection based on GPA and leadership
   Beta Theta Pi Fraternity Scholarship Ring for members who earn a 4.0 GPA

University of Wisconsin/Platteville—Seville, Spain   Fall 1994

EXPERIENCE
MCI, Inc., Sergeant Bluff, IA   May 1994–August 1995
Computer System Consultant
  - Computer system operator for "Friends and Family" sales and marketing division
  - Initiated direct contact with 40–50 customers per week

Wells Dairy, Inc., LeMars, IA   May–August 1993
Warehouse Packager and Coordinator
  - Assisted in complex warehouse system distribution and delivery system
  - Required extensive knowledge of freezer product packaging

L & L Construction Co., Sioux City, IA   June–August 1992
Construction Assistant
  - Labored on public school building development. Hung dry wall and painted walls

World on Wheels Skating Rink, LeMars, IA   January–May 1991
Safety Inspector and Disc Jockey
  - Monitored skaters for rough play and provided music entertainment for skaters

ACTIVITIES
Bering Straits Eskimo Missionary Team   1995
  - Member of five-person volunteer team which served in Savoonga, Alaska; worked on school and housing developments and conducted Bible classes

I.S.U. Honors Program   1991–1995
  - Coordinated lectures, honors seminars, and poster presentations with University Scholarship Office

Alpha Kappa Psi Professional Business Fraternity   1991–1995
  - Pledge Class President; Organized fund-raisers and community service event

Enjoy weightlifting, running, biking, computers.
Extensive travel throughout Europe, North Africa and Middle East in high school and college.

ADMISSIONS

Sample Résumé #2

This applicant is working on a master's degree and has listed the dates of her employment as seasons rather than months because most of her experience is part time.

Name
Address
City, State, Zip
Phone

EDUCATION
Lesley College, Cambridge, Massachusetts
M.Ed. Moderate Special Needs, expected August 1994
Certification: Nursery through Ninth Grade

B.S. Elementary Education   May 1993
Certification: Grade 1 through Grade 6
Specialization: Reading

TEACHING EXPERIENCE
Substitute Teacher, Nursery through Sixth Grade   Academic year 1993–94
Brookline School System, Brookline, Massachusetts
Concord Children's Center, Concord, Massachusetts
- Maintained a flexible schedule

Volunteer Tutor, Third Grade   Spring 1993
Peabody School, Cambridge, Massachusetts
- Assessed and tutored an individual student in reading
- Developed lessons addressing student's problem areas
- Assisted teachers with lesson plans

Student Teacher, Third Grade   Spring 1992
Wollaston School, Quincy, Massachusetts
- Instructed entire class, small groups and individuals in all subject areas
- Designed and implemented a science unit on oceanography
- Employed cooperative learning techniques and demonstrative activities

Student Teacher, Fourth Grade   Winter 1992
Wibsey First School, Bradford, England
- Instructed entire class, small groups, and individuals in all subject areas
- Formulated a science unit on the metric system
- Implemented hands-on activities using manipulatives

Pre-Practicum Teacher, K–1   Fall 1990
Lowell School, Watertown, Massachusetts
- Instructed entire class and individuals in all subject areas
- Taught biological and physical science
- Used computers in the classroom

RELATED EXPERIENCE
Municipally Funded Job Training Program Counselor
Emergency Shelter Intern, tutored children in reading and math
Child care helper for a Boston family (three days per week)

INTERESTS
Travel, reading and outdoor activities, including bicycle riding

Completing Your Application

Sample Résumé #3

This applicant has chosen to highlight her job titles and has listed her extracurricular activities as a separate section. She has listed courses she took at Montgomery College to show her preparation for law school.

Name
Address
City, State, Zip
Phone

Education
Skidmore College, Saratoga Springs, NY
BA, Psychology Major, Political Science Minor,   June, 1995
    Working knowledge of Spanish
    Proficient in Microsoft Word

Montgomery College, Rockville, MD
Enrolled in various pre-law courses in fall, 1995, including
    Contracts
    Basic Constitutional Law
    Introduction to Legal Research and Writing

Experience
Teacher's Assistant   January 1995–March 1995
John Peters, Statistics, New York, NY
    Elementary statistics and behavioral sciences aide. Held
    weekly office hours to counsel students on course material. Graded weekly homework and major exams.

Waitress and Cocktail Server   October 1993–January 1995
Hilton Hotels, Purchase, NY
    Duties included: opening and closing of the restaurant
    bar, taking customer orders, and dealing with customer
    complaints.

Head Counselor   June 1993–August 1993
Camp Valley Stream Seneca, MD
    Implemented teaching program. Trained junior counselors and cared for seven horses on a daily basis.
    Instructed beginning horseback riding and supervised
    other instructors.

Salesperson   Seasonal Employment 1988–1992
The Gap, Washington, DC
    Communicated with customers, received orders, created
    and delivered holiday baskets. Solicited new customers
    from mass mailing lists.

Extracurricular Activities
Volunteer, Senior Class Council

Volunteer, Humane Society, Saratoga Springs, NY

Member, Washington Hebrew Congregation Youth Group, Washington, DC

Member, Upstate New York Prelaw Society

Interests and Skills
Avid horseback rider. Enjoy hiking, travel, reading books about current medical techniques.

ADMISSIONS

Sample Résumé #4

This applicant has no full-time work experience, yet submitted a résumé anyway to highlight his entrepeneurial background.

Name
Address
Cty, State, Zip
Telephone
E-mail Address

EDUCATION

University of Michigan, Ann Arbor, MI
January 1994–Present
B.S., Business Administration with an emphasis in Finance
- GPA, 3.8
- Dean's List, 1994–Present
- Member, Phi Beta Kappa and Golden Key National Honor Societies
- Awarded the Newman Corporation Memorial Scholarship, October 1995

University of Illinois at Champaign-Urbana, Champaign, IL
August 1992–December 1993

EMPLOYMENT

Office Temps, Chicago, IL
Secretary and Administrative Assistant
July 1995–August 1995
- Performed services for retail, manufacturing, engineering and wholesale food firms.

ACME Tutoring, Ann Arbor, MI
Founder
January 1995–May 1995
- Started a tutoring business that served upper division economic students.
- Developed extensive marketing campaign, including campus flyers and seminar reviews.

University of Michigan, Ann Arbor, MI
Various Employment Opportunities:
August 1994–March 1995
- Teaching Assistant for Finance 101.
- Game Room Coordinator for the Office of Student Activities.

Hot Diggity Dog Vending Cart, Chicago, IL
Entrepreneur
June 1994–August 1994
- Rented a vending cart and purchased goods.
- Serviced 150 clients daily in a twelve-square-block area.
- Developed schedule to regularly service local business employees in their offices.

THEATER and DANCE ACTIVITIES

Ballroom Dance, Univ. of Michigan
January 1995–May 1995

Theater, Univ. of Michigan
January 1994–October 1994

Asian Music and Dance, Univ. of Illinois
January 1993–April 1993

PART FOUR

Financing Your Law Degree

CHAPTER 10

Planning Your Investment

Very few people would think about making a major purchase without first making some plans to finance it. If you were purchasing a car, you wouldn't ignore the issue of its cost until after you signed the contract to purchase it.

Unfortunately, many applicants ignore their own common sense when planning for law school, and delay thinking about the financing part until late in the process—perhaps after they've received their acceptance letter. This is a bad idea. Putting off thinking about

> **Keep in Mind**
>
> In your financial planning, keep in mind that law school is usually a 3- to 4-year commitment.

your finances virtually guarantees that you'll encounter difficulties that could have been prevented or minimized. We'll describe some of those pitfalls in this chapter, and tell you how to avoid them.

Financing Your Law Degree

Paying for law school requires the same kind of careful planning that you used to get admitted. When you're thinking about applying to law school—optimally, 15 to 18 months before you plan to enroll—you should also be considering how you're going to pay for your education.

Think Long Term

Construct a financial plan that takes the long view. After all, depending upon whether you enroll full or part time or pursue a joint degree, law school is a three- or four-year proposition.

KAPLAN 111

FINANCING YOUR LAW DEGREE

Start Planning Early

In addition to planning ahead to your second, third, or even fourth year of school, you need to start planning early. Don't wait until your first tuition payment is due, a few weeks prior to the start of fall term.

Get Your Personal Finances in Order

Applying for financial aid may be important to your plans for financing your law degree, but it is only one aspect of a successful financial plan. You also need to have other aspects of your finances in order. If you don't have the skills necessary to manage your finances, you'll need to develop them. Don't bring out the excuse that you're not good with money or don't have a head for finances. To help you understand how you spend your money compared to others, take a spending personality assessment. The Web address is www.ns.net/cash/selftest. The habits you have now will affect your financial future.

Read!

Here's some suggested reading to get a better handle on your finances. Invest in them or borrow them from your local library:

- Siegel, Shim, and Hartmann. *Dictionary of Personal Finance.* New York: Macmillan, 1992.
- Kenneth M. Morris and Alan M. Siegel. *The Wall Street Journal Guide to Understanding Personal Finance.* New York: Simon & Schuster, 1992.
- Christine Dugas. *Fiscal Fitness.* Kansas City: Andrews and McNeel, 1995.
- Beth Kobliner. *Get a Financial Life.* New York: Simon & Schuster, 1996.
- Carol Keefe. *How to Get What You Want in Life With the Money You Already Have.* Boston: Little Brown, 1995.

Take the Long View

A common error applicants make is to think only about how to pay for the first semester, or even the first year, of law school. This shortsighted view may have long-term consequences if problems arise. It's kind of like starting a long trip with just enough money for the first week of expenses. Even if you can't anticipate every circumstance, financial or otherwise, that you'll encounter in law school, considering your options ahead of time will give you more choices later. What do we mean about planning ahead? Here are some comments from real law students who didn't:

- "I didn't understand what a horrible effect missing a few credit card payments would have on my credit record."
- "If I'd realized how expensive it would be to live alone, I would have tried to find a roommate to share costs."
- "Why did I buy this car last year? The payments are killing me and I can't sell it for what I owe on the loan."

Planning Your Investment

Students can sometimes make poor choices—for example, overspending on some item only to regret it later. By thinking ahead, you can avoid many of these problems.

It's never too early to get your own finances in order—about the time you start thinking about the options for preparing for taking the LSAT, you need to be thinking about your finances. That's right, 15 to 18 months before you actually enroll in law school, your financial decisions should reflect your future major purchase: a legal education.

> ### How Do You Rate?
> Why do some people manage their money more effectively than others? Find out your spending personality at www.ns.net/cash/selftest.

Get out your pencil—here's a brief checklist to assess your financial health in preparation for enrolling in law school. Remember, no one will "grade" this exam but you, so be honest.

Rate Your Financial Health

1. I am living within my means (i.e., I do not finance living expenses with credit cards and/or cash advances).	❏ yes	❏ no
2. I am able to pay off my credit card charges in full (not just the minimum payments) at the end of each month.	❏ yes	❏ no
3. I have not made any major purchases (such as a car, furniture, wedding, vacation, etcetera) that will not be fully paid for before I start law school.	❏ yes	❏ no
4. I consider saving for law school as the primary use for any discretionary income I may have.	❏ yes	❏ no
5. No matter how tight my finances, I manage to have some discretionary income at the end of each month.	❏ yes	❏ no
6. If you have previous student loans, are you up to date on the payments?	❏ yes	❏ no

Scoring

If you answered yes to 5–6 questions, give yourself an A.

If you answered yes to 4 questions, give yourself a B.

If you answered yes to 3 questions, give yourself a C.

FINANCING YOUR LAW DEGREE

> ### It's the Law
> Federal law prohibits you from using financial aid for expenses you incurred before attending law school.

If you answered yes to fewer than three questions, consider deferring your enrollment to law school until you can get your finances in order. (And a C grade may indicate you need some tutorial work on your finances.)

Students who enroll in law school with monthly obligations that are beyond the costs associated with their current living expenses can quickly find themselves in a tight spot. Federal law prohibits students from receiving aid for expenses that occurred before law school. If you have car and credit card payments of $200–500 per month in addition to current law school costs, common sense tells you that you will run out of money. This can occur at the least advantageous time—say, in December, when you should be studying for your first law school exams. You don't need this aggravation! Not to mention that you're spending too much on law school to blow the first semester with poor grades. Plan ahead, be honest with yourself about your costs and resources, and make certain you don't find yourself in this situation.

> ### Dial 911
> Emergency funds are sometimes available from a school's financial aid office to get you over a tight spot—but don't count on it!

It Really Happened!

One law school administrator told of a recent situation with a first-year law student who came to the financial aid office just before spring term final exams. The student was about to be evicted for missing three months of rent. It turned out that the student owed payments on ten credit cards and had managed to make the minimum payments on all of them for most of fall term, but was accumulating a deficit as each month went by. During spring term things really fell apart. Running short of money, the student not only had missed several months of credit card payments, but stopped paying rent as well. If the rent was not paid within three days, the student would be evicted.

In this case, the financial aid office was able to obtain emergency funds from the university (not always an option) and help the student keep his apartment. The student found it difficult to concentrate during the exam period and did not do as well as he hoped. He had to take the next year off and work to repay the emergency loan and get back in a "current" status with his creditors. As a result of the problems with credit cards, he could not receive all of the loans he needed to enroll full time and ended up transferring to the evening division. Because of his financial difficulties, his graduation date was delayed by two years.

Assess Your Money Situation

As you plan for law school, you can't forget about your current expenses. They won't go away just because you've enrolled in law school. Recent studies show that graduate students (including law students) have more than $7,000 worth of credit card debt on which they are making payments while enrolled. Few can afford more than the required minimum monthly amount. If you haven't already done so, add up your monthly credit obligations. Figure out which are charging the highest interest rate and pay those off, if possible. If not, reduce the balance as much as possible. Don't make any purchases that send your debt back up.

> **On the Edge?**
>
> If you have more than two credit cards with balances that remain unpaid at the end of the month, you are, by definition, teetering on the edge of financial trouble.

Helpful Tips

Here are some quick suggestions to help you start getting a grip on your personal expenses.

Pay Down Your Consumer Debt

Financial advisors tell us that credit card debt should not exceed ten percent of a person's monthly pay. To extrapolate that to a student's situation, the cost should not exceed ten percent of the amount the school budgets for monthly living expenses. If it exceeds that amount, how are you planning to manage the payments? You can't just ignore your debts. Imagine spending three or four years hard at work in law school, only to be prevented from sitting for the bar exam because the bar examiners have noted your poor credit record? Lawyers are supposed to exhibit a responsible financial attitude. How people handle their own finances says something about how they'd manage funds entrusted to their care.

Avoid Major Purchases

Now is not the time to incur major expenses or make any major purchases. Be honest with yourself. Will you really need a car to get to and from school, or is it simply nice to have?

> **Don't Wait**
>
> Now is the time to develop good financial management habits. Don't wait until graduation to become fiscally reliable.

Ask For Help If You Need It

If you need help developing a manageable budget and assistance with creditors, contact the Consumer Credit Counseling Service, a free nationwide service by calling (800) 388-2227 to learn the location of the office nearest you. The agency works with people whose bills exceed their resources, to develop spending plans and negotiate repayment terms with creditors.

FINANCING YOUR LAW DEGREE

Obtain a Copy of Your Credit Report

How good or bad is your credit file? There are three national credit agencies, all with web sites that contain helpful information about credit and finance. They also describe the process of requesting a report. The three credit bureaus are:

www.experian.com
www.transunion.com
www.equifax.com

Avoid nasty surprises by getting a copy of your report well in advance of when you plan to enroll. Credit errors take a while to correct. And if you've missed payments, it takes time to get your payment history back on track.

Strategies for Affording Law School

If you have expenses other than the costs normally associated with daily living, can you pay off the obligations or reduce them significantly before entering law school? Rarely, if ever, would a school increase institutional aid for these costs. But you may still be able to attend law school even if, for example, you owe court-ordered payments such as alimony or child support, liens, or payments on loans previously in default. You'll just have to use your ingenuity.

Bargain Law Schools

School	In-State-Tuition	Out-of-State Tuition
U. of Arizona	$4,060	$10,712
Brigham Young University (UT)	$4,950	$7,430
Georgia State U.	$3,748	$11,844
U. of Colorado	$4,954	$16,172
U. of Illinois	$6,538	$16,610
Indiana U. at Indianapolis	$6,017	$14,618
U. of Kentucky	$4,620	$12,460
U. of North Carolina at Chapel Hill	$2,881	$14,743
Northern Illinois U.	$5,038	$10,076
U. of Oklahoma	$3,600	$11,238
U. of South Dakota	$2,970	$8,610
U. of Tennessee	$4,204	$10,496
Texas Southern U.	$3,960	$7,860
U. of Utah	$4,685	$10,503
U. of Washington	$5,388	$13,293
West Virginia U.	$5,062	$12,104
U. of Wisconsin	$5,710	$15,442

Take Out Extra Loans

In certain cases, financial aid officers will allow you to add your extra expenses to your budget. And although you probably won't get extra grant money from your school, you might be able to take out additional loans for these expenses.

Create a Separate Savings Account

If you have savings, you could set aside the amount needed for these annual payments in a separate account. This is one way of making sure you always have the money for these mandatory expenses.

> **First Aid**
>
> Consumer Credit Counseling Service, at (800) 388-2227, can help you plan your way out of personal debt.

Live Cheap

You may be able to afford law school payments by a combination of savings and by keeping your living costs below the expenses of other students.

Attend School Part Time

If you can't eliminate your expenses or reduce your costs to a manageable level, consider enrolling in law school on a part-time basis. A large number of law schools offer part-time programs, with evening classes for students with full-time jobs. This option has many advantages, assuming you're earning enough to cover your living expenses while you're in school. Even with a decent salary, you're eligible to obtain financial aid—usually loans—for tuition, books and other school-related expenses. Your salary may affect the type of loan you can receive, but you are eligible for the funding.

Attend a Low-Cost School

There are some schools where you might still be able to write the check yourself! For schools with in-state tuitions currently below $6,000 per year, check out the list on the previous page.

Work and Save Now

Planning to go to law school next fall? If you are, this is not the time to forego a summer job or quit your job early and take a tour of Europe or participate in some other high-priced adventure. You can only afford one dream at a time. If law school is that dream, you cannot also afford an expensive jaunt. Instead, you need to be saving your available resources for future law school expenses, or at the very least, not running up your credit card debt beyond what you can pay off before you begin law school.

FINANCING YOUR LAW DEGREE

It Really Happened! (Reprise)

Recently, a prospective student came crying to a financial aid officer at a certain well-known law school. The student said he was needier than other students because he had no summer savings, and further, owed large credit card bills. He also had no money to pay the airfare to get to school. When the officer asked him what had occurred, he responded, "I was in Europe this summer. Do you know how bad the exchange rate is? My credit cards are charged up to the maximum." With three weeks left before the start of the term, he hadn't yet applied for financial aid. This student did not receive funding from the school, and he did not enroll. Very few aid officers would be sympathetic to this sort of appeal, even if they had the funds to assist the applicant. There are few successful financial aid applicants who can afford to forego a summer job to take this kind of trip.

CHAPTER 11

Applying for Financial Aid

The reality is that few students (or their parents) can write the check for law school themselves. You'll join many of your future classmates in applying for financial aid. When you apply, try to be as thorough as when you apply for admission. Complete your application on time or early, keep records of everything you send out, read all the information you receive, and ask questions when you don't understand something. Sound difficult? Don't worry. We'll take you step-by-step through the financial aid application process in this chapter.

Financial Aid Basics

Financial aid is part of a successful financial plan for most students. The aid itself can take many forms. Options include scholarships or grants, usually funded by the law school, federal and privately funded loans, and work programs. These terms can sometimes be confusing, especially if you never applied for financial aid before. Let's take a look at each of these financial aid options.

> **Give Yourself a Scholarship**
>
> One of the surest ways to get a "scholarship" of about $1,000 per year is to get a roommate. Students can save $150–200 per month by sharing housing.

> **Digging for Gold**
>
> What's the best approach to receiving financial aid for law school? Research all of the possibilities carefully and apply early.

FINANCING YOUR LAW DEGREE

> **Fund Your Future**
>
> KapLoan™, The Kaplan Student Loan Information Program, can help you get information and advice about loans for law school. Call 1-888-KAP-LOAN or visit the Kaploan Web site at http://www.kaploan.com.

Grants and Scholarships

The terms *grant* and *scholarship* will be used interchangeably in this chapter. Basically, a grant or scholarship is "free money" that does not have to be repaid. Unfortunately, there's not much federal funding available in the form of grants for law students. The primary source of grants and scholarships are the law schools. Since the schools themselves are giving out the money, they set their own criteria for awarding funds. The schools also establish their own application processes and set their own deadlines. Carefully read the admissions booklet for each school you're applying to. Learn about its policies and procedures for awarding scholarships.

Loans

Loans for law school basically work like other types of loans. They're available from a variety of sources.

Federal Programs

The federal government is a significant source of loans for law students. The Federal Stafford Subsidized and Unsubsidized Student Loan Programs are the largest sources of funds for law students nationwide. The smaller Federal Perkins Loan program is also available at some law schools.

Institutional Loans

In addition to federal sources, some law schools have small loan programs for their students. Check with the school's financial aid office to see if this type of loan is available.

Private Loans

Several private organizations lend funds to law students as a supplement to the federal programs. Two private loans used by many law students are the Law Access Loan and the LawLoans program.

Work Programs

The Federal Work-Study program funds the majority of jobs for law students. Federal work-study allows students to work part-time during the school year. Participants are paid an hourly wage and receive a paycheck for the hours worked. Schools differ in the amount of funding they have available for work-study. Schools participating in the Federal Work-Study program are now required by law to provide off-campus employment opportunities meeting community service guidelines. Usually, you'll need to have completed a year of coursework to be eligible for one of these off-campus positions. These jobs can be used to gain valuable legal experience. Your eligibility for a Federal Work-Study job is based on financial need.

Not all law schools participate in the Federal Work-Study program, though. And funds are limited at the schools which offer the program.

Federal Aid Basics

Federal aid for law students takes the form of loans and work-study. To be eligible for federal financial aid, you must:

> **Read the Book**
>
> Admissions application booklets have a section on financial aid. If you haven't noticed this information, go back now and read the details for each school you're interested in attending.

- Be a U.S. citizen or permanent resident
- Not be in default on any federal student loans borrowed previously
- Not owe a refund on prior federal grants you may have received
- Be registered for the Selective Service (men only)

This criteria is not just relevant to federal loans and work-study. Many law schools also restrict their own financial aid to students who meet the above criteria. If you don't meet all of the criteria, don't panic. You have time to address these problems. (We're assuming that you're reading this chapter at least eighteen months in advance of when you plan to enroll in law schools.)

If you're in default or owe a refund, you should correct this situation as soon as possible. See the section entitled Help for Loan Defaulters in chapter 12 for information on how to rectify this situation. Realize that you must correct these deficiencies before you enroll, or your access to funding sources will be severely limited. Also, thinking very far ahead, loan defaults or debts owed to the federal government could disqualify you from sitting for the Bar Examination—an obvious hindrance to the aspiring attorney!

Federal Aid Application Form

In order to have your eligibility for federal aid determined, you must file a FAFSA application. The FAFSA, or Free Application for Federal Student Aid, is a document that collects information about:

- Your income and assets
- Your spouse's income and assets
- Your family size
- Your marital status

This and other information is used to calculate your federally-determined "effective family contribution" (in plain English, the amount of money you should be able to contribute to your school costs).

Need analysis is the official term for the process of determining your aid eligibility through the use of federally determined formulas. We'll describe need analysis in detail, and show you how to calculate your eligibility later in this chapter. In addition to the FAFSA, some schools require students to complete a second need analysis form, usually Financial Aid PROFILE, administered by the College Scholarship Service, or Need Access, administered by The Access Group.

How to Get a FAFSA

FAFSA forms are available from public libraries, college and university financial aid offices, and by calling a U.S. Department of Education hotline at (800) 4FED-AID. The forms are usually available by December 1 each year. Federal regulations require you to mail the FAFSA no sooner than January 1 of the year before the fall term when you plan to enroll in law school. You can also obtain a copy of the FAFSA and complete it online at www.fafsa.gov. This is the quickest method to complete the application because it eliminates a delay in having the data entered at a processing center.

> **Foreign Aid**
>
> If you're an international student, you may find your choices of financial aid very limited. The law school may offer you a limited amount of scholarship assistance or a job on campus.

Renewal FAFSA

If you completed a FAFSA form for the prior academic year, whether or not you enrolled in school or received aid, a "renewal FAFSA" application will be mailed to your permanent address in December. While the renewal form asks the same questions as the FAFSA, some data about you is already filled in, which saves you time when completing the application. Either a FAFSA or a renewal FAFSA is acceptable when applying for federal financial aid for your first year of law school.

Applying for Grants

Unfortunately, the idea that "millions of dollars of financial aid goes unclaimed every year" is truly a myth. When students look at the high costs of college or law school, they immediately hope someone is out there waiting to give them a full tuition ride. This is wishful thinking.

The most likely source of "free money," grants or scholarships that do not have to be paid back, are the law schools themselves. The best way to receive the funds is to apply for them. Start by reading the application brochure or viewbook. This is a revolutionary concept for some applicants. All accredited law schools describe their financial aid and scholarship policies in their application materials, although some disclose more than others. Deadlines will be spelled out in the application brochure, so once again, be sure to actually read that information. And be sure to follow the deadlines: The free money goes first.

Some schools do offer merit scholarships to applicants whose credentials exceed that school's median LSAT scores and GPAs. But being selected for a scholarship for which you don't apply, but are simply "picked" is not very common. Don't rely on being "discovered" in this way.

Law School Funds

To be considered for law school funds at most schools, you'll probably be required to complete the FAFSA form as well as some other applications. Exceptions would be schools that award grant or scholarship funds based solely on merit. Don't wait until you've been accepted by a law school to begin applying for financial aid. If you delay, you'll just be playing catch-up.

You can learn what a school's procedures are by reading the admissions application booklet for each school. Read through the application materials sooner rather than later. Deadlines and application guidelines are usually quite specific and rigid. Follow these procedures and deadlines. Schools rarely make exceptions.

Institutional Applications

Often a school will have an institutional application which is completed and returned directly to the school. Sometimes the application is in the admissions booklet and should be completed by all applicants for admission. Other schools provide the application only to accepted prospective students. In either case, follow the process outlined for the particular school you're interested in.

> **Assets**
>
> Assets are financial holdings, such as checking and savings accounts, stocks, bonds, trusts and other securities, loan receivables, home and other real estate equity, business equipment, and business inventory.

Supplemental Applications

Many schools also use a supplemental application form to award their own financial aid. The two applications currently in use are the Financial Aid PROFILE sponsored by The College Board (the same people who administer the SAT) and the Need Access application, processed by the Access Group. Once again, each school's application booklet should specify which applications are required and deadlines for filing the forms.

PROFILE and Need Access application procedures are similar. Both allow you to complete a standardized application and pay to have it sent to the schools from which you hope to receive aid. The deadlines for these applications are determined by each school. Generally, the deadlines are in February or March. But realize that just as admission decisions at most schools are made on a rolling basis, so are financial aid decisions. The sooner you complete your financial aid file, the sooner you will learn the results of your request, assuming you're accepted for admission.

> **Good Form**
>
> The Free Application for Federal Student Aid (FAFSA) form is always required to apply for any federal financial aid.

At peak processing times, allow four to six weeks for the schools to receive the results of your application. Once your results arrive at the school, it'll take another one to four weeks to have your financial aid file reviewed, depending upon the volume of applications received at the same time. You see why it's important that you don't wait until the due date to submit your application. Also, before mailing off any FAFSA and PROFILE or Need Access application, make a copy for your personal financial aid file. The severe winter storms during the winter of 1996 caused applications to be lost. It could happen again. So be prepared. A copy will help you complete the next year's form. So keep it in mind.

Other Aid Sources

Although the millions aren't out there, there may be some scholarship sources you're overlooking. If you belonged to a local chapter of any national social or service organization in college, this is one of the first places you should look for scholarship assistance. Often, these organizations will offer small ($500–2,000) one-time awards to former members who plan to pursue graduate study. If you've lost track of the address of your group's national organization, contact your undergraduate school. Most deadlines for any scholarships offered by these organizations are in January or February of the year before you plan to enroll.

If you do find some scholarships you think you qualify for, think of them as bonuses, rather than as sure things. Remember that there are lots of law students, just as eager as you, that are scouring the same places to find free funds. Most organizations receive a large number of applications each year. The competition is tough, and the more general the eligibility criteria, the larger the number of people applying.

To Search or Not to Search

There is a myth, which could be classified as an "urban legend," that has helped make small fortunes for people who are clever enough to prey on hopeful students who pay $39, $59, or $79 for a computerized scholarship search. Some states, such as New York, have closed down a number of these computerized search services for fraudulent business practices.

The myth is that there is $6.6 billion dollars, or $8 million, or some other astronomically high number of dollars, of unclaimed scholarships each year. The source of the $6.6 billion number was testimony at a U.S. Congressional hearing in 1983. However, it refers to an estimate of the number of unused employee education benefits offered by companies.

Very few of these "unclaimed" scholarships can be located by paying for a computer scholarship search. To locate these unclaimed "billions," you should peruse books on the best companies to work for in the United States. Most will offer employee educational benefits. Then you have to get a job at one of these companies, or be the son or daughter of an employee whose company offers benefits to employee's children to receive the benefits. Not a very likely path to a full scholarship, is it? Your time is better spent making certain you meet the application deadlines for the law school to which you're applying.

Some undergraduate financial aid offices offer legitimate scholarship search services either for free or at very low cost. But even these services provide little assistance for graduate students, including law school students. The reason is that most scholarships are set up by private organizations to address a need in their communities, and the focus is on assisting students trying to earn an undergraduate degree. The common sentiment of most scholarship donors is that once you earn your bachelor's degree, you are an adult and on your own. Instead of spending your money on a scholarship search service, save it, or use it to pay off your credit card debts.

Calculating Your Need

The calculation of how much you and your family can contribute toward your legal education always seems the most incomprehensible part of the financial aid process. It's actually quite straightforward once you know the guidelines and rules.

Basic Aid Guidelines

The first concept to understand is financial need. Think of it as simple subtraction:

Cost of Attendance − Expected Family Contribution = Financial Need

The cost of attendance is determined by the school and consists of the tuition and fees, room and board, books and supplies, transportation, and personal expenses. The Expected Family Contribution (EFC) is determined through use of a federal formula called Federal Methodology (FM). The federal processor runs your FAFSA figures through this formula and produces a family contribution. The federal processor is a selected firm under U.S. government contract which uses the methodology approved by Congress to calculate your contribution.

Don't let the term *family contribution* concern you. As a graduate student, you're automatically considered independent of your parents, even if you live with them. But if you're married, your spouse or partner is considered part of your family and his/her income and assets will be assessed in the calculation of your family contribution. On the other hand, if you have children, your expected family contribution will be reduced.

> **Free Web Site Scholarship Search**
>
> The address for a free scholarship search sponsored by the National Financial Aid Association is http://www.finaid.org.

For federal aid eligibility (Federal Stafford, Federal Perkins, and Federal Work-Study), the income and assets of your parents will not be assessed. However, many law schools require students to submit parental information when applying for institutional grants or scholarships. Generally, if parental information is required, and the analysis shows that the parents have the ability to contribute,

FINANCING YOUR LAW DEGREE

a parental contribution is factored into the assessment of an applicant's eligibility for school-based aid, whether the parents plan to assist the student or not.

Many financial aid administrators will acknowledge this is a very unpopular policy at their schools. Most will also confirm that faculty policy dictates how school aid is awarded; requiring parental information is not something an administrator can waive at will. The schools look at it this way: There are far more applicants requesting aid than resources available, and many aid applicants look exactly the same—little income, no assets. You can see why family resources enter the equation when trying to award funds to those with the most need.

> **Parent Factor**
>
> Keep in mind that a school might factor in a parental contribution when analyzing your eligibility for school-based aid—whether your parents plan to help you or not.

Every law school determines its awarding policies for its own aid. Some schools require parental information, others do not. Requirements for parental information are explained in the financial aid section of the admissions application booklet for each school. Check it out if obtaining parental information is a problem for you. Schools' policies in this regard may affect the list of the schools to which you apply.

What are some of the components reviewed in assessing family contribution? They include:

- Total family income from the previous calendar year (base year income)
- Net value of any assets (value minus debt)
- Taxes paid (federal, state, and local)
- Asset protection for retirement
- Number of family members
- Number of family members in college at least half time
- Costs associated with two people working
- Income protection allowance (IPA) for basic living expenses

To understand how your contribution will be calculated, you need to understand the components listed above and why they are considered.

Base Year Income

The formula in Federal Methodology uses your income from the previous calendar year to determine your contribution. This means that if you enroll in fall 1998, you'll be asked to provide your calendar year 1997 income. This is because, for most people, the best predictor of what their income will be in any given year is their income from the year before.

Income Protection Allowance (IPA)

This allowance provides for basic living expenses not included in the standard student expense budget. This allowance will vary according to the number of family members and the number in college at least half-time. For a single student with no dependents, the IPA is $3,000; a married student with no dependents other than a spouse is allowed $6,000; for students with dependent children, the amount varies depending on the number of family members.

Asset Protection Allowance

The formula includes an allowance for protection of assets, depending on your age. This means that a portion of your assets will not be considered in the calculation because they're protected for your retirement. The older you are, the more your assets are protected.

Employment Allowance

The concept of an employment allowance grows from the realization that it costs to have both members of a married couple work outside the home. The formula allows 35 percent of the lower income, up to $2,800, to be deducted as an allowance against total income.

Federal Methodology (FM)

The formula used in need analysis to determine eligibility for most federal financial aid programs has been written into law by the U.S. Congress. Congress reviews this formula every several years and recommends changes to it. The federal formula was established to set objective standards that would be uniformly applied to all applicants.

Broadly, FM follows this procedure:

- Your household income is looked at
- Taxes that you've paid are subtracted
- The cost of maintaining your other family members is subtracted
- A portion of your household's assets is added
- A percentage of the result is calculated, and this is the expected family contribution

Although this formula may not take into account all the vagaries of an individual student's situation, it produces generally comparable data on all students applying for financial aid. The financial aid officer at the school then has the option of adjusting data elements (through professional judgment) to make the contribution realistic for the individual student.

> **Federal Methodology (FM)**
>
> FM is a need analysis method developed by the U.S. Congress and used to calculate the Expected Family Contribution (EFC), which determines eligibility for federal student aid programs.

> **Independence Day**
>
> For federal aid eligibility, the income and assets of your parents will not be assessed.

FINANCING YOUR LAW DEGREE

If you have Internet access, you can also complete the FAFSA online in a simulated environment to see what the federal analysis will be. While the site is not sponsored by the Federal government, the results of the simulated FAFSA analysis are said to closely parallel the actual FAFSA analysis. The Web site address is: http://www.finaid.org.

CHAPTER 12

Borrowing the Money

Loans to finance some or all of your law school expenses are in your future unless you're able to:

- Write the check yourself, or find someone to write it for you
- Attend a very low-cost school and work your way through
- Receive a merit scholarship that covers everything

Probably, you'll need a loan. Why not take the smart approach to loans, rather than the typical unprepared one many students take? This chapter will help set you up with the right strategies and information.

Basic Borrowing Strategies

Too often, students want to avoid the topic of loans because they view loans as too onerous and too complicated to think about. Unfortunately, not thinking about loans won't help you. You need to be smart about this key financial issue.

Take Control

Students have more control over their debt than they think. But a lot of students simply sign up for all the loans they are eligible to receive, often whether the funds are needed or not. In the long run, though, it makes more sense to do the financial planning needed to make intelligent choices.

FINANCING YOUR LAW DEGREE

Look for Loans with the Best Terms

As with any form of financing, student loans come in various types with different eligibility criteria. Your goal will be to take advantage of the loans with the best terms, to the fullest extent possible, borrowing as little as you can.

Think About Repayments

Don't borrow more than you actually need, and don't borrow any extra "just in case." If you have it, you'll find a reason to spend it. And don't adopt the attitude, "What's another $1,000, $2,000 or even $3,000 extra per year when I'm already borrowing so much?" For one thing, it could add $100 per month or more to your payments, depending on the terms of the loan.

> **Rule of Thumb**
>
> Every $10,000 borrowed equals payments of approximately $130 per month at today's interest rates, assuming a standard ten-year repayment.

Recent default data shows that graduates who default are those who overborrowed as law students. Often the borrower is living a lifestyle in law school that is difficult to sustain on a first-year associate's salary when student loan payments and other start-up costs are added in. Recognize the limitations loan debt has on future career and living style choices. Plan to borrow less than the approved student budget at the school you attend, not more.

Don't Go Wild

Borrowing too much has other pernicious effects which students too often realize only when they look back after the money is spent. Extra funds seem to encourage students who don't have a clear financial plan to spend beyond that extra $1,000 or $2,000. It's like getting a raise—sometimes your spending habits immediately get ratcheted up in anticipation of the higher pay. So by the time the raise shows up on your paycheck, you hardly feel the benefits. In the world of students, the extra $2,000 can sometimes give license to other expenditures that wouldn't have been contemplated if the extra money hadn't been there in the first place.

Compare Loan Programs

In all cases, the terms of federal loans are more advantageous than non-federal ones. Only the federal government can afford to:

- Charge minimal loan fees
- Cap the interest rate
- Subsidize the interest for some loans
- Extend your repayment beyond the normal ten years without charging an additional fee
- Cancel or forgive your loan under certain conditions

In order to help you compare programs, here's an overview of your federal and private loan options.

KapLoan, the Kaplan Student Loan Information Program

Through KapLoan, students can get information and advice about how to meet the cost of law school. Affiliated with one of the nation's largest student loan providers, KapLoan directs you to the financing you need to reach your educational goals. Why KapLoan? Information and guidance is provided through seminars, written materials, and online services. Additional KapLoan benefits include:

- Student loan experts are available to answer questions seven days a week, twelve hours a day, at 1-888-KAP-LOAN.
- Application editing is available. KapLoan experts will thoroughly review all entries, signatures, and figures on your application to ensure accuracy and eliminate certification delays due to missing information.
- The Second Look™, KapLoan's credit reevaluation program, guides previously denied borrowers through the process of clearing incorrect and/or outdated credit report listings and, if possible, reverses a credit-denied status.

Federal Loan Programs

The two U.S. federal loan programs available to law school students are generally considered the core loan programs, since they carry certain attractive features defined by law. These features include a low interest rate, low fees, and defined deferment provisions. The two programs are:

- Federal Stafford Student Loan Program
- William D. Ford Federal Direct Student Loan Program

The terms of these loan programs are similar. The eligibility criteria, interest rates, fees, grace period, deferment and cancellation provisions, and other terms are all basically the same. There are, however, minor differences in the application process and certain repayment options.

The key difference lies in who provides the loan funds. The Federal Stafford Student Loan is part of the Federal Family Education Loan Program (FFELP), through which loans are made by a private lender (such as a bank, a savings and loan association, a credit union, or an insurance company) and are insured by a state or private guarantee agency sponsored by the U.S. federal government. Under the William D. Ford Federal Direct Student Loan Program, the U.S. federal government is the lender.

> **One to a Customer**
>
> The school you attend will participate in one of the two U.S. federal loan programs (Federal Stafford or the Ford Direct). Most schools participate in the Stafford program.

FINANCING YOUR LAW DEGREE

Most schools participate in the Stafford program, but some participate in the Ford Direct program. The school you attend will determine which of these two loans you can apply for.

Eligibility for either of these programs is the same. You must:

- Be a citizen, a permanent resident, or eligible noncitizen of the United States
- Be enrolled at least half time (usually six credits per term)
- be in good academic standing, making satisfactory progress toward the degree (as defined by the school)
- Not be in default of any previous loans without being in an approved repayment program
- Have progressed a class year since receiving your last Federal Stafford Loan
- How financial need based on the information provided on your FAFSA in order to qualify for the interest subsidy

Federal Stafford Student Loans

The Federal Subsidized Stafford Loan Program provides two types of loans: subsidized and unsubsidized. The subsidized loans are a better deal, but you have to meet the government's financial need criteria. For either type of loan, you may defer payments of principal and interest until you graduate or drop below half-time enrollment. There's a grace period of six months before you'll have to start repayment.

Federal Subsidized Stafford Loans are available to all students who meet the "financial need" criteria. A federally mandated needs analysis, based on information provided on the FAFSA, determines a student's Federal Subsidized Stafford Loan eligibility. Students who don't qualify for the subsidized loan or need to borrow beyond the limit can take out a Federal Unsubsidized Stafford Loan.

> ### Cutoff
> The maximum Federal Subsidized Stafford Loan you can borrow is $8,500 per year. You can borrow up to $18,500 per year in the Federal Unsubsidized Stafford Loan program, minus any Federal Subsidized Stafford Loan approved.

Borrowing Limits

Graduate students may borrow up to their demonstrated need with a maximum of $8,500 per year in the Federal Subsidized Stafford Loan Program. The total borrowing limit, including undergraduate Federal Stafford Loans, is $65,500. The Federal Unsubsidized Stafford Loan Program allows an eligible student to borrow up to $18,500 per year, minus any Federal Subsidized Stafford Loan approved. The total cumulative maximum is $138,500 (including the Federal Subsidized Stafford Loan).

Interest Rate

As the program's name indicates, the U.S. federal government subsidizes the interest on the Federal Subsidized Stafford Loan. You're not required to pay interest on these loans until after you leave school.

If you have a Federal Unsubsidized Stafford Loan, you're responsible for the interest while you're in school, but most lenders will allow you to capitalize the interest, and not pay it until you leave school. Capitalization means that the interest accrues while you're still in school and is added to the principal at a predetermined time (often at the point of repayment). The interest rate on these loans has a cap of 8.25 percent. Applications and information about current interest rates and repayment schedules are available at participating lending institutions.

Federal Stafford Student Loans are made through participating banks, savings and loan associations, credit unions, and insurance companies. You can now arrange a Federal Stafford Student Loan through Kaplan's student loan information program, KapLoan.

> **Pay Later**
>
> *Capitalization* means that you don't have to pay interest on your loan while you're in school. Interest accrues and is added to the principal later, usually when you start to repay the loan.

Application Procedures

To apply for a Federal Stafford Student Loan, you should first complete the Free Application for Federal Student Aid (FAFSA) and mail it to the federal processor. You'll receive a Student Aid Report (SAR) in three to four weeks. It'll give you the results of your application and your eligibility. The schools that you originally listed on the FAFSA will receive your eligibility information electronically.

> **Promissory Notes**
>
> Terms of repayment are explained in your promissory note. Be sure that you understand them. Keep the promissory note; it's your contract with the lender.

Fill out a loan application.

Obtain one from a participating lender (bank, credit union, or savings and loan). Submit the completed application to the Financial Aid Office at the school that you plan to attend.

Your school processes the application.

Once you've submitted any additional required documentation, the school calculates your eligibility for the subsidized and/or unsubsidized portion of the loan, certifies your loan, and mails the application directly to the lender.

The loan is processed.

Once the loan is approved, the lender then either mails the school a check payable to you and the school, or transmits the funds to the school via Electronic Funds Transfer (EFT).

> **There Are Limits**
>
> Federal loans may cover no more than two consecutive semesters, or three quarters.

Please take this timetable into account when applying for a Federal Stafford Loan:

FINANCING YOUR LAW DEGREE

- It takes three to four weeks for the federal processor to process your FAFSA.
- Depending on the lender and the time of the year, you may not receive any money until eight to 12 weeks after completing the loan application.

Repayment

The amount of your monthly payment will depend on the total amount you borrowed, the number of months in the repayment schedule you chose, and whether you elected to pay interest on any unsubsidized loans while in school. The maximum repayment period is usually ten years, unless you opt for federal loan consolidation, which is described in more detail in the section called Loan Repayment Options later in this chapter.

If you don't meet the repayment terms of the loan, you go into default and the entire balance of the loan becomes due. If your loan goes into default, you must rehabilitate the debt before you'll be eligible for additional federal aid, including loans. See the section called Help for Loan Defaulters later in this chapter.

> ### Payback Time
>
> The Federal Stafford Loan Program and the Ford Federal Direct Loan Program share a standard repayment plan: equal monthly installments over a maximum of ten years, with a minimum monthly installment of $50.

Deferments

Under certain circumstances you may be able to defer, or postpone, the payments of your Federal Stafford Loan. For example, you may qualify for a deferment of principal and/or interest on your federal loan if you are:

- Studying at least half time at a postsecondary school
- Studying in an approved graduate or postgraduate fellowship-supported program or in an approved rehabilitation program for the disabled
- Unable to find full-time employment
- Experiencing economic hardship

Keep in mind that deferments aren't automatic; you must apply for a deferment according to the procedures established by your loan holder.

Forbearance

You can request forbearance in situations that aren't covered by normal deferments, such as those listed above. Forbearance means the lender agrees to grant you a temporary suspension of payments, reduced payments, or an extension of the time for your payments.

William D. Ford Federal Direct Loan Program

In this fairly new program, individual schools, rather than banks or other financial institutions, originate the loans. This program includes two types of loans: the Federal Direct Stafford/Ford Loan and the Federal Direct Unsubsidized Stafford/Ford Loan.

The eligibility criteria, borrowing limits, interest rate, fees, grace period, and deferment and cancellation provisions are the same as for the Federal Stafford Loan Program. The Ford Federal Direct Loan Program has different application procedures and repayment options.

Application Procedures

The FAFSA and the other required documents that were discussed earlier must be completed. Usually, the Ford Federal Direct Loan will be offered as part of your financial aid package. If you accept the loan, your school will electronically request approval from the federal servicer. Once it receives approval, the school can disburse the first semester portion of your loan (minus fees) to your student account. The entire process—from loan certification to disbursement of the check—can take less than a week.

Repayment

Most of the conditions of repayment are the same as for the Federal Stafford Loan Program, such as the standard repayment plan which involves fixed payments for up to ten years. Ford Federal Direct Loan borrowers have three additional repayment options: the extended repayment plan, the income contingent repayment plan, and the graduated repayment plan. Federal Stafford borrowers can take advantage of these repayment options by applying through the Individual Education Account option offered by the U.S. Department of Education. See the section called "Loan Repayment Options" for details.

No matter what repayment option you select, the plan will be explained in the promissory note you sign. Repayments will be made to a federal loan servicer contracted by the United States Department of Education.

Private Loans

Private, commercial loans are often taken out by students at schools where the costs exceed $18,500 (the maximum federal loan amount). These loans are fairly easy to obtain. Usually, there's no requirement for a cosigner or collateral. The lenders assume that you'll be able to repay in the future. However, the loan terms are less advantageous than the federal programs. Interest accrues from the time the funds are

---

A Good Read

For more information about federal student financial aid programs and how to apply for them, send for a copy of *The Student Guide*, a free publication of the U.S. Department of Education.

Federal Student Aid
Information Center
P.O. Box 84
Washington, DC 20044-0084

FINANCING YOUR LAW DEGREE

disbursed. The fees are higher, and so is the interest rate charged. Applicants also must have "clean credit" to be eligible.

The definition of clean credit varies by lender. The most lenient loan program reviews an applicant's credit history for the past twelve months. During that time, the student cannot have had more than one payment that was between 60 and 90 days late. Also, the late payment can't be outstanding when you apply.

In addition, you can't have discharged student loans through bankruptcy proceedings within the last seven years, and you can't have any outstanding liens or charge-offs reported to the credit bureau. Other lenders look back 24 months, reject loans if there is any late payment of more than 59 days during that time, and check whether the borrower has applied for more than six forms of credit in the three months prior to submitting the loan application.

Every year when you apply for a commercial loan, your credit history will be reviewed. Don't make the mistake of missing credit card payments while you are in school because you think they won't matter. You could be denied loans for your second or third years if you start skipping payments while in school.

When students first start using credit cards they are often inexperienced at managing money, and do it badly. Missed payments or checks written with insufficient funds are problems students can fall into if they're not careful about how they handle their finances. You should realize that a clean credit file is an important asset. Treat your credit history as carefully as you treat your grade point average. Just as a GPA takes several semesters to recover from one bad semester, it takes quite a while to bring credit back into clear status again after a single stumble. And the negative marks remain on your credit report, just as the grades from the bad semester do.

Private Loan Programs

As the economic environment changes, new private loan programs are added and some older programs are discontinued. Check with the individual programs for their current provisions.

TERI Supplemental Loan Program

This is a private educational loan program designed to help students make up the difference between their cost of education and their grants or loans. Approval is based on the creditworthiness of the applicant. For more information, call the toll free kaploan hot line at 1-888-KAP-LOAN.

Other private loan options include:

- Law Access Loan program—sponsored by the Access Group
- LawLoans program—sponsored by the Norwest Bank and HEMAR
- GradEXCEL/EXCEL—sponsored by Nellie Mae, a private loan agency
- Citibank Advantage—contact Citibank for more information

Loan Repayment Options

For most federal loans, the standard repayment plan is ten years. In this age of much higher loan debt, the amount that students borrow for college is equivalent to what students used to owe for college and law school combined. It's a relief to learn that there are a number of strategies available to help make the payments more manageable. Make no mistake, a loan is a loan, and even if you're able to stretch the payments out to make them easier to afford, a loan is still an encumbrance of future income. The payment might have an effect on the career decisions you make and the jobs you pursue, as well as other life choices.

The obvious way to reduce the loan payments you'll have to make after you graduate is to borrow less while you're in law school. Review chapter 10, "Planning Your Investment," for tips on how to borrow less. In addition, the following options are available to make loan payments more affordable:

- Federal Loan Consolidation
- Income Contingent Loan Repayment

Federal Loan Consolidation

Federal Loan Consolidation programs allow students with substantial debt to combine several federal loans into one larger loan with a longer repayment schedule. They also help resolve the problem of having multiple lenders. One key restriction, however, is that these programs apply only to federal loan programs—not private loans.

There are two federal loan consolidation programs: one is funded by private lenders (FFELP Consolidation Loan Program), and the other is funded by the federal government (Federal Direct Consolidation Loan Program). Under both programs, you execute a new promissory note with your consolidating lender, who in turn pays off your earlier loans. You have the option of deciding which loans to consolidate. Often, students consolidate their higher interest loans, but keep their Federal Perkins Loans separate since the interest rate is so low. The new loan has an interest rate based on the weighted average of the rates of the consolidated loans.

Normally, to qualify for federal loan consolidation, you must be in your grace period or in your repayment period. If in repayment, you should be no more than ninety days delinquent in making your payments (under the Federal Direct Loan Consolidation Program you may be in default status, provided you have made satisfactory arrangements for repayment).

The table below will give you a sense of how much of an extension to the repayment periods you can secure by consolidating your loans. For example, if you have federally sponsored loans with two different lenders, each totaling $6,000, you would have ten years to pay off each loan. But if you consolidated these loans into a single $12,000 loan, you would have up to 15 years to repay the debt. While you'll reduce your monthly payments, there's a trade-off: The longer you take to pay, the more interest you'll end up paying.

FINANCING YOUR LAW DEGREE

Just as there are differences in the two core federal loan programs, there are differences in the two consolidation loan programs. But the principle is the same: to help students repay their educational loans. You should check out the details of the consolidation loan programs as you approach graduation or the beginning of the repayment period. Find out if your student loan lender participates in the consolidation program. If your lender doesn't participate, you can shop around and arrange a consolidation loan through a lender that does.

The chart below shows what your monthly payments would be like under the Federal Consolidation Loan program, using various repayment schedules. We're assuming an interest rate of 8.25 percent, which is fairly typical for Federal Consolidation loans.

Income Contingent Loan Repayment

Since January 1995, the William D. Ford Federal Direct Loan Program, through its Individual Education Account (IEA), has allowed graduates to have federal Stafford and unsubsidized Stafford loan payments based on after-graduation earnings. There are three other repayment options offered as well, and graduates can choose to move between the programs as their financial circumstances change.

In addition to the standard ten-year repayment plan for federal loans, borrowers have the following options:

Option 1: Extended Repayment.
Similar to the standard repayment plan, it allows the student to repay a fixed amount over a period longer than ten years.

Option 2: Income Contingent Repayment.
You pay a percentage of your salary no matter how much you've borrowed. If you have a high debt, this option could require many more years of repayment than the standard ten years. As your salary increases, so would your loan repayments. The drawback to this option is that the longer you take to repay, the more interest you pay on the loan. Indeed, if your payment doesn't cover the current interest due, unpaid interest will be capitalized, increasing the amount of principal you owe. If you are married, your spouse's income is included in the calculation used to determine your monthly payment.

Option 3: Graduated Repayment.
This allows you to opt for lower payments at the beginning of the repayment cycle when your salary is lower. The payments automatically increase as the years progress. The repayment term remains ten years but the payments are more manageable in the beginning when you probably will have a lower salary.

At no obligation to the borrower, the program offers a free service to project loan payments under the various direct loan consolidation options.

Help for Loan Defaulters

One additional aspect of the Federal Income Contingent Loan Program is that it offers previous loan defaulters a way to bring their loans into "current" status so that the borrower is eligible for federal aid to fund future education.

A borrower with a defaulted loan can enter into an income contingent repayment agreement and have their aid eligibility restored as a result. Prior to this program, loan defaulters were required to make monthly payments for at least six months before they could apply for additional federal aid.

> **Don't Despair**
>
> Are you facing default on your student loans? Explore the various options available to you to keep your loans "current."

Once in the income contingent repayment program, the student must continue making payments on the loan even while enrolled in law school. The process requires at least 90 days to arrange. If you are in default on a prior federal loan and hope to enroll in law school at the beginning of fall term and receive federal aid, you should begin making arrangements to participate in the income contingent loan program at least six months before in order to allow sufficient time for your defaulted loan to be brought current and your new application to be processed.

Loan Repayment Assistance Programs (LRAPs)

For graduates interested in pursuing a career in public service, a number of law schools and a few states offer loan repayment assistance programs, called LRAPS. Approximately 50 law schools offer some form of LRAP assistance to their graduates. There are state-based LRAP programs in Arizona, Florida, Maryland, Minnesota, North Carolina, and Tennessee. Contact the bar associations of these states for more details.

> **Look Before You Leap**
>
> Not all LRAPs are created equal. Some schools have very small programs where only one or two graduates receive a small award for a year or two. Be certain to check out the details of the LRAPs if you are counting on this program to help you pay your loans while you work in a public interest job.

There are as many variations on LRAPs as there are law schools, so if this type of program piques your interest, get the details on the program offered by each school you are planning to attend. Each has its own definition of public interest and its own formula for determining benefits. NAPIL, the National Association of Public Interest Law, periodically surveys law schools to find out what additional schools have added LRAP programs and tracks the changes schools make in their programs. They publish a manual on LRAPs, available to students for $23 per copy (includes shipping and handling). To order, send a check to NAPIL Publications, 1118 22nd Street N.W., Third Floor, Washington, DC 20037.

FINANCING YOUR LAW DEGREE

Tips for Completing Your Aid Applications

Applicants often want to know how to "position" themselves for the best financial aid. Any financial aid officer will tell you that honesty is the best policy, but don't lose your head. You can actually cheat yourself by ignoring or misreading the directions that accompany the application forms.

Document Your Applications

The federal government requires you to honestly and accurately report your assets when you are applying for financial aid. During the process of evaluating your FAFSA, the federal processor may identify your application as one that the school is required to follow up on, in a process called "verification." During this certification process, you'll be asked to document your taxable income from the prior year and your assets as they existed at the time you filed your application. In other instances, school procedures may require that you document the data provided on the form. The normal documentation is a signed copy of the prior year's federal tax return. You might also be required to provide proof of the value of assets such as bank accounts and investments. The verification process could also require you to provide documentation of your marital status and size of your household. If your income was so low that you didn't file a return, you may be asked to provide a written statement outlining your sources of income for the previous year.

Accurately Report Your Assets

When completing your applications, assets must be reported in all instances. There's one type of asset you shouldn't report, though. Applicants for law school who are current students sometimes err when listing the proceeds of student aid that is intended to meet expenses for the current academic year. Don't overstate your resources.

But don't forget about your resources, either. If your tax return shows income from interest or dividends, many financial aid offices will review your financial statement to see if you've reported the corresponding asset from which the income was earned. If you spent these assets after the end of the prior tax year but before you applied for financial aid, you should retain the documentation of their sale to document why the asset was omitted from the financial aid application. Otherwise, you may have to obtain documentation of their sale after the fact from your bank or broker if your school financial aid office questions the absence of these resources.

Don't Automatically Spend Down Your Assets

Sometimes students will ask whether they should spend down their assets to make themselves more eligible for financial aid. The definitive answer is, "it depends." It depends upon the

- Amount of your assets
- Aid policies for the schools you hope to be accepted to

- Other purposes you might have for the assets
- Way you feel about debt

Let's assume that your resources (whether it is your income, your resources and family contribution, or some combination of these) disqualify you from receiving aid from the school. Or perhaps you don't receive any funding based on merit. The question then becomes, "Should I spend all of my resources and then apply for aid?"

In general, you should always apply for financial aid before deciding whether to spend down your assets. (Again, if you have internet access, you could use several "what if" scenarios to see what impact your assets would have on your eligibility for financial aid. The address is http://www.finaid.org/.) Learn what impact your assets have on your eligibility for aid. Depending upon your age and whether you are single and/or have dependents, a portion of your assets may be sheltered from any contribution for school expenses. For federal purposes, any asset that you are living in—whether a condominium or house—is ignored when determining your eligibility for federal aid. (Note, however, that institutional policies concerning home equity vary widely, and may be viewed as a resource for determination of school-funded assistance.)

Other assets, whether invested in a C.D. with a future expiration date, a mutual fund, or in stocks, must be reported at the current market value when you complete the financial aid application. Sometimes students prefer to spend all of their funds before obtaining financial aid. Perhaps they are able to finance the first year entirely themselves, then take loans for the remainder of the time. This may not be the best strategy.

Consider Your Salary from Last Year

Since your eligibility for some types of federal financial aid, namely Federal Stafford Loans, Federal Work-Study, and Perkins Loans, is based on your prior year taxable income, you may initially have difficulty qualifying for these funds if you were employed full time last year. However, in all cases, you would still be eligible for the Unsubsidized Federal Stafford loan for up to $18,500 per year or up to the annual cost of attendance, whichever is less.

Depending upon your income and assets and the cost of the school you wish to attend, the salary you earned last year might reduce your chances of receiving these funds. When you receive your aid award from the law school(s) which you are considering, check the figure the school listed as your student contribution.

If you aren't eligible for a Federal Stafford loan ($8,500 annually), which is the most widely available federal loan program, it's possible that the aid determination you received was based on your salary from the previous year. Assuming you're leaving your job and enrolling as a full-time student, or are relocating to attend a part-time program, you should contact the law school financial aid office and request a review of your file. Under certain conditions, the aid office can exercise "professional judgment" and use projected year income rather than prior tax year data.

CHAPTER 13

Your Financial Aid Package

Your hard work has paid off. Your moment of decision is here. In this chapter, we'll lead you through the process of comparing aid packages and selecting the law school you'll actually attend.

You Get Your Award Letter—Now What?

After you complete the application process for financial aid, you will receive an official notice from the schools that have admitted you. This notice, called an "award letter" in financial aid language, lists the funds that the law school has awarded you from their own resources (if any, assuming you meet their grant/scholarship criteria) along with federal aid for which you qualify. The award letter also lists the student expense budget used to determine your award, and the expected contribution from you and your parents, if applicable.

Read this information and any accompanying materials carefully. Read it a couple of times if you are new to the whole concept of financial aid. Even if you're one of those people who didn't go to business school because you wanted to avoid any more math, you can't afford to take that attitude toward your finances.

Although a decision to choose one law school over another should never be based solely on financial reasons, financial considerations do play a role in your decision of what school to attend. Sometimes these considerations include things like which school is likely to provide the best employment prospects in the fields and region of the country in which you have an interest. This information is difficult to quantify. But one easy thing to do is assess how much it will cost you to attend. Use the Financial Aid Package Comparison worksheet on page 146 to compare your net expenses at each school.

FINANCING YOUR LAW DEGREE

Don't just compare the amount of grant or scholarship money you are awarded. It's important, but it doesn't tell the whole story.

Comparing Awards

"What should I do? I got a scholarship from my third-choice school and not enough money from my first choice!" First of all, congratulate yourself that you have gotten into the schools you selected. This means you have taken the process seriously, analyzed your choices thoughtfully, and followed through on what you needed to do to get admitted. Now, the financial choices confront you.

Suppose you got a better aid offer from your third- or fourth- choice school. What should you do? It never hurts to contact the second school to let them know what other offers you are considering. You need to be tactful in your approach; very few schools respond positively when an applicant "demands" the same offer from a second school.

Different schools will have different responses to your inquiry. Their responses are largely governed by how they award aid.

- Is financial need a factor (or perhaps the criterion)?
- Does parental ability to pay enter the equation?
- Is the money awarded solely upon merit?
- Are your credentials above the median at one school but average for another?

The general information on scholarship and grant policies is discussed in every law school's admissions brochure. Read this information before you make your phone call.

If School Y awards its aid solely on financial need, its staff will review your file to make certain no errors were made when your award was determined. They will also ask if any changes have occurred since you provided the information which would increase your eligibility for aid. Beyond that, they usually do not enter into "bidding wars" with other schools. Because each school determines its own criteria for awarding institutional aid, each school's response is likely to be different.

A financial officer explains, "When a student contacts my office with the news that Law School X gave him or her a full-tuition scholarship, half-tuition, living stipend, or whatever, and that our school provided much less, I tell the student to think carefully before turning the other school's offer down. The worst thing a student can do is spend their law school career second-guessing their choice of one law school over another. No school's offer of significant assistance should be rejected until it is carefully considered."

A student who is offered merit funds might have very competitive credentials for the school that is recruiting him or her, and has a high probability of doing well there academically. Since good grades are important for law graduates, a stellar academic record is an invaluable asset. There are widely differing opinions about whether excellent grades at a lower ranked school are more valuable than lower grades at a school with a better academic reputation. That's a personal decision each prospective student must make. The questions below may help frame your thinking.

Ask These Questions

Obviously, you want to look at whether you received grant or scholarship aid and in what amounts. Some other things you should consider when comparing award offers:

- In each case, what is your student contribution?
- Is a parent contribution listed, and if so, for what amount?
- How much are you expected to borrow?
- What are the terms of the loans? Does interest accrue while you are enrolled?
- What are the requirements for the grant aid to be renewed, or is it a multiyear award commitment?
- If you have to maintain a certain grade point average, how difficult is that going to be? (Remember that the competition in law school is generally much tougher than what you experienced as an undergraduate.)

The Financial Aid Package Comparison on the next page will help you compare and evaluate the various awards you have received. You should also complete the estimate of what you may need to borrow and what the monthly payments will be after you graduate. If you're accepted by more than three schools, photocopy the worksheet.

FINANCING YOUR LAW DEGREE

Financial Aid Package Comparison

Step 1: Estimate Your Resources

Contribution from Assets $ _____
Contribution from Summer Savings $ _____
Parental Contribution $ _____
Spouse/Partner Contribution $ _____

Your Estimated Total Resources: $ _____

Step 2: Compare School Expenses and Financial Aid Awards

Schools: 1. _____   2. _____   3. _____

1. Tuition and Fees $ _____ $ _____ $ _____
2. Living Costs
3. Long-Distance Travel
4. Total School Expenses (Add 1–3)
5. Your Estimated Total Resources (From Step 1)
6. School Estimate of Your Total Contribution
7. Difference (Subtract 6 from 5)
8. School Analysis of Your Financial Need
9. School-Based Grant/Scholarship
10. Other Grants
11. Other Grants
12. Total Gift Aid (Add 9–11)
13. Federal Perkins Loan
14. Federal Stafford/Federal Direct Loan
15. Federal Unsubsidized Stafford/Direct Loan
16. Private Educational Loans
17. Total Loans Per Year (Add 13–16)
18. Federal Work-Study
19. Total Financial Aid (Add 12, 17, 18)
20. Total Unmet Need (Subtract 19 from 4)

Step 3: Calculate Your Total Loan Debt and Monthly Payments

Schools: 1. _____   2. _____   3. _____

21. Your Estimated Total Debt Per Year (Item 17) $ _____ $ _____ $ _____
22. Total Estimated Debt*
    Multiply yearly debt by number
    of years in program (Item 21 x 3 or 4)
23. Total Estimated Monthly Payment
    Multiply total debt (Item 22) by $.0122

*If you will take out loans that have interest accruing while you are in school, add approximately $800 per year for each $10,000 borrowed. (This assumes an 8% interest rate.)

The figure you arrive at in Item 23 of the worksheet will give you an idea of what your monthly loan repayments will be like after graduation if you accept a school's financial aid package. Only you can decide if the cost is worth it.

Case Study: She Could Have Planned Differently

Let's look ahead and take the example of Serene Student. She has savings of $18,000 and attends a state school with costs of $12,000 annually. She does not qualify for grant assistance, so she will be paying the costs through her savings and student loans. She decides to pay the entire cost for the first year from savings, leaving $6,000 for her last two years. She spends the remaining $6,000 in year two and borrows the other $6,000 from the Stafford Loan program. For her final year, she has no savings, and finances the cost of her third year through the federal loan programs. She takes an $8,500 Stafford loan and a $3,500 unsubsidized Stafford to finance her costs. Upon graduation, Serene owes $14,000 in Stafford loans and $3,500 in unsubsidized Stafford funds, where interest has accrued from the date the funds were disbursed. She has no savings left.

There were several ways of arranging her finances that might have been less costly. And Serene would have had more alternatives after law school if she'd thought ahead. For example, she could have prorated her $18,000 in savings over the three years, borrowing a $6,000 Stafford loan each year to supplement her savings. Or, she could have borrowed an $8,500 Stafford loan each year (the annual maximum available), spending $3,500 each year from her assets, saving the remaining $7,500 to meet other "life after law school" expenses.

She could have either prepaid a part of the Stafford loan during the six-month grace period, with no prepayment penalty, or used all or some of her assets for after law school costs. Many students fail to plan ahead to bridge the gap between law school graduation and when their first job begins. During the summer following graduation, students are feverishly studying for the bar exams, held in the later part of July. It is difficult to both work and adequately prepare for the bar exam; students want to pass the exam on the first try. Keeping some of your savings for this purpose is good long-range planning and keeps you from spending on items that have fleeting value.

In the worst of all worlds, Serene borrows the full cost of education each year, uses her assets to supplement the loans, lives "the good life" while in law school, and ends up with $36,000 in student loans and no savings to cover living expenses during the bar. If you don't think ahead, or you follow the pathway of many law students before you, you could find yourself making the same poor choices.

Right about now you're probably thinking, I haven't even gotten in yet—give me a break! Even though you may be at the very beginning of the financial aid application process, it is not too soon to be thinking about how you manage your money and its impact on your life during and after law school.

There are some things that cannot be quantified which you need to take into consideration before you decide to accept a school's aid offer and enroll. We'll discuss these issues next.

FINANCING YOUR LAW DEGREE

More than Tuition

When you're looking at the cost of law schools, remember to look beyond the cost of tuition. The tuition expense is a major item, there's no question about that. Depending upon whether you choose an urban environment, which is usually more expensive than a rural setting, or if the university or law school offers subsidized student housing, your living costs can vary significantly. Also consider whether transportation to and from law school and your permanent residence is reasonable. If you have to pay for plane tickets to return home, you need to add that cost to your expenses. Are you going to have to buy additional clothes for a different climate? If you have lots of belongings, moving them can be very expensive unless you do it yourself.

The Long View

As with many decisions related to your attendance at law school, you need to take the long view when choosing which law school to attend. This is hard to do since you haven't yet had the experience. But you need to think beyond law school when deciding where to enroll. Questions like "Where do I want to live after law school?" are important.

Lower-ranked schools generally have less portable credentials. If you plan to practice in the region where the school is located and it has a good reputation locally, with job opportunities for its graduates, then going to that school could be an excellent choice. Attending the school and doing well, making job contacts through part-time academic year employment and building relationships with professors can go a long way to ensuring your successful career path. However, if you have no interest in living in the region where the school is located and choose it primarily because of the financial incentives, you may be making a mistake.

This is particularly true if the aid you receive is insufficient to meet all your costs and you still have to borrow loans for living costs. Trying to find a job outside the region where a school is known can be extremely difficult. And making loan payments without a job or generous family support is extremely tricky. The Career Services Office at your school may be ill equipped to assist you with your search and you could find yourself trying to create your own connections.

If you plan to relocate to a city, you should know that most major metropolitan areas are attractive to a large number of hopeful law graduates. This is especially true if any law schools are located there. It is very difficult to break into that kind of market with few job contacts and a law degree from a little-known school. We've heard from many graduates who are pursuing an LLM. degree at a school in a major city where they've settled. They realize that they need to upgrade their credentials in the eyes of prospective employers because the degree they earned, while it could be of high quality, is an unknown quantity in that particular metropolis. We've heard stories like this from Washington, D.C., New York, Boston, Chicago, Philadelphia, San Francisco, Miami, and Los Angeles. In short, choose your law school for more than just the immediate financial incentives it offers.

Ask the Right Aid Questions

Now that you're gotten admitted and you've received your financial aid offer, you need to gather some more information before you decide to accept the aid and enroll.

> **Travel Light**
>
> Try to pare down what you'll take with you to law school. It'll cost you less to move and keep your life less complicated.

The questions on the next page are not exclusively in the domain of the law school financial aid office. However, they have an important bearing on the future direction your road to law school will take. Try to obtain reasonable answers for the questions that interest you.

If the law school does not have its own financial aid office, contact the admissions office. Some of these questions can also be referred to the Office of Career Services. This list may encourage you to think of some of your own questions, too.

While many of these questions are not strictly financial aid questions, they have a potential bearing on your financial future during and after law school. Get your answers before you decide to commit to law school—not halfway through or afterwards.

If You Miss the Aid Deadline

First of all, if you're reading this book, you shouldn't let that detour happen. Don't bother to concoct exotic excuses! A late financial aid application is a late application, and it really doesn't matter why, as painful as that might be for the applicant.

All law schools have a finite amount of resources to award. If you apply after all the funds have been given out, the only way to assist you is to take it away from another aid recipient. The financial aid office at your school cannot do this, for obvious reasons. Avoid the problem by applying on time. But if you do find yourself applying late for whatever reason, be thorough in your preparation:

- Follow the application procedures.
- Make an appointment with a financial aid counselor at the school after the school has received your results, and ask for suggestions about how to supplement the loans you will be eligible to receive.
- If you meet the law school's eligibility for grants but the school ran out of funds before you completed your application, see if the aid office maintains a "wait list." Try to make certain your name is on that list so that you can be considered for any funds that are returned or de-obligated by another applicant.

FINANCING YOUR LAW DEGREE

Financial Questions to Ask Law Schools

- ☐ What are the terms for renewing my grant/scholarship from the law school? Does aid policy change for upperclassmen?

- ☐ What has the average annual tuition increase been over the last couple of years? What is it likely to be in the future?

- ☐ What is the average indebtedness of students who graduated last spring? What is the typical monthly payment necessary to pay the average debt off within ten years?

- ☐ What is the default rate for your graduates? Are there any loans your students cannot obtain because of problems with repayment of your school's graduates?

- ☐ What percentage of your graduates have legal employment by graduation? How many have legal employment within six months of graduation?

- ☐ What is the most common type of legal employment your graduates obtain right after law school?

- ☐ What is the typical starting salary for those graduates?

- ☐ I am interested in public interest/government employment/teaching/corporate work/_____ (you fill in the blank). What percentage of your graduates typically enter this field?

- ☐ What services does your school provide for students who are unemployed after graduation?

- ☐ Does your school have a loan repayment assistance program to assist graduates in low paying and/or public interest jobs?

- ☐ What is the eligibility criteria for receiving benefits?

- ☐ What are the benefits?

- ☐ How many graduates participate in the program annually?

Loans Are Always Available

There is always money for aid applicants, although it may not be in the form the applicant is hoping for. Under current federal programs, the Stafford and Unsubsidized Stafford Loans are available even to late applicants. Assuming your credit record is not a barrier, you are also eligible to borrow supplemental funds through private commercial programs up to the cost of education.

Summing Up

We hope that this section on financing law school has made you realize that there's a lot more to getting into law school than just taking the LSAT. A successful journey to law school requires substantial planning and a great deal of time and effort on your part. If you're not prepared to make that kind of commitment, maybe you should look seriously at how committed you are to going to law school in the first place. It's not a place for the unmotivated or the weak-hearted.

But if you're prepared to make an effort to follow the above advice, you will be well prepared and will put forward the best possible case for yourself. And for most of you, three years of law school and a lifetime as a lawyer will be your reward. Good luck.

PART FIVE

Special Considerations

CHAPTER 14

Older Students: Three Myths

Everything we have said about weighing the decision to pursue a legal education, and engaging in a careful school selection process applies to an even greater degree to older students. Just who exactly is an "older" student? I would define an older student as anyone who has been out of undergraduate school for more than five to seven years. Clearly, this very general definition covers a broad range of people. Older law students are a diverse group, with a wide variety of backgrounds, aspirations, and concerns. Keep in mind that not everything in this chapter will apply equally to everyone who could be categorized as a older law student.

Many Motives for Studying Law Later

Although there is no single reason that people return to school to pursue a legal education, there are some typical scenarios. A nontraditional law student might be someone who has had a successful career in another field, and who has decided to retrain in another area after taking early retirement. A nontraditional student might be someone who has reached a dead end in her current career and wants to strike off in a completely different direction. Or, in contrast, an older student might be planning to enhance his current career through training in the legal aspects of his field.

Stats on Age

For information on the average age of students at all 180 ABA-approved law schools, check the Law Schools section at the back of this book.

SPECIAL CONSIDERATIONS

One example of a second-career person comes to mind. A few years ago, a man in his early fifties enrolled at Georgetown Law Center after a career in the military. He was trying to avoid the fate that had befallen many of his fellow workers. The scenario went like this: A colleague would leave the service and obtain employment with a government contractor, based on his potential contacts and ability to generate business for the company. After a few years, those contacts moved on and the recent retiree lost his job with the contractor. This fellow had a diffent future in mind for himself. "As the sun sets on the Navy, I see it rising on law school and the life I can create for myself with my degree," he told me.

Sometimes an older student is someone who is tired of her current job and sees the law as a relatively short academic program culminating in brighter financial prospects. For some students, this would be an accurate assessment. For other students, it would not.

Whatever their situations, potential returning students should carefully consider all the options and opportunities law school has to offer. In making a realistic appraisal, they should avoid some common myths.

Myth Number One

"With all my years of work in the X field, I'll be really valuable to a potential law firm."

This myth can lead to disappointment. Many students think that years of experience will be recognized in a potential employer's evaluation of a law student's attractiveness to the firm. This is not always the case.

Generally, potential employers place value on experience that is related to the potential area of specialization within the firm. For example, a geneticist applying to a firm that specializes in scientific patent work could capitalize on her knowledge base in genetics. But if the geneticist wants to go into an entirely new area of the law, she needs to have course work in the new area, competitive grades, and part-time work experience that demonstrates an interest and competency in the new topic. She will not be hired simply because the skills she has in one field are "transferable" to another area. Work experience that is not legally related will not have the same value to an employer as legal work experience, even if the legal experience is only for the summer or part time during the year.

Myth Number Two

"With all my great work experience, grades don't matter as much when a law firm is considering hiring me."

The legal profession is a competitive one. Grades matter, and they matter a lot, no matter which law school a student attends. An older student cannot hide behind great work experience when his or her academic performance doesn't meet the stated grade requirement for potential job applicants.

If you're an an older student returning to school after an absence of many years, consider taking classes in some other degree program part time for a semester or two to get your academic "sea legs" back. (A graduate program will give you the best sense of the kind of competition you'll likely face.) While you're at it, you can also use the time to get yourself in shape mentally to return to school. You'll probaly need to upgrade your computer skills, relearn how to study, write papers, and reacquaint yourself with a library. If you try to combine any of these tasks with attending law school, you are doubling the challenge you will already face. Doing well in law school is a big enough task in itself.

Myth Number Three

"I should attend the 'best' school I get into, regardless of the cost."

First of all, you need to get beyond the rankings provided by the various media. Consider what you want to do with your degree. What do the schools you're considering offer in your areas of potential interest? Don't decide on ABC law school because it has a better national name if you want to specialize in environmental law and ABC school has only one professor who teaches one class a year on the subject. Don't ignore nearby DEF law school just because it has a lower ranking, when DEF has a well-known faculty offering a number of interesting classes on this topic each semester, along with a legal journal focusing on environmental issues.

You need to research the strengths of the schools you're considering, after carefully assessing your own areas of interest. Don't assume that the glib summaries of law schools in a magazine can replace your own careful review.

SPECIAL CONSIDERATIONS

Consider the experience of one graduate of a well-known law school, who had returned to law school full time after a career as a teacher. He told me that he firmly believed in every person's right to screw up his own life. By that, he meant that he had made some bad financial decisions to finance law school. He had taken out too many student loans. Then law school did not work out exactly as he had imagined. He had not been in the top third of the class and had not found good summer jobs. Upon graduation, he had been unable to find a legal job that paid better than teaching. Saddled with student loans, he concluded that returning to teaching was his best option. At least he got summers off, he rationalized. Gradually, he did make connections through the parents of some of his students, finally landing a job as an attorney. But his success came after several lean years in which his teacher's salary had to stretch to cover student loan payments in addition to living expenses. His low teacher's salary was part of what had motivated him to go to law school in the first place.

There is at least one very good reason to attend a nationally known law school. If you plan to relocate after law school, a nationally known law school might serve your needs better than a school with an excellent regional reputation. National law schools generally have graduates in every major city and many countries around the world. But if you plan to practice in the local area and there are two schools in the region, one nationally known and the other considered more regional, find out which law school helps its graduates with local jobs.

For example, let's say you are interested in legal issues on a state government level. You're considering two schools; one of them is nearby, with a good local reputation. The other school you're considering is nationally known. Suppose the local school is known as the feeder for people who work in the state attorney general's office, whereas the nationally ranked school focuses on employment opportunities at traditional law firms and local corporations. The regional school might have great part-time employment leads to help you get the all-important work experience you'll need to round out your résumé. The other school might not emphasize those options.

Whatever your interests are, you'll need to do your own careful research. Find out what the schools have to offer by talking to the offices of career services and by contacting recent graduates. You're efforts will be rewarded. You'll turn up information that you'd never be able to find on a chart in a magazine.

Bottom Line

If you are an older student considering applying to law school, take the time to assess why you're going, which schools are the best fit, and how you will finance your education. Older students who take the time to do the assessment make the best decisions and have the greatest options after law school. Make sure you're one of the smart ones.

CHAPTER 15

Minority Students

by Everett Bellamy

First, the good news. Although you often hear of a "glut" of lawyers in the United States and that there are more lawyers per capita in the United States than in any other country in the world, there is still a need for more minority attorneys.

A recent survey contains the following statistics: "In 1970, only one percent of all attorneys were people of color. In 1990, that figure had risen to seven percent." However, this figure is well below the national population average (for example, African Americans are approximately 12 percent of the United States population but make up less than three percent of all the lawyers in this country). The survey continues, "Nationwide, close to half of all law firm offices—45.9 percent—had no minority partners, and over one-fifth—22.4 percent—had no minority associates. Fewer than one-fifth of offices reported having five percent or more minority partners, and not quite 30 percent reported minority representation of 13 percent or more among associates."

The survey also indicated that firms of 100 or fewer employees were most likely to have no minority representation among partners and associates, while large firms of 250 or more were most likely to fall into the categories of highest representation.[1]

So, if you are interested in becoming a lawyer, and you are a student of color, you should pursue your dream.

Ideally, preparation for law school admission involves careful planning throughout one's academic life. In the next few pages, I will discuss the steps you should consider taking for a successful matriculation into a law school of your choice, with a particular focus on the minority student applicant.

SPECIAL CONSIDERATIONS

Minorities on the March

Total overall enrollment at ABA-approved law schools grew from 123,198 in 1987 to 134,949 in 1996, an increase of 9.5 percent. Proportionally, enrollments by minorities jumped during that period. Some examples of the gains by various minority groups:

- African American students: up by 58.3 percent, from 6,028 in 1987 to 9,542 in 1996.

- Mexican American students: up by 47.7 percent, from 1,644 in 1987 to 2,429 in 1996.

- Asian or Pacific Islander students: up by 190 percent, from 2,656 in 1987 to 7,706 in 1996.

- The total population of minority students increased by 90 percent, from 13,250 in 1987 to 25,279.

Source: American Bar Association, *ABA Approved Law Schools*, 1998

Prelaw Preparation

Frequently, educators paraphrase the title to the book *All I Really Need to Know I Learned in Kindergarten*. There is some truth in this statement with respect to preparation for law school. That's because the skills that you need to develop in order to get into and succeed in law school happen to be academic fundamentals. Those skills—reading, writing, and critical thinking—are at the heart of the lawyering process. Therefore, students who are planning on applying (and going) to law school should start developing those skills as soon as possible. You can do this by either selecting a major where the development of these skills is part and parcel of that particular major or taking elective courses that require these skills.

Seek out those professors who require substantial amounts of reading that involve critical analysis of the material and not a restatement of what you've read. Whether you major in African American Studies or Political Science—be sure to read and write as much as you can.

Write On!

For some, writing comes easy. But for most, writing is a laborious process. Most students have to work at it in order to be successful. But don't despair, you can achieve success with the aid of a thoughtful teacher who takes the time to comment on your writing word by word, paragraph by paragraph. Perhaps most important, students should keep in mind the late Justice Louis Brandeis's comment, "There is no such thing as good writing but only a good rewrite."

As a future law student and lawyer, you should develop the time and skill of rewriting. From, say, the first draft, which is put aside for a while before editing, to the rewrite.

If you are a minority student who has to make up for attending a less competitive high school with limited resources, it's imperative that you hone these skills while in college. Find a mentor, a willing professor in your department, who can guide you through the maze of course offerings so that you can get the most out of your years in college.

Find out as much as you can about the resources—academic and counseling—that are available to you. In other words, be an educated consumer. Get the most of your college experience, while laying the foundation for a successful career in the law.

Critical Thinking

Upon entering law school, you will hear the phrase *getting students to think like a lawyer*. What is meant by this phrase is the ability to analyze a set of facts or a legal problem and fashion arguments for or against a certain result. Your arguments must be based on sound legal reasoning. In other words, you must support your arguments by comparing or contrasting them to similar facts that lead to the same result you seek.

Unfortunately, many undergraduate courses simply require that you understand the material and restate it on the exam. Few courses will demand that you take a body of material, analyze it, support one position or another, and explain your reasoning. If you have the opportunity while in college, seek these courses out; find the professors who require this type of critical thinking of their students and enroll in their courses. You will benefit tremendously when you are in law school.

Prelaw Summer Programs

For some, attending a summer program is the best way to prepare for law school. There are two national, nonprofit programs—the Council on Legal Education Opportunity Program and the Charles Hamilton Houston Preparatory Law Institute. (Both can be reached at the addresses listed at the end of this chapter.) Both organizations are geared toward providing minority students and students from low income backgrounds an opportunity to prepare for the rigors of law school. Their summer programs consist of approximately six weeks of instruction. Students are taught the basics of legal reasoning and writing. The programs allow students to focus on their strengths and weaknesses and to take law school exams before enrolling in law school.

Some law schools have their own programs. Students should contact any law school they are interested in attending and inquire as to the availability of a summer program. If a school does have a summer program, attendance may be a condition of admission. In other words, you are invited to attend the summer program based on certain admissions criteria, and if you do well you are admitted.

Selecting a Law School

Recently, there has been much debate about the ranking of law schools, and how those rankings can (or should) be used in selecting a law school. The argument for ranking law schools, using some sort of survey that measures a set of criteria, is that applicants will be better educated consumers. The argument against rankings is that they are unreliable.

SPECIAL CONSIDERATIONS

The bottom line, is that minority students, like all students, should do their homework with respect to selecting a law school.

Factors that should be considered include:

- Academic support program
- Diversity of the students, faculty and senior administrators
- Student body size
- Geographic location (i.e., small town, urban, rural)
- Course offerings
- Financial aid
- Opportunity to interact with the local bar, specifically minority attorneys and judges
- Clinical programs
- Faculty-to-student ratio

For many students the question may come down to: Should I attend a good regional state law school or a more prestigious national law school? Of course, it is possible to have you cake and eat it, too, so to speak, by attending a prestigious state law school.

Minority applicants should read as much as they can about the law schools they are interested in—material supplied by the schools, as well as information from other sources (American Bar Association, Section of Legal Education, for example). In addition, applicants should call the law schools and ask for the names and telephone numbers of current minority students and alumni who they can call and ask questions about various aspects of the law school.

> **Studying Civil Rights Law**
>
> For a list of law schools that report an academic specialty in civil rights law, see part B of the Law Schools section in the back of this book.

Finally, there's nothing better than to kick the tires and take the car for a drive to use an often stated metaphor. Go visit the campus. Walk around. Talk to students, faculty and staff. Sit in on a class. Meet with leaders of student organizations.

Most law schools invite accepted applicants to campus in the spring for an open house. You should take advantage of these opportunities, and you should also arrange your own visit. Your ultimate goal is to get as much information as you can before you make a decision.

Game Plan

Organization is the key. Being very methodical in your planning can have a positive affect on your results. Law school applicants should start the planning process at least 12–18 months before they plan to matriculate. Most law schools accept applicants for matriculation only in the fall semester. Therefore, deciding when to take the Law School Admissions Test (LSAT), which is only offered four times a year, in February, June, September or October, and December, is very important.

When is your academic schedule and personal life less hectic? When will you have more time to study, take a review course and be at your optimal performance? These factors, as well as when you plan to start law school, should help determine when you take the LSAT. Some students, including minority students, rely on the application deadline (February or March) as the due date for submitting all of the admission material. However, most law schools accept students on a rolling basis. That is, when an application is complete, a decision will be made. Consequently, an applicant can place himself or herself at an disadvantage by applying too late. In other words, your applications should be in the mail by November or early December.

Being realistic in selecting the schools that you apply to is an important part of your game plan. Most students will apply to five or more law schools. Regardless of how many law schools that you apply to, you should include law schools from your wish list (top choices), alternative list (if you don't get any of your top choices) and so called fall-back schools (law schools where you can get a good education even though they're not your first or second choice). Of course, it's better that you apply only to ABA-approved schools. (Currently, there are 180 J.D.-granting ABA-approved law schools.)

Minority students may want to increase their chances of being accepted by applying to schools that have a low minority applicant pool. Moreover, such schools may offer more generous financial awards.

Most law schools are confronting the issue of affirmative action. As a result of Proposition 209 and *Hopwood v. Texas*, state law schools located in Texas and California cannot take race into consideration when making admission decisions. Although *Hopwood* was a 5th circuit court decision, Louisiana and Mississippi are under separate court orders to remedy the effects of past discrimination. (The 5th federal court circuit consists of Louisiana, Mississippi, and Texas.)

Private law schools, as of yet, are not affected. Most legal scholars agree that *The Board of Regents of the University of California v. Bakke* is still good law. The United States Supreme Court stated in *Bakke* that race can be one of many factors in making admission decisions. However, more law suits are probably likely.

Consequently, most law schools are actively seeking diversity in their student body. It's worth mentioning that seeking diversity is different from having a quota system, whereby a certain number of slots in each class are set aside exclusively for minority students.

By referring to the ABA guide to approved law schools[2] (or some similar publication), minority students can ascertain the minority enrollment of any ABA-approved law school. The minority applicant can then speak to the director of admissions of the law school she is interested in to find out how that figure compares to the minority applicant pool. In this way, minority applicants can find out which schools

SPECIAL CONSIDERATIONS

have a low minority applicant pool. This fact-gathering may increase the odds of admission at schools that profess to having a problem finding qualified minority applicants.

All law students should find a law school that is a good fit, but this may be of special importance to minority students attending predominately nonminority law schools. What are some of the factors of a good law school for minority students?

- A supportive environment (at a minimum, nonhostile)
- Minority faculty and senior administrators
- An active minority alumni group who are willing to mentor current students
- Low attrition rate for all students, including minority students
- A proven track record of having minority students active in academic extracurricular activities (ie., law journals, moot court)

Minority students can rate a school on these factors by visiting the campus and meeting with senior members of the administrative staff in the offices of admissions, career services, alumni affairs, and academic affairs. Minority students should also ask for the names and telephone numbers of currently enrolled minority students as well as recent minority graduates. In order to ensure that the view points are objective, minority students should conduct their own random survey of students' opinions when visiting the campus.

Minority Scholarships

Some law schools offer merit-based scholarships in order to attract minority students. Similar to attacks on affirmative action, law schools have been sued for scholarships set aside exclusively for minority students. However, by having private funds contributed to support this effort, schools have been able to limit their liability while pursuing diversity.

If a minority student has a stellar academic record the law schools that offer merit based scholarships will, in all likelihood, seek him or her out. The best thing to do, however, is to ask for a list of all scholarship sources, particularly minority scholarships. In other words, rather than sit back and wait take a proactive role. The key is: Apply early!

Race Matters

As mentioned earlier, the U.S. Supreme Court ruled in *Bakke* that race can be a factor in striving for a diverse student body. Therefore, minority applicants should not hide their race. If you participated in a minority student organization, list it in your application. Acknowledging that you are a member of a minority group could help; it certainly shouldn't hurt you.

In fact, if there is something unique or of special interest as regards your race or ethnicity, whether it relates to your personal or professional development or illustrates how you would add a unique or different perspective to the student body, include it in your personal statement.

Is there a negative side to being a minority student at a predominately white law school (even one with a supportive environment)? Remember, American law schools are, by and large, a microcosm of American society. Will a professor treat me differently because of my race? How about my classmates? Will I be expected to be the spokesperson for the entire race? It is possible that if you are a minority law student attending a predominately white law school you will encounter racism in law school, subtle or overt. Certain courses may lend themselves to a frank and open discussion of race and the legal system (e.g., criminal law). This discussion need not be racist, however. Much will depend on how the professor conducts the class. Here are a few suggestions regarding race matters and the legal academy.

- Remember, you were admitted, so you have a right to be there like everyone else.
- You are being trained to think like a lawyer—think and speak rationally, with well-reasoned arguments.
- The deans and other administrators are there to assist you if you feel you are being mistreated based on your race or ethnicity.
- Don't feel compelled to speak out on race matters, but remember, learning the law is an active, not a passive, process.

Life After Law School

As a recent article in *The National Jurist*[3] highlighted, Minority associates say that even today they are subjected to racial slurs, marginalization, lack of leadership opportunities, and other forms of bias. Although there is a demand for minority lawyers based on the low percentage of those now practicing, there are still obstacles. Minority lawyers in large firms may experience a less than hospitable environment. Therefore, it's important to know why you want to be a lawyer. You should think through your options—large, medium, or small firm practice; in-house corporate lawyer; or sole practitioner.

You may not know the type of law you want to practice when you enter law school, but make sure you do all that you can to gain insights from practicing attorneys and career counselors while in law school.

Conclusion

There is no one way to prepare for law school. And, there is no magic formula for success. There are, however, certain skills that are crucial to be a successful law student and lawyer. These include the development of critical thinking and reading skills; the ability to write in a concise, thorough manner; and to analyze complex material. Minority students, like all law students, should lay the foundation for developing these skills before law school, and work hard in law school to develop them to their optimal level.

SPECIAL CONSIDERATIONS

Sources

1. *ABA Commission on Opportunities for Minorities in the Law* (American Bar Association, 1997).

2. *Official American Bar Association Guide to Approved Law Schools* (MacMillan, 1999).

3. T. Stabile, "Law Firms in Black and White," *The National Jurist*, p. 22–27. (May/June 1998).

Resources

Council on Legal Education Opportunity
American Bar Association Building
740 Fifteenth Street, N.W., 7th Floor
Washington, D.C. 20005

Charles Hamilton Houston
Law School Preparatory Institute
P.O. Box 75484
Washington, D.C. 20013

American Bar Association
Section of Legal Education and Admissions to the Bar
750 North Lake Shore Drive
Chicago, IL 60611

CHAPTER 16

Women Students

Can women have successful careers in law?

The answer is a decided "Yes."

Have they been making the progress they might have hoped for in the mid-seventies, when law schools began opening their doors to women in greater numbers? The answer to this question depends upon whom you talk with, and what kind of progress the women you speak with would like to be making.

More than ever before, women hold leadership positions within the legal world. The most highly visible success stories include Janet Reno as Attorney General of the United States, and Supreme Court Justices Sandra O'Connor and Ruth Ginsberg. The achievements of these women have assured us that women are capable of performing excellently at the top of the legal profession. But how does this assurance translate to the normal female law student who simply aspires to a satisfying job with decent pay and reasonable promotion prospects? Someone who, furthermore, hopes to receive fair treatment in law school as she works towards her goal?

> **Women's Law Group**
>
> The Women's Law Group of Vermont Law School seeks to promote the full and equal participation of women in the legal profession and the equal application of the law to all women. Their Web site at http://www.sover.net/~subrosa/ is a resource for those who have an interest in women's legal issues.

SPECIAL CONSIDERATIONS

Doing the Math

The best advice for the woman with these concerns fits many other situations as well: Pick your law school carefully. Many law schools now have almost fifty-fifty enrollment parity between men and women. But that doesn't mean necessarily that women are accorded credit for the talents and attributes they bring to law school. One very good indication of the values that inculcate a school is the number of women on the faculty. And beyond numbers, how are female professors used? Are they teaching courses throughout the curriculum or are they confined to the typically "female" areas of the course offerings such as family law? Does it seem as if there's just a token number of women who were able to leap the hurdle of XYZ Law School's "high standards" for faculty?

> **Women on the Rise**
>
> Total overall enrollment at ABA-approved law schools grew from 123,198 in 1987 to 134,949 in 1996, an increase of 9.5 percent. During that period, the enrollment of Women Students rose by 16.8 percent, from 48,920 in 1987 to 57,123 in 1996.
>
> Source: *ABA-Approved Law Schools*, 1998.

The ABA publication *ABA-Approved Law Schools* provides a wealth of information about the percentage of women and men in each law school, along with the gender and racial composition of the faculty. If women are not well represented in both the student body and faculty, it is very likely that the climate for you and other women will be less supportive than it should be. Faculty might not value your potential and could be reluctant to hire women as research assistants, recommend them for jobs after law school, and be generally less likely to see them as effective future members of the profession. These messages can be communicated in a variety of ways, particularly in the large lecture classroom, where Women Students often find themselves at a disadvantage because of a difference in learning styles.

Women and the Law School Experience

Although legal education in the '90s certainly includes innovation, and a number of creative approaches have been developed to present the traditional curriculum, it is still very often true that the majority of male professors favor the assertive student, who is, most often, a man. Law schools have been brought to task for this phenomenon, most recently through the writings of Lani Guinier, professor of law at the University of Pennsylvania. She has noted that women at her law school are underrepresented among students who rank in the top ten percent of their class. Professor Guinier takes issue with this ranking. As she has pointed out, women's objective admissions credentials are comparable to those of men admitted to the same school. Yet they make up only 25 percent of the top ten percent of academic performers.

Professor Guinier's study is not without its critics. One could argue about the methodology of her study as well as its conclusions. But it nonetheless should be a reminder to women that a successful law school experience happens because of a careful selection process, where you look beyond the rankings of law schools in the national magazines, as none of the indices used to rank law schools assess such factors as the academic climate for women.

> **Info on Women**
>
> For statistics on the percentage of women enrolled in various law school, see part A of the Law Schools section in the back of this book. Part B of that section contains a listing of schools that report offering an academic specialty in women's rights law.

It is true that law school is only a three-or four-year experience, depending upon whether a student enrolls full time and/or pursues a joint degree. But it is also true that how one performs in law school has a powerful influence on the job opportunities available after graduation. Like it or not, grades have a disproportionate influence on the first position after law school, and that in turn opens up, or shuts off, future options.

The joke in medical schools is:

"What do you say to a doctor who graduates in the bottom half of the class?"

"Yes, doctor."

"What do you say to a law school graduate who graduates in the bottom half of the class?"

"I'll take fries with that hamburger."

It stands to reason that you need to select a school that offers opportunities and an academic environment in which you and others like you, can succeed. Do your homework: Look beyond the magazine ratings to find a school that meets your needs.

CHAPTER 17

Gay and Lesbian Students

by Janice Austin

As a gay or lesbian person interested in applying to law school, you will consider the same criteria that every individual considers when selecting and applying to school. The reputation of the school, cost of attendance, the academic program, and potential career opportunities will all factor into your decision making. Whether you are openly gay or not, I hope this chapter provides additional insight that will assist you in selecting schools to apply to and perhaps enroll in.

Reasons for Going to Law School

Every applicant to law school must do some soul searching and consider her reasons for wanting to attend law school early in the process. You will need to provide a thoughtful answer to yourself and others as you journey towards your educational goals.

Many gay and lesbian applicants will feel a strong desire to empower themselves and their communities by becoming members of the legal community. Indeed, many of today's major legal issues involve the rights of gay people. Sexual orientation has been a pivotal issue in nondiscrimination policies and ordinances, equal-protection clauses, military service, access to employment and educational opportunities, child adoption, and the recognition of same-sex marriages. Gays and lesbians may view the law as a powerful mechanism that can legislate or promote social change, a weapon in the fight for equality.

The desire to obtain a legal education in order to be actively involved in the struggle for gay rights is a legitimate reason for any gay or lesbian person to apply to law school. However, gay or lesbian applicants should not feel predisposed or compelled to believe that "gay rights law" might be their only area of professional practice.

SPECIAL CONSIDERATIONS

Finding Gay-Friendly Law Schools

Wouldn't it be wonderful if you could find such an environment? What would you consider a gay-friendly law school to be, and how important is it to you? Will the environment provide an atmosphere allowing you to reach your full potential as a student? Here are some tips that will help you to find the best schools for you as a gay law school candidate.

Evaluate a School's Representation

In your attempt to identify a gay-friendly law school, begin with evaluating the way that a school represents itself. A school's representation includes the people associated with the school whom you encounter, as well as publications from the school. How do you feel about the people and the printed materials representing a school?

Let's say you meet an admissions staff member from a particular school at a Law School Forum. Would you consider discussing your concerns about gay and lesbian issues with him? How would you gauge his reaction or response? An admissions person's frankness, or lack of it, might not be enough for you to add or delete a potential school from your list, but it should feature prominently in your final decision making.

While reviewing printed material or a school's Web site, check to see if the school publishes a nondiscrimination policy that includes sexual orientation or sexual preference. If the policy is not readily available, you should ask the school to send you a copy. Though the nondiscrimination policy might appear to be just another federal government-mandated requirement, in reality it might serve as a window into the culture of the school.

Check on Key Policies

Here's a tactic you might want to try, though it's a bit more dicey: Ask about the school's employer policies, and about military recruiting on campus. Recent changes to federal law has sent some shock waves regarding military recruiting on law school campus. You might wish to check with schools to find out the current status of this practice. Continue your perusal of the publications. Would you consider the descriptive language and photos depicting the law school as inclusive? Sure, some photos will be staged shots of a group of smiling diverse individuals, but the omission of inclusive imagery might be more telling indeed.

Inquire about other law school or central university policies. Is there a policy that provides same-sex partners of employees (faculty and staff) with domestic partners benefits? Though these benefits (health/life insurance, access to campus facilities such as libraries, fitness centers, residence halls) are usually available for same-sex partners of employees, some benefits maybe available to the partners of current students. The definition of and eligibility of partners will be left up to the institution to determine. You will find that today more and more public and private educational institutions and corporations are offering comparable benefits to gay and lesbian employees. A number of major law firms have begun to offer domestic partners benefits too. Everyone wants to maintain their competitive edge of attracting and hiring outstanding people.

What about financial aid policies or policies allocating other nonmonetary resources. Is marital status given any advantage? If so, are students in committed same-sex relationships disadvantaged somehow? You'll have to check with the policies at the various schools and discuss this matter with the appropriate administrator.

The existence of any policies that mandate equitable treatment of all students and employees does suggest that the law school is committed to supporting gay and lesbian people.

Quantify the "Level of Outness"

The most reliable barometer to identify a gay-friendly law school is to quantify the "level of outness." Are there members of the law school community who are out? This includes faculty, administrators, support staff, and of course, current students. Regardless of their position within the law school hierarchy it is important to understand and respect that different levels of outness will exist for different individuals. As in the large gay community, everyone has to determine their own comfort level and importance of being out. However, a critical mass of "out" members of the community and supportive nongay people will foster an environment where regardless of their sexual orientation every person is valued.

Check out the listing of courses. Are there any that specifically address gay issues? What about other courses will the instructor be introducing any discussion or hypothetical involving gay and lesbian people? Is there a gay or lesbian student organization already in place or will you have to organize one? What about other student organizations—inclusive (gay friendly) or exclusive (homophobic)?

Is there a gay or lesbian law school alumni group or a professional group within the local bar association chapter? Personally and professionally, you will find that networking within both the law school and larger legal community to be a necessity.

Look Beyond Campus

Make sure to continue your search for community beyond the law school environment. Of course the law school culture is important but many gay and lesbian law school applicants will be equally concerned about the extended law school community. Is the law school affiliated with a larger central university or college, if so, is there a gay and lesbian student center or campus organization(s)?

"Location, location, location" is still the most important factor when purchasing real estate, and it may be even more crucial when selecting which law school to settle into for a few years. Is there an estab-

SPECIAL CONSIDERATIONS

lished gay and lesbian community or if not, is that okay with you? We know that New York, San Francisco, Los Angeles, and Washington, DC have large and diverse gay communities. Don't overlook other cities, small towns, or rural settings that have smaller and less visible gay communities. You might be just as content there.

See for Yourself

Lastly, visit the school. Walk the corridors, attend a class and by all means speak with current gay and lesbian students. You should be able to contact students through a LGB organization, the admissions office, or an office of student affairs. Speaking with current students may provide insightful information that will prove to be your best resource helping you to identify gay-friendly schools. Your inability to contact gay students may not be good sign.

To Come Out or Not: The Admissions Process

Every applicant to law school is repeatedly told to use your personal statement to tell the admissions committee about yourself. Each year I tell countless applicants, "As an admissions professional I consider your personal statement to be your short story, therefore, tell me who you are and why your file is on my desk."

For many gay and lesbian applicants, their sexual orientation and their desire to pursue a legal education maybe so closely connected that they will feel compelled to be "out and proud" in their personal statement. Other gay and lesbian applicants will decide that their orientation has nothing to do with their decision to apply to law school and will feel no compulsion to be out.

Clearly, it is very personal decision to decide to be out on your application and ultimately, in law school. You may find yourself being out on some applications and not on other applications. There is no right or wrong answer as to whether or not to be out. Many applicants will discover that who they are and articulating what they have or hope to accomplish can not be suddenly camouflaged or omitted.

Often gay and lesbian applicants will submit resumes that demonstrate extensive involvement with and commitment to lesbian and gay communities. These involvements may include leadership roles in campus organizations such as the gay student group. Applicants might have volunteer work or professional experience with other gay rights organizations such as Lambda Legal Defense Fund or the Human Rights Campaign. However, it would be unwise and inappropriate for the admissions committee to assume someone is gay because the applicant presents a "gay resume." On the flip side, such a demonstration of an involvement with gay-related issues might be the applicant's way to be comfortable with their own level of "outness," without stating their orientation explicitly in the personal statement.

Gay and Lesbian Students

Like all applicants to law school, gay and lesbian candidates will give some thought, regardless of how fleeting, as to who is actually reading their application material. Sure, it would be comforting to know if the reader was that gay or gay-friendly admissions person you encountered at the Law Forum. Usually, admissions committees are comprised of admissions professional staff, faculty and perhaps current students. Good admissions practices suggest that all readers will be able to set aside their personal opinions in order to subjectively evaluate an applicant to their law school. I believe that admissions offices conduct their processes in very fair and impartial ways. Apart from law schools that adhere to religious doctrines, as gay and lesbian applicants you should be confident knowing that your candidacy will be evaluated on the merits, and not with discrimination or bias.

Law schools must provide an intellectual environment where all individuals regardless of their sexual orientation feel empowered to fully participate in the institutional mission of learning the law without the fear of alienation, or reprisal. Every law school reports that they value diversity (as they define the term) in the classroom. The exchange of ideas should not be limited to law school students who offer racial and ethnic diversity. The perspective and opinions of gay and lesbian law students will be valued in the classroom and ultimately, in the legal profession.

It is my hope that gay and lesbian law school applicants will add some of the ideas outlined in this chapter to their selection criteria when considering which law school to apply to.

CHAPTER 18

Students with Disabilities

by Chris Rosa

In the late 1970s, the political and social landscape was rapidly changing for people with disabilities. The Education for All Handicapped Children's Act of 1972 guaranteed equal access to elementary and secondary education, and the first generation of students with disabilities to reap the benefits were coming of age. A new civil rights consciousness was emerging among people with disabilities and was galvanized through their efforts to implement Section #504 of the 1973 Rehabilitation Act—the first comprehensive civil rights law ever enacted for people with disabilities. This landmark legislation would ultimately provide unprecedented access and opportunity to Americans with disabilities in post-secondary education. It was in this context that a young Steve Mikita pursued his dream of going to law school.

As a person with a neuromuscular disability, Steve was used to being a pioneer, used to being "the first." The first freshman ever to use a wheelchair on Duke University's campus, Steve graduated magna cum laude. He had managed to achieve this success without requiring much in the way of reasonable academic adjustments, by taking classes that were flexible regarding attendance, and which required papers rather than in-class exams. In this way Steve was able to balance the demands of his college course work against the physical demands of living with a disability. Confident that he could employ the same approach to achieve similar results in law school, Steve entered Brigham Young University Law school, his school of choice. He became only the second wheelchair user to attend BYU's Law School.

However, within his first few weeks at BYU, it became painfully apparent to Steve that law school would be very different than college. He had never fallen behind in his reading as an undergraduate and now, despite his best efforts, he was consistently behind in reading law books which were impossible for him

SPECIAL CONSIDERATIONS

to lift, let alone peruse. He found law school exams long and physically grueling; for the first time, he was forced to request extended exam time in a separate setting. Confronted with this very sobering reality, Steve was forced to make two very difficult admissions. He had not been physically and emotionally prepared for the rigorous lifestyle of law school, and he would have to reduce his course load, which meant he would miss graduating with his class.

Undaunted by these trying circumstances, Steve quickly regrouped and mobilized all the resources that would make it possible for him to put in the long hours of study that law school demands. He graduated in four years and got a job in the Utah attorney general's office, where he now serves as the Assistant Attorney General. As an expert on the Americans with Disabilities Act, Steve has conducted trainings for educational institutions to help ensure that they are accessible to people with disabilities. He currently serves as a visiting professor at BYU Law School where he teaches a seminar on disability law.

Because of trailblazers like Steve Mikita, people with disabilities are applying to law schools in unprecedented numbers today. For these people, legal training is not only a means to preserve their legal rights, but also a way of gaining access to well-paying jobs and key resources for affluence and influence. This chapter will attempt to guide you through the constellation of unique factors that have a bearing on your choice of law schools when you are a person with a disability.

Are You Ready?

The decision to go to law school involves a major commitment of time, money, energy, and the development of a professional sense of self. It is an enormous commitment for any individual, but especially for individuals with disabilities. In choosing a law school, people with disabilities commit the same personal resources that all students devote to the law school endeavor. And in addition, people with disabilities must also realign the access resources they rely on for independence and success in other parts of their lives in order to support their efforts in law school. This reallocation of independent living resources to support legal training often significantly diminishes people with disabilities' quality of life in other life domains. If one is truly ready for law school and chooses the right program, these sacrifices are surely worth it. However, in order to avoid regrettable decisions, candidates with disabilities must understand what it takes to be ready academically, logistically, physically, and emotionally for the rigors of law school; they then must be willing look at themselves critically and ask, "Am I really ready for this?"

The Right Stuff

Like all candidates for law school, students with disabilities must ensure that their candidate profiles meet the criteria for admission to the programs to which they apply and that their profiles are sufficiently attractive to merit serious consideration from admission committees. In constructing applicant profiles, people with disabilities should consider disability issues that will affect the way they present themselves as candidates.

It's Academic: Undergraduate Performance

Candidates' performance in undergraduate courses will be a significant factor in whether or not they are admitted to their programs of choice. But your GPA doesn't have to decide your fate. If your undergraduate performance was affected by a disability issue such as an undergraduate institution's failure to adequately meet your needs for reasonable accommodation, or a learning disability that went undiagnosed throughout most of a college career, use your personal statement, letters of reference, admissions committee interviews, etcetera to "explain away" a lower grade point average. While such explanations may improve your chances for admission, they often do so at the cost of disclosing your identity as a candidate with a disability.

To Tell or Not to Tell: Disclosing a Disability

While personal statements, letters of reference, LSAT scores, and interviews with admissions committees offer candidates with disabilities the opportunity to demonstrate the richness of their backgrounds and strengths as applicants, these dimensions of the candidate profile are fraught with opportunities for others to learn about one's status as a candidate with a disability. For those concerned about disability disclosure, these aspects of your candidate profile must be carefully managed. Here are some tips on managing disability disclosure in the admissions process:

- The decision of whether or not to disclose a disability in a personal statement is a very difficult, very personal one. This decision pits people's pride in their disability identity against their concerns that lingering cultural biases against people with disabilities will cause candidates who have disclosed their disabilities to be perceived as somehow less viable by admissions committees. If you are at all concerned about disability disclosure, unless it is central to your personal statement's thesis or to your ability to "explain away" a subpar undergraduate performance, follow this general rule: When in doubt, leave it out!
- Speak to those providing you with letters of reference who are aware of your disability and let them know how you feel about disability disclosure so that they do not unwittingly disclose information that you're uncomfortable with in their reference letters.
- If you have a disability and are at all concerned with the implications of disability disclosure, do not volunteer any information about your disability during interviews with admissions personnel or program representatives. While the asking the question, "Do you have a disability?" is illegal in most admissions contexts, if asked such an inappropriate questioning during an interview, asserting your Americans with Disabilities Act right to confidentiality will probably not help your admissions chances. If asked about your disability, you might consider simply and honestly informing the interviewer that you have a disability that, with the necessary reasonable accommodations, in no way limits your ability to be successful in graduate school.

SPECIAL CONSIDERATIONS

The "Maris Effect" and the LSAT

In 1961, the New York Yankees' Roger Maris hit home runs at a torrid pace that enabled him to eclipse Babe Ruth's single season record for round-trippers, a record that the experts swore would never be broken. In breaking Ruth's record of 60 home runs, Maris was the subject of much controversy and criticism among contemporaries who thought his accomplishment was less valid because he hit his 61 homers during a 162 game schedule, while Ruth reached 60 home runs in only 154 games. As a result of this controversy, Baseball Commissioner Ford Frick placed an asterisk next to his home run total of 61, which forever stigmatized and diminished Maris' record-setting total. When candidates with disabilities take the LSAT under accommodative conditions, they run the risk of experiencing the "Maris Effect."

Even though reasonable exam accommodations do not provide testers with disabilities a distinct advantage over standard exam takers, the LSAT includes a statement in exam reports indicating that accommodative exams were taken under nonstandard conditions. This distinction may cause even the highest LSAT scores to be considered less valid and may serve as a red flag, alerting programs to candidates' status as applicants with disabilities. Those who are concerned about the issue of disability disclosure should beware of the "Maris Effect" and weigh the potential costs of disclosing their disabilities through this process against the benefits of accommodative testing when considering taking the LSAT under nonstandard conditions.

Taking the LSAT Under Accommodative Conditions

Reasonable accommodations in the exam setting may be available for individuals with documented disabilities who wish to take the LSAT. These accommodations may include testing material in alternative, accessible formats, provision of wheelchair-accessible testing sites, amanuensis services, and extended exam time. The provision of reasonable accommodations is triggered by a formal request to Law Services. This request must be comprised of:

- A completed LSAT Accommodation Form for Candidates with Disabilities
- A completed Candidates Form
- A Specialist Form to be completed by a certified/licensed professional
- A completed Authorization to Release Information Form (if you wish accommodations information to be released to the schools to which to apply)
- Accompanying disability documentation which, if documenting a cognitive disability, must adhere to LSAC's official guidelines

Get your request for exam accommodations in early! It is important to submit all accommodations information, along with LSAT registration, to Legal Services by the appropriate deadline for the exam you wish to take. In most instances, Legal Services will process your request for accommodations within two weeks of its receipt. Legal Services is not required to consider requests for accommodations received after the deadline for late registration, since doing so would constitute an undue administrative burden for LSAC. You must submit a completed LSAT Accommodations Form for Candidates with Disabilities each time you wish to take the LSAT in an accommodative setting. You should submit the rest of the "accommodations packet," i.e., documentation, etcetera, only if your accommodations needs have changed from prior LSAT administrations.

Requests for Additional Time

Taking the LSAT under most accommodative conditions will have no impact on your admissions profile; they will be reported like other exams taken under "standard conditions" and will offer no "red flags" of your disability status. However, if you receive extended test time as an accommodation, LSAC will send a statement with your LSDAS Law School Reports indicating that your scores should be interpreted with "great sensitivity and flexibility." Such scores are reported individually, are not averaged with standard-time scores, and therefore, percentile ranks are not available for these scores and will not be reported. Scores reported in this manner may serve as an indication that you are a candidate with a disability to admissions committees; if you are concerned about disability disclosure, you must weigh the potential costs of disclosing your disability against the potential benefits of taking your exam in the most accessible setting. Individual law schools may waive the LSAT requirement for candidates with disabilities, so if you wish to explore this possibility, discuss this option with law schools you are considering.

Assessing Accessibility

Once you've narrowed the field and have a short list of law schools you're interested in, you'll have to make some tough choices. But before doing that, there's more work to be done. Here are the main factors to consider in judging how accessible the law schools on your short list are to people with disabilities.

Ramps, Raised Dots, and TTYs: Physical Access

The architectural and technological accessibility of a campus should play a significant role in your evaluation of law schools. The following questions will help you to evaluate the physical accessibility of a school.

1. What is the campus terrain like? Is it hilly or flat?
2. What is the campus infrastructure like? Are walkways and roadways well paved or littered with cracks and potholes?
3. Are the buildings in which all aspects of the law student experience are housed accessible to students with mobility-related disabilities? If not, what is the institution's policy regarding moving classes and other law student activities to accessible sites to accommodate students with disabilities?
4. Are the assistive technologies that you need available and are the academic computing facilities accessible to students with disabilities?

SPECIAL CONSIDERATIONS

5. The school's law library will play a central role in your legal education. How accessible are its facilities and services to students with disabilities? What kind of assistive technologies are available?
6. Many law schools have clinical components that allow students to try out their legal skills representing clients in a variety of community and institutional settings. Are these clinical settings and their facilities accessible to people with disabilities?

Get with the Program: Programmatic Access

For all students with disabilities, but particularly for students with learning, sensory, and psychiatric disabilities, the programmatic accessibility of law schools will play a significant part your choice of schools. When assessing the accessibility of law programs from an academic perspective, keep the following questions in mind:

1. Law schools invariably demand large volumes of assigned and unassigned reading. What are the institution's policies regarding the provision of reading and other course materials in accessible formats?
2. What are the institution's policies on the provision of reader, note taker, and sign language interpreter services?
3. What are the law school's policies on incomplete grades and leaves of absence?
4. What are the institution's policies on accommodative testing?
5. Where does the institution keep confidential student disability documentation? It should not store such records in your law school student files, which are not strictly confidential.

Office of Services for Students with Disabilities

Effective services and accommodations for law students with disabilities is usually an indicator that an institution has a high quality Office of Services for Students with Disabilities (OSSD). Effective OSSDs will work closely with you and law school faculty and administration to ensure that your accommodation needs are met. It's a good sign if the school established an office dedicated solely to coordinating the provision of reasonable accommodations and support services to students with disabilities, as opposed to assigning this responsibility to a person or office with many other responsibilities. The commitment of significant resources to accommodate students with disabilities through an OSSD is often indicative of an institution's larger commitment to equal access and opportunity for individuals with disabilities in all aspects of law student life.

PART SIX

Experiences from the Real World

CHAPTER 19

What Law School Students and Grads Say

You've progressed a long way down the road to law school. You've learned how to gain admission to a program that fits your needs. You've explored how to find the money to pay for your legal education. But you may still have many questions. What's law school really like? Will my investment be worth it? Of course, your own answers to these questions lie in the future. In the meantime, however, we can show you how people who have been down the road to law school would answer.

Our survey included law school students, recent graduates, and established lawyers. Their responses offer perspective on what to expect and how to get the most out of law school. One piece of advice was offered by many of our interviewees: Get as much practical exposure as possible. Exposure to legal work while in law school will help you uncover your likes and dislikes, and create opportunities for the future. Most of the grads we interviewed had participated in clinics, held summer jobs with law firms, and/or participated in mock trial groups. For most grads, these real-world tastes were highlights of the law school experience. But we'll let our survey group speak for themselves.

Born Lawyer

J.D., Southwestern U., 1977

I can remember even when I was young I wanted to be a criminal lawyer, to have what I thought would be an exciting life. It was the only thing I ever wanted to be. I applied to between six and ten schools and went to the only one that accepted me.

EXPERIENCES FROM THE REAL WORLD

The first emotion that comes to mind regarding law school was feeling overwhelmed. Looking back now, it seems they were trying to intimidate us. There was a lot of energy—you became obsessed. The entire grade could be based on one exam, and this produced a lot of pressure. I would have certainly preferred more exams. The constant first-year fear was feeling that one bad grade could get us kicked out of the program. But I think as a whole, the positive outweighed the negative.

After I graduated, I started out with an insurance defense firm. I left to do trial work and eventually went into partnership with one of the attorneys I was working with. He ended up leaving and now I run my own firm, which specializes in defense work in the civil arena. I think going to law school was the best thing that ever happened to me. It makes you more critical and disciplined; it makes you appreciate how you speak, how you structure your thoughts. I still enjoy being a lawyer, and I hope to expand my firm while continuing to do more and different things in litigation.

I recently hired two lawyers who had both just graduated from law school. They were both heavily in debt. What I would tell prospective students today is to ask themselves if they really want to be $100,000 in debt because they want to be a lawyer. I don't know that many rich lawyers.

Do Your Research

First-year student, CUNY—Queens College

I was always good at debating, and I was interested in politics. The event that shaped my desire to go to law school was a football accident in which I was disabled, and then the process of going through a related lawsuit. I believed that I wasn't represented very well. As an African American and a disabled person, I felt that I was a member of two cultures that needed more representation in the legal profession. I'm in my first year, and in my particular program it's the second year, which is supposed to be harder, where you get the tougher core courses. I'm enjoying it right now. It's more time-consuming than college, but I can still take one day off a week and watch a ball game without feeling guilty. You need to do this or you'll go crazy. The key is good time management and prioritization.

Do your research on each law school you apply to and know what you're getting into. CUNY has great public interest clinics which align with my desire to be a disability lawyer. Students here help each other and interact more than at other schools, because of the pass-fail system used as opposed to the traditional Socratic tier grading. This program is interested in teaching future lawyers how to practice. And they have been very accommodating with regards to my disability, willing to deal with new questions as they arise in order to make my life here productive and successful. However, the school operates on a state budget and we're suffering now as the new governor's cutbacks are depriving us of resources.

Night School

J.D., Fordham, 1994

Why did I go to law school? Honestly, everyone else in my family is a lawyer, and I felt I had a precise mind—that made me a good prospect.

I started out at St. John's. I couldn't get into an Ivy League program, and since I wanted to practice in New York, it was really just as good anyway. The program at St. John's was geared toward details that would help you pass the local bar exam. After my first year, I transferred to Fordham. Being more of a nationally oriented program, you were really encouraged to think more about theoretical questions concerning the law. I preferred this approach, though I think it's St. John's approach that really gets you past the bar. I really don't think law school and undergrad school are that different in terms of difficulty. You don't have to be a genius to get through law school. You just need a strong work ethic.

I think I could have gotten more out of law school academically, but I was working full time as a press spokesperson for the local Office of Public Affairs. I went to school at night. But I think my achievements on the job and the connections I made then helped me getting my job as an Assistant District Attorney. I love what I'm doing now. I was able to start trying cases my first day on the job instead of moving depositions around for seven years as a cog in a big firm. Right now I'm happy as a clam making no money, trying cases in court. I know that at some point, if I want to raise a family, I have to see myself making more money, probably in a litigation firm.

What you do in law school has a direct impact on whether you will get a good job. Don't mortgage your future if you are not dead serious.

A Terrific Education

J.D., Cornell, 1968

My father was a lawyer. I like that sort of work and I wanted to help people. I was accepted to three schools but I had a fellowship to study in France for a year; Cornell was the only school that would take me without my having to reapply the following year. I found law school to be a very positive experience. I made a lot of friends and enjoyed it, but it's an awful lot of work—it's a job. It was a terrific education, though I'm not sure it made me more analytical and all the rest of the things you are supposed to be after having gone through law school.

I started out in private practice right away. While I was trying to establish my practice, I had to support myself by working at some other jobs as well. I worked part time as an assistant D.A., a law clerk, and a corporation counselor for five years before really establishing my practice. This is a tough job—a lot of hard work, a lot of pressure. I don't think anyone realizes how much time is involved. The law is a jealous mistress; it's very difficult to balance your personal and professional lives. I once knew a family court judge who had a quote hung on his wall that I still think is significant: "It's nice to be important, but it's more important to be nice." I think what he was getting at was that people need answers; you have to be a good listener, you must have empathy and compassion.

Law school students need internships to understand how things really work. In law school, you spend hours coming up with theory—in practice you need concrete answers in five minutes. You have to find your niche—for example, big city law or nonprofit. Not everybody works at a big firm; many go on to practice in a smaller setting. Take active steps to do different things in law school; take advantage of summer jobs and internships. Economics will be a factor. Can you afford to take a non-paying internship that will reward you with valuable experience? In the long run, I think you're better off, but with the cost of tuition these days, can you afford to do it?

To Change the Future

J.D., Widener, 1995

I wanted to effect long-term change for the public interest. In other professions, whether you're a sociologist or working in a soup kitchen, you can make an immediate impact on people's daily lives. What drew me to law school was that I believed—and I'm not so convinced now—that the law was a vehicle to better people's lives over the long haul.

For me, law school was a means to an end. It doesn't have a lot to do with the real world, so you just get through it. At least half the students at my school were going to work for their fathers. If you have this kind of connection, you really don't have to stress out in law school, you can just get by. Otherwise, to get a job, you have to be in the top of your class or figure out some other way to put yourself in an elite category.

I spent a year in my school's civil law clinic, not the usual semester, and went on to become a supervisor the following year. The great thing about clinics is you have the benefit of actually applying the law while simultaneously being able to draw on faculty advice, which is not something you can get working a summer job at a law firm. It opened up an immense amount of opportunity for me. This is certainly not the norm, but I actually got a chance to argue in federal court and won. I think it was instrumental in finding a job.

I am currently working as a law clerk for a presiding county judge. I love it; it's the best thing ever. I'm involved with child support issues, and domestic violence; I feel like I'm making a real difference in putting these sorts of offenders away.

What Law School Student and Grads Say

Defining a Career

J.D., Western New England, 1994

I didn't see myself doing much with my B.A. degree, and they pushed graduate education at the liberal arts college I attended. I wasn't a good enough writer to do anything in that direction and I just felt that I had to do something else. I applied to several schools, and was admitted to a couple of programs. I decided to accept a scholarship at Western New England, where I could also live with my parents while I was in school. I occasionally regretted not going to the best program to which I had been accepted, but it's a tough job market no matter where you go—and I don't have loans hanging over my head.

I liked law school. Still, I think it can't help but make you a little more cynical about things. You just see how contentious people are. Every time there's money in a family, you can see a battle for the estate emerging; everything is a lawsuit waiting to happen. As for the academic side of things—I don't want to sound clichéd—I found the third year boring. I was champing at the bit to get out and do something. If you have a clinic, you still spend a lot of time in class—and you can't always even get into a clinic. If you're in a big city, there may be more opportunities for internships and jobs than where I went to school. I think that's something to consider when you're applying to schools.

Experience Counts

During my second year, I was a staff member at my school's law review. I wrote a long, boring note that was eventually published. I then became a note editor and I looked at other people's long, boring notes. If you get published it's a nice feather in your cap when you are looking for a job, and you do get valuable experience through the process of producing a formal document. I guess I would do it again even though I complained about it a lot at the time.

When I got out of school, I clerked for a year. Without being in the top of your class at Harvard or having family connections, expect to take a clerkship to make connections and acquire professional references. You can try to do this while you're in school, too. Check your school paper for positions in firms doing research and that kind of thing. If you perform well while you're there, there's always the chance they might hire you when you graduate. My clerkship eventually helped me land a position in the firm where I work now, handling bankruptcy creditor's rights. I draft motions, talk with clients. There is nothing special about what I do; it's pretty straightforward legal work, but I find it satisfying. Of course, there is a lot of time pressure and other pressures, but when you finish a job there is always that sense of satisfaction.

Great Fun

J.D., University of Florida, 1994

I went to law school because I had lost a job due to budget cuts, was 40, and decided it would be fun. I wanted to see if all my friends who were lawyers—who talked about how grueling law school was—were right. Actually, I got interested for two more reasons: (1) I attended the obscenity trials related to 2 Live Crew, the rap group, and became interested in the legal process; and (2) In 1989, I was at a party and talking to someone about the possibility of a deep recession or depression. I said I probably would do well because I was used to scraping by as a writer, college adjunct, etcetera. He sneered that people like me were totally expendable, but since he was a lawyer he would always have a job. He was an associate in a big Manhattan law firm. (When he moved to be with his new wife in Philadelphia in 1991, it took him over a year to find a new job, I later found out.)

Law school was great fun. It was intellectually challenging, more so than grad school (I have master's degrees in English and creative writing and a lot of graduate credits in education). It was my first time living in a university town. All the students were very nice, I thought. We had a nice mix of people, mostly young, but also some my age (40 to start) and in between, and everyone seemed to mix fairly well. I was impressed with most of my professors. The work was very hard at first—like learning a whole new way of thinking—but there was a lot of camaraderie, as if you're in a shared experience. I remember on the first day my Civil Procedure teacher quoted Lou Reed: "Welcome to the start of a great adventure." Since I didn't care that much about grades, I didn't feel the pressure other students did. I ended up doing very well, graduating in the top three percent of my class.

I liked the "learning" part of law school. I liked having a lot of books to read all the time. I liked being with other people who were having the same experience. On the other hand, I guess I disliked the narrow focus that law schools have, the kind of forced bonding. In Professional Responsibility, I was one of the few people who would criticize lawyers and bring up the fact that 30,000 of them leave this profession every year. I'm old enough to know that lawyers steal. They never said in Professional Responsibility, Don't steal, which is probably 90 percent of the ethical problems attorneys have. Instead, we had these intellectual debates. I guess it was assumed everyone in the class was honest, but I know that some of my classmates will end up disbarred. In my opinion, there's far too much self-congratulation in law school.

Using a J.D. Without Practicing Law

I am currently a Visiting Assistant at the Center for Governmental Responsibility, a public policy institute/think tank at the school where I went to law school. I am on a grant to study legal issues in educational technology, but I do other things as well. I don't practice law, but I research the law, write legal memoranda that are published as documents by the state Education Department, and I keep up with developments in the exploding field of computer law and cyberlaw. I also read law review articles that interest me. I have worked a little on other projects, like editing an historic preservation model code for a colleague, and I help supervise ten law students who work as fellows and are placed at public interest law firms or organizations like my job. I make my own hours, have a lot of freedom, and I don't have to dress up most days.

I got the job by answering a national ad in the *Chronicle of Higher Education* that I found on the Internet. It helped that my past experience teaching teachers how to use computers and my law school courses were a perfect match for the grant-funded position. It didn't hurt that I was a student of the head of the committee which interviewed me.

From the Trenches
First-year student, Benjamin N. Cardozo School of Law

I was interested in obtaining a higher degree, and I think a law degree is more versatile than an M.B.A., more practical than a doctorate. I chose Cardozo based on the quality of its faculty, its strong entertainment and finance specialties, and its location.

As far as first impressions go, I thought it would be a lot of uptight people, but I have found a lot of different backgrounds, and very focused, very motivated people. There are some pompous knuckleheads, but no more so than anywhere else in life. I like the course material and the faculty in general, though I'm far from enthralled by the fact that the profs rely on you teaching yourself; the old sink-or-swim approach. It is constant work—you'll never be ahead because there is so much to do. I've heard a lot of talk about it being horrible, but it is manageable.

I think law school changes you—and it's going to change me a lot more as I go through, I can tell. It forces you to become more analytical. You're encouraged to be able to play both sides of the coin. The motto runs something like: "If the facts are against you, use the law. If the law is against you, use the facts. If the law and the facts are against you, argue."

Part-Time Flexibility
J.D., Brooklyn Law School, 1993

I got interested in applying to law school because my father was a lawyer—he tried to talk me out of it—and I was interested in politics and the running of the government. Being a person with a disability, I also needed a career that uses my intelligence; I mean, I'm not going to be performing any brain surgery. I only applied to a few schools because I wanted to go to Brooklyn and was pretty sure I could get in. Brooklyn had the best part-time program in the metropolitan area, and I didn't know if I had the stamina to go full time. Part time also gave me a more flexible schedule and liberty when it came to weekends.

I was a member of the Student Bar Association. It's partly a popularity club, but you do learn things. You set policy, administer a budget, and work with other student groups. People involved here tend to get involved in government in the future. You can make good contacts and dealing with people in this sort of environment is going to help you in the future. I also worked for the court attorney at the county Surrogate Court, writing memoranda, making recommendations, and briefing the judge on cases. He

EXPERIENCES FROM THE REAL WORLD

was kind of a bully, and it was a powerful feeling for me, because he was listening to what I said. I felt like a real participant in the practice of the law.

Clinical programs are really the key. There are schools that coach you to pass the bar, and others that are theoretical, and still others that emphasize the practical side of things but that will not necessarily help you pass bar. Look at a law school's clinical programs, which is where you learn how law works in the field. They can tell a lot about a school. They are also vital in making connections to the job market and making the adjustment from the academic world to the professional world. The danger is you can get obsessed with your clinic and that can eat into the time you need to spend on your other classes. You have to be careful to balance it out; it can become a quagmire.

I had my problems with law school. I think an emphasis is placed on the stars of the school. If you are in the top 25 percent, they want you to succeed. They don't care about the bottom quarter of the class and beat you over the head about how you aren't going to pass the bar. Most of my friends and I were in the bottom of the class, and we all passed the bar. I also found school far too theoretical, not focusing enough on practical considerations, i.e., how the law works in the real world. The bar itself is an exercise in futility. It is nothing like what you are supposed to be doing in real practice. Yes, you need to know the various laws, but a testing situation demands an immediate answer while in the real world you're expected to research a case.

There are times when I'm glad I made the investment in law school and there are times when I'm not. Two months ago, when I was unemployed, I was not. Now I'm working as a legislative liaison and systems advocate—basically a lobbyist for disability rights—meeting with various local government bodies. I also do research on the side. So, I'm doing fairly well and am pretty happy. I feel a little tied down in that I can't take my law degree anywhere out of the state without having to take the bar again.

My advice when it comes to law school is to make sure you are a good student before you go. What you study is not so important; just work until you are comfortable working hard. I did really well as an undergraduate, but in law school everyone is smart. Coming in, I was just another one of the kids with a 4.0 grade average. And you have to be ready to fall on your face.

Family and Career

J.D., Hastings, 1984

I decided to go to law school after working in a legal aid office. I really enjoyed the strategy involved in legal work—the intellectual challenge. Hastings became my choice for a couple of reasons. It was a decent school, I could afford it, and it's in a city—I'm definitely a city person. I paid my way through with loans, mostly. I also worked some part-time legal jobs that also proved to be great experiences.

My school was very ethnically mixed, but most students were Californians. I think the biggest factor in my law school experience was the faculty, some of whom were great, and some of whom weren't. I was already aware of the "unprincipled" association with lawyers, so I wasn't surprised by the money-grubbing side of things. In general, law school gave me more confidence. I had gone to public schools all my life, and I was surrounded by people who had gone to private schools—people who had always intimidated me for some reason. I did really well in law school, and it made me realize I was every bit as good as those people. Looking back, I would say try to stay relaxed and concentrate on what you need to know, not how you appear to others around you.

I worked in a low-income clinic while I was in school. You work the whole case, interviewing the client and making recommendations. I did well on my cases and found it very rewarding. Everyone should work at a clinic. If you really hate it, it's better to know early on and get involved with corporate transactions or some other form of law where you don't have to do that sort of work.

The law can be very consuming, taking over your personal life. When I got out of school I was prepared to work the long hours. Today, I'm the mother of two children. I work for the State Department on diplomatic privileges and international immunities issues. My job is much more manageable and I can't envision searching out that sort of all-consuming job now, although I hope to find the time to publish some of the material I'm working on. I love being a lawyer and wouldn't want to do anything else.

PART SEVEN

Law Schools

The law school data in this section was provided by the Midwest Association of Prelaw Advisers (MAPLA). A software (Windows) version of this data is available from MAPLA; see the copyright page for more information. MAPLA does not endorse or acknowledge the effectiveness or utility of any commercial test preparation or advising program.

Directory of U.S. Law Schools

How to Use the Information

School Name and Contact Information
Here you'll find the information you need to contact each school by mail, phone, and fax.

Characteristics of Entering Class 1997
This section provides statistics on how many and what kind of students attend the school. The first number given after the category of Minority is the percentage of the fall 1997 entering class that was classified as minority (African American, Asian American, Latino, etcetera). The second number (the one following the slash) is the percentage of the entire student body that was categorized as minority.

Academics
Information on the academic programs offered by the school is contained in this section.

Finances
In this section you'll find information that will help you determine how much attending the school will cost and how good your chances are of getting a scholarship. The tuition figures provided are for the 1997–1998 academic year. We have listed both in-state and out-of-state tuition amounts; most state schools have a lower tuition for in-state residents, but most private schools have no such distinction.

LAW SCHOOLS

Admissions Requirements
The deadline for application for admission in the fall semester is given in this section. Some schools also accept applicants mid year; those schools are noted. Contact the school for application deadline dates for midyear admission. Also be aware that some special programs at a law school might have deadlines earlier than the one listed here.

Selectivity
The information printed in this section will help you determine your chances of being accepted by the school. For most schools, the information is for the fall 1997 entering class.

A

UNIVERSITY OF AKRON

School of Law
Akron, OH 44325-2901
Phone: (800) 4-AKRONU
Fax: (330) 258-2343
E-mail: lawadmissions@uakron.edu
Web Site:
http://http://www.uakron.edu/law
**Characteristics of Entering Class
1997:** Full-time students: 130. Part-time students: 71. In-state: 78%. Minority: 11%. Women: 45%. Average Age: 29.
Academics: Evening program. No summer program offered.
Finances: Tuition: $12,083. Students receiving scholarships: 37%.
Admission Requirements: Application deadline: 04/01. Admissions: fall term only.
Selectivity: Applications received: 1,198. Students accepted: 587. Students enrolled: 201. Median undergraduate GPA: 3.18. Median LSAT: 152.

UNIVERSITY OF ALABAMA

School of Law
Box 870382;101 Bryant Drive East
Tuscaloosa, AL 35487-0382
Phone: (205) 348-5440
Fax: (205) 348-3917
E-mail: admission@law.ua.edu
Web Site: http://www.law.ua.edu
**Characteristics of Entering Class
1997:** Full-time students: 204. In-state: 90%. Minority: 10%. Women: 40%. Average Age: 24.
Academics: No evening program. Summer program offered.
Finances: In-State Tuition: $3,758. Out-of-State Tuition: $8,382. Students receiving scholarships: 25%. Students receiving loans: 65%.

Admission Requirements: Application deadline: 03/01. Admissions: fall term only.
Selectivity: Applications received: 757. Students accepted: 326. Students enrolled: 204. Median undergraduate GPA: 3.34. Median LSAT: 157.

ALBANY LAW SCHOOL

80 New Scotland Avenue
Albany, NY 12208
Phone: (518) 445-2326
Fax: (516) 445-2369
E-mail: admissions@mail.als.edu
Web Site: http://www.als.edu
**Characteristics of Entering Class
1997:** Full-time students: 232. Part-time students: 18. In-state: 85%. Minority: 16/17%. Women: 54%. Average Age: 26.
Academics: No evening program. No summer program offered.
Finances: Tuition: $18,795. Students receiving scholarships: 43%. Students receiving loans: 87%.
Admission Requirements: Application deadline: March 15. Admissions: fall term only.
Selectivity: Applications received: 1,199. Students accepted: 849. Students enrolled: 250. Median undergraduate GPA: 3.08. Median LSAT: 150.

AMERICAN UNIVERSITY

Washington College of Law
4801 Massachusetts Avenue, N.W.
Washington, DC 20016
Phone: (202) 274-4101
Fax: (202) 274-4107
**Characteristics of Entering Class
1997:** Full-time students: 286. Part-time students: 15. Minority: 28%. Women: 60%. Average Age: 24.
Academics: Evening program. No summer program offered.
Finances: Tuition: $21,554. Students receiving loans: 80%.

Admission Requirements: Application deadline: March 1. Admissions: fall term only.
Selectivity: Applications received: 4,482. Students accepted: 1,912. Students enrolled: 381. Median undergraduate GPA: 3.27. Median LSAT: 156.

UNIVERSITY OF ARIZONA

College of Law
1100 E. Speedway
Tucson, AZ 85721
Phone: (520) 621-3477
Fax: (520) 621-9140
E-mail: admissions@nt.law.arizona.edu
Web Site: http://www.law.arizona.edu
**Characteristics of Entering Class
1997:** Full-time students: 151. In-state: 75%. Minority: 28/25%. Women: 44%. Average Age: 25.
Academics: No evening program. No summer program offered.
Finances: In-State Tuition: $4,060. Out-of-State Tuition: $10,712. Students receiving scholarships: 60%. Students receiving loans: 80%.
Admission Requirements: Application deadline: March 1. Admissions: fall term only.
Selectivity: Applications received: 1,459. Students accepted: 442. Students enrolled: 151. Median undergraduate GPA: 3.41. Median LSAT: 160.

ARIZONA STATE UNIVERSITY

College of Law
Armstrong Hall
Tempe, AZ 85287-7906
Phone: (602) 965-7896
Fax: (602) 965-5550
E-mail: wanda.decrow@asu.edu
**Characteristics of Entering Class
1997:** Full-time students: 158. In-state: 70%. Minority: 30/26%. Women: 47%. Average Age: 27.
Academics: No evening program. No summer program offered.

LAW SCHOOLS

Finances: In-State Tuition: $4,059. Out-of-State Tuition: $10,711. Students receiving scholarships: 40%.
Admission Requirements: Application deadline: March 1. Admissions: fall term only.
Selectivity: Applications received: 1,754. Students accepted: 391. Students enrolled: 158. Median undergraduate GPA: 3.3. Median LSAT: 159.

UNIVERSITY OF ARKANSAS—LITTLE ROCK

School of Law
1201 McAlmont
Little Rock, AR 72120
Phone: (501) 324-9903
Fax: (501) 324-9433
Characteristics of Entering Class 1997: Full-time students: 81. Part-time students: 50. In-state: 89%. Minority: 10%. Women: 41%. Average Age: 26.
Academics: Evening program. Summer program offered.
Finances: Students receiving scholarships: 11%. Students receiving loans: 63%.
Admission Requirements: Application deadline: April 1. Admissions: fall term only.
Selectivity: Applications received: 460. Students accepted: 234. Students enrolled: 131. Median undergraduate GPA: 3.23. Median LSAT: 152.

UNIVERSITY OF ARKANSAS—FAYETTEVILLE

School of Law
Leflar Law Center
Fayetteville, AR 72701
Phone: (501) 575-3102
Fax: (501) 575-3320
Web Site: http://www.law.uark.edu
Characteristics of Entering Class 1997: Minority: 9/10%. Women: 45%. Average Age: 26.
Academics: No evening program. No summer program offered.

Finances: In-State Tuition: $3,604. Out-of-State Tuition: $7,780. Students receiving scholarships: 25%. Students receiving loans: 77%.
Admission Requirements: Application deadline: N/A. Admissions: fall term only.
Selectivity: Applications received: 675. Students accepted: 317. Students enrolled: 131. Median undergraduate GPA: 3.26. Median LSAT: 153.

B

UNIVERSITY OF BALTIMORE

School of Law
1420 N. Charles Street
Baltimore, MD 21201
Phone: (410) 837-4459
Fax: (410) 837-4450
E-mail: lwadmiss@ubmail.ubalt.edu
Web Site: http://www.ubalt.edu/http://www/law
Characteristics of Entering Class 1997: Full-time students: 220. Part-time students: 83. In-state: 76%. Minority: 18%. Women: 54%. Average Age: 28.
Academics: Evening program. Summer program offered.
Finances: In-State Tuition: $7,812. Out-of-State Tuition: $13,940. Students receiving scholarships: 7%.
Admission Requirements: Application deadline: April 1. Admissions: Fall term only.
Selectivity: Applications received: 1,684. Students accepted: 902. Students enrolled: 303. Median undergraduate GPA: 2.98. Median LSAT: 151.

BAYLOR LAW SCHOOL

P.O. Box 97288
Waco, TX 76798
Phone: (254) 710-1911
Fax: (254) 710-2316
E-mail: Law_Support@Baylor.edu
Web Site: http://www.baylor.edu/~Law
Characteristics of Entering Class 1997: Full-time students: 75. In-state: 73%. Minority: 6%. Women: 37%. Average Age: 22.
Academics: No evening program. No summer program offered.
Finances: Students receiving scholarships: 40%. Students receiving loans: 97%.
Admission Requirements: Application deadline: March 1. Mid-year admission allowed.
Selectivity: Applications received: 797. Students accepted: 310. Students enrolled: 75. Median undergraduate GPA: 3.54. Median LSAT: 160.

BOSTON COLLEGE

Law School
885 Centre Street
Newton, MA 02159
Phone: (617) 552-4350
Fax: (617) 552-2615
E-mail: bclawadm@bc.edu
Web Site: http://www.bc.edu/lawschool
Characteristics of Entering Class 1997: Full-time students: 289. In-state: 33%. Minority: 22/20%. Women: 55%. Average Age: 24.
Academics: No evening program. No summer program offered.
Finances: Tuition: $22,300. Students receiving scholarships: 35%. Students receiving loans: 80%.
Admission Requirements: Application deadline: March 1. Admissions: fall term only.
Selectivity: Applications received: 4,090. Students accepted: 1,237. Students enrolled: 289. Median undergraduate GPA: 3.5. Median LSAT: 161.

Boston University

School of Law
765 Commonwealth Avenue
Boston, MA 02215
Phone: (617) 353-3100
Fax: (617) 353-2547
E-mail: bulawadm@bu.edu
Web Site: web.bu.edu/law

**Characteristics of Entering Class
1997:** Full-time students: 326. In-state: 22%. Minority: 20/17%. Women: 43%. Average Age: 24.
Academics: No evening program. No summer program offered.
Finances: Tuition: $21,970. Students receiving scholarships: 45%. Students receiving loans: 80%.
Admission Requirements: Application deadline: March 1. Admissions: fall term only.
Selectivity: Applications received: 4,103. Students accepted: 1,651. Students enrolled: 326. Median undergraduate GPA: 3.28. Median LSAT: 161.

Brigham Young University

Law School
340 JRCB, Box 28000
Provo, UT 84602-8000
Phone: (801) 378-4277
Fax: (801) 378-3595
E-mail: wilcockl@lawgate.byu.edu
Web Site: http://www.law.byu.edu

**Characteristics of Entering Class
1997:** Full-time students: 140. In-state: 61%. Minority: 14%. Women: 34%. Average Age: 26.
Academics: No evening program. No summer program offered.
Finances: In-State Tuition: $4,950. Out-of-State Tuition: $7,430. Students receiving scholarships: 62%. Students receiving loans: 80%.
Admission Requirements: Application deadline: February 1. Admissions: fall term only.

Selectivity: Applications received: 685. Students accepted: 226. Students enrolled: 140. Median undergraduate GPA: 3.6. Median LSAT: 160.

Brooklyn Law School

250 Joralemon Street
Brooklyn, NY 11201
Phone: (718) 780-7906
Fax: (718) 780-0395
E-mail: admitq@brooklaw.edu
Web Site: http://www.brooklaw.edu

**Characteristics of Entering Class
1997:** Full-time students: 275. Part-time students: 210. In-state: 7,085%. Minority: 21/20%. Women: 46%. Average Age: 25.
Academics: Evening program. Summer program offered.
Finances: Tuition: $20,640. Students receiving scholarships: 35%. Students receiving loans: 79%.
Admission Requirements: Application deadline: None. Admissions: fall term only.
Selectivity: Applications received: 2,826. Students accepted: 1,396. Students enrolled: 485. Median undergraduate GPA: 3.33. Median LSAT: 157.

University of Buffalo—SUNY

School of Law
312 O'Brian Hall
Buffalo, NY 14260
Phone: (716) 645-2907
Fax: (716) 645-5940
Web Site: http://www.buffalo.edu/law

**Characteristics of Entering Class
1997:** Full-time students: 217. In-state: 96%. Minority: 22/19%. Women: 49%. Average Age: 26.
Academics: No evening program. No summer program offered.
Finances: In-State Tuition: $7,350. Out-of-State Tuition: $12,000. Students receiving scholarships: 13%. Students receiving loans: 71%.

Admission Requirements: Application deadline: February 1. Admissions: fall term only.
Selectivity: Applications received: 944. Students accepted: 500. Students enrolled: 217. Median undergraduate GPA: 3.2. Median LSAT: 154.

C

University of California—Berkeley

5 Boalt Hall
Berkeley, CA 94720-7200
Phone: (510) 642-2274
Fax: (510) 643-6222
E-mail: admissions@boalt.berkeley.edu
Web Site: http://www.law.berkeley.edu

**Characteristics of Entering Class
1997:** Full-time students: 268. In-state: 71%. Minority: 20%. Women: 51%. Average Age: 24.
Academics: No evening program. No summer program offered.
Finances: Students receiving scholarships: 60%. Students receiving loans: 75%.
Admission Requirements: Application deadline: February 1. Admissions: fall term only.
Selectivity: Applications received: 4,171. Students accepted: 820. Students enrolled: 268. Median undergraduate GPA: 3.76. Median LSAT: 166.

University of California—Davis

School of Law
King Hall
Davis, CA 95616-5201
Phone: (530) 752-6477
Fax: (530) 752-6125
E-mail: admission@lawadmin.ucdavis.edu
Web Site: http://www.kinghall.ucdavis.edu

LAW SCHOOLS

Characteristics of Entering Class
1997: Full-time students: 172. In-state: 86%. Minority: 20%. Women: 65%. Average Age: 25.
Academics: No evening program. No summer program offered.
Finances: In-State Tuition: $10,843. Out-of-State Tuition: $19,827. Students receiving scholarships: 76%. Students receiving loans: 81%.
Admission Requirements: Application deadline: February 1. Admissions: fall term only.
Selectivity: Applications received: 2,095. Students accepted: 805. Students enrolled: 172. Median undergraduate GPA: 3.49. Median LSAT: 160.

UNIVERSITY OF CALIFORNIA—HASTINGS

College of Law
200 McAllister Street
San Francisco, CA 94102
Phone: (415) 565-4623
Fax: (415) 565-4863
E-mail: admiss@uchastings.edu
Web Site: http://www.uchastings.edu
Characteristics of Entering Class
1997: Full-time students: 311. In-state: 88%. Minority: 25/31%. Women: 51%. Average Age: 25.
Academics: No evening program. No summer program offered.
Finances: In-State Tuition: $11,172. Out-of-State Tuition: $19,564. Students receiving scholarships: 69%. Students receiving loans: 80%.
Admission Requirements: Application deadline: February 16. Admissions: fall term only.
Selectivity: Applications received: 3,605. Students accepted: 1,287. Students enrolled: 311. Median undergraduate GPA: 3.33. Median LSAT: 162.

UNIVERSITY OF CALIFORNIA—LOS ANGELES

School of Law
71 Dodd Hall Box 951445
Los Angeles, CA 90095-1445
Phone: (310) 825-2080
E-mail: admissions@law.ucla.edu
Web Site: http://www.law.ucla.edu
Characteristics of Entering Class
1997: Full-time students: 381. In-state: 76%. Minority: 35/37%. Women: 46%. Average Age: 24.
Academics: No evening program. No summer program offered.
Finances: In-State Tuition: $10,916. Out-of-State Tuition: $19,900. Students receiving scholarships: 8%.
Admission Requirements: Application deadline: January 15. Admissions: fall term only.
Selectivity: Applications received: 3,957. Students accepted: 1,007. Students enrolled: 381. Median undergraduate GPA: 3.59. Median LSAT: 162.

CALIFORNIA WESTERN

School of Law
225 Cedar Street
San Diego, CA 92101
Phone: (619) 525-1401
Fax: (619) 685-2916
E-mail: admissions@cwsl.edu
Web Site: http://www.cwsl.edu
Characteristics of Entering Class
1997: Full-time students: 292. In-state: 54%. Minority: 33/29%. Women: 52%. Average Age: 27.
Academics: No evening program. Summer program offered.
Finances: Tuition: $19,750. Students receiving scholarships: 17%. Students receiving loans: 75%.
Admission Requirements: Application deadline: April 11. Midyear admission allowed.
Selectivity: Applications received: 1,779. Students accepted: 1,277. Students enrolled: 292. Median undergraduate GPA: 3.05. Median LSAT: 150.

CAMPBELL UNIVERSITY

School of Law
P.O. Box 158
Bules Creek, NC 27506
School did not submit data.

CAPITAL UNIVERSITY

Law School
303 E. Broad Street
Columbus, OH 43215
Phone: (614) 236-6510
Fax: (614) 236-6970
E-mail: law-admissions@capital.edu
Web Site: http://www.capital.edu/law/law/htm
Characteristics of Entering Class
1997: Full-time students: 166. Part-time students: 116. In-state: 73%. Minority: 11/12%. Women: 46%. Average Age: 26.
Academics: Evening program. Summer program offered.
Finances: Tuition: $14,993. Students receiving scholarships: 30%. Students receiving loans: 81%.
Admission Requirements: Application deadline: N/A. Admissions: fall term only.
Selectivity: Applications received: 857. Students accepted: 600. Students enrolled: 282. Median undergraduate GPA: 3.0 Median LSAT: 150.

BENJAMIN N. CARDOZO SCHOOL OF LAW

55 Fifth Avenue
New York, NY 10003
Phone: 212-790-0274
Fax: 212-790-0345
E-mail: lawinfo@ymail.yu.edu
Web Site: www.yu.edu/csl/law

Directory of U.S. Law Schools

Characteristics of Entering Class 1997: Full-time students: 329. Minority: 28%. Women: 49%. Average Age: 23.
Academics: No evening program. No summer program offered.
Finances: Tuition: 19,780. Students receiving scholarships: 53%. Students receiving loans: 74%.
Admission Requirements: Application deadline: April 1. Midyear admission allowed.
Selectivity: Applications received: 2,330. Students accepted: 1,074. Students enrolled: 329. Median undergraduate GPA: 3.3. Median LSAT: 157.

Case Western Reserve University

School of Law
11075 East Blvd.
Cleveland, OH 44106
Phone: (216) 368-3600
Characteristics of Entering Class 1997: Full-time students: 225. In-state: 46%. Minority: 15%. Women: 40%. Average Age: 25.
Academics: No evening program. No summer program offered.
Finances: Tuition: $17,500. Students receiving scholarships: 25%. Students receiving loans: 75%.
Admission Requirements: Application deadline: April 1. Admissions fall term only.
Selectivity: Applications received: 1,940. Students accepted: 803. Students enrolled: 225. Median undergraduate GPA: 3.29. Median LSAT: 159.

Catholic University of America

The Columbus School of Law
Office of Admissions, Cardinal Station
Washington, DC 20064
Phone: (202) 319-5151
Fax: (202) 319-4498
E-mail: sokatch@law.cua.edu
Web Site: http://www.law.edu

Characteristics of Entering Class 1997: Full-time students: 219. Part-time students: 83. Minority: 25%. Women: 52%. Average Age: 23.
Academics: Evening program. No summer program offered.
Finances: Tuition: $21,918. Students receiving scholarships: 11%. Students receiving loans: 93%.
Admission Requirements: Application deadline: March 1. Admissions: fall term only.
Selectivity: Applications received: 2,161. Students accepted: 1,080. Students enrolled: 302. Median undergraduate GPA: 3.1. Median LSAT: 155.

Chicago-Kent College of Law

See Illinois Institute of Technology.

University of Chicago

Law School
1111 E. 60th Street
Chicago, IL 60637
Phone: (773) 702-9484
Fax: (773) 834-0942
E-mail: r-badger@chicago.edu
Web Site: http://www.law.uchicago.edu
Characteristics of Entering Class 1997: Full-time students: 175. In-state: 18%. Minority: 22/23%. Women: 46%. Average Age: 24.
Academics: No evening program. No summer program offered.
Finances: Tuition: $23,748. Students receiving scholarships: 39%. Students receiving loans: 79%.
Admission Requirements: Application deadline: None. Admissions: fall term only.
Selectivity: Applications received: 2,520. Students accepted: 631. Students enrolled: 175. Median undergraduate GPA: 3.67. Median LSAT: 169.

University of Cincinnati

College of Law
P.O. Box 210040
Cincinnati, OH 45221-0040
Phone: (513) 556-6805
Fax: (513) 556-2391
E-mail: admissions@law.uc.edu
Web Site: http://www.law.uc.edu
Characteristics of Entering Class 1997: Full-time students: 123. In-state: 72%. Minority: 16%. Women: 52%. Average Age: 25.
Academics: No evening program. No summer program offered.
Finances: In-State Tuition: $7,245. Out-of-State Tuition: $14,076.
Admission Requirements: Application deadline: April 1. Admissions: fall term only.
Selectivity: Applications received: 1,008. Students accepted: 406. Students enrolled: 123. Median undergraduate GPA: 3.42. Median LSAT: 160.

City University of New York

School of Law
65-21 Main Street
Flushing, NY 11367
Phone: (718) 340-4210
Fax: (718) 3404372
E-mail: perez@maclaw.law.cuny.edu
Web Site: http://www.law.cuny.edu
Characteristics of Entering Class 1997: Full-time students: 167. In-state: 56%. Minority: 42/40%. Women: 61%. Average Age: 29.
Academics: No evening program. No summer program offered.
Finances: In-State Tuition: $5,700. Out-of-State Tuition: $8,930. Students receiving scholarships: 10%.
Admission Requirements: Application deadline: March 15. Admissions fall term only.
Selectivity: Applications received: 1,441. Students accepted: 543. Students enrolled: 167. Median undergraduate GPA: 3.09. Median LSAT: 147.

LAW SCHOOLS

CLEVELAND STATE UNIVERSITY

Cleveland–Marshall College of Law
1801 Euclid Ave.
Cleveland, OH 44115-2223
Phone: (216) 687-2304
Fax: (216) 687-6881
E-mail: mmcnally@trans.csuohio.edu
Web Site: http://www.law.csuohio.edu

Characteristics of Entering Class 1997: Full-time students: 188. Part-time students: 99. In-state: 81%. Minority: 16%. Women: 41%. Average Age: 27.

Academics: Evening program. Summer program offered.

Finances: In-State Tuition: $7,104. Out-of-State Tuition: $14,208. Students receiving scholarships: 40%. Students receiving loans: 70%.

Admission Requirements: Application deadline: April 1. Admissions: fall term only.

Selectivity: Applications received: 1,330. Students accepted: 786. Students enrolled: 283. Median undergraduate GPA: 3.08. Median LSAT: 150.

UNIVERSITY OF COLORADO

School of Law
Campus Box 403
Boulder, CO 80309-0403
Phone: (303) 493-5706
Fax: (303) 492-2542
Web Site: http://www.colorado.edu/LAW

Characteristics of Entering Class 1997: Full-time students: 187. In-state: 51%. Minority: 17/18%. Women: 52%. Average Age: 26.

Academics: No evening program. No summer program offered.

Finances: In-State Tuition: $4,954. Out-of-State Tuition: $16,172. Students receiving scholarships: 29%. Students receiving loans: 80%.

Admission Requirements: Application deadline: February 16. Admissions: fall term only.

Selectivity: Applications received: 1,846. Students accepted: 650. Students enrolled: 187. Median undergraduate GPA: 3.54. Median LSAT: 161.

COLUMBIA UNIVERSITY

School of Law
435 West 116th Street
New York, NY 10027
Phone: (212) 854-2674
Fax: (212) 854-7946
Web Site:
http://www.columbia.edu/cu/law

Characteristics of Entering Class 1997: Full-time students: 358. In-state: 32%. Minority: 35/36%. Women: 45%. Average Age: 24.

Academics: No evening program. No summer program offered.

Finances: Tuition: $25,128. Students receiving scholarships: 25%. Students receiving loans: 75%.

Admission Requirements: Application deadline: February 15. Admissions fall term only.

Selectivity: Applications received: 5,080. Students enrolled: 358. Median undergraduate GPA: 3.6. Median LSAT: 169.

UNIVERSITY OF CONNECTICUT

School of Law
55 Elizabeth Street
Hartford, CT 06105
Phone: (860) 570-5100
Fax: (860) 570-5153
E-mail: admit@law.uconn.edu
Web Site: http://www.law.uconn.edu

Characteristics of Entering Class 1997: Full-time students: 140. Part-time students: 55. In-state: 57%. Minority: 19%. Women: 51%. Average Age: 25.

Academics: Evening program. No summer program offered.

Finances: Tuition: $22,420. Students receiving scholarships: 32%. Students receiving loans: 75%.

Admission Requirements: Application deadline: March 15. Admissions: fall term only.

Selectivity: Applications received: 1,245. Students accepted: 482. Students enrolled: 195. Median undergraduate GPA: 3.3. Median LSAT: 158.

CORNELL LAW SCHOOL

Myron Taylor Hall
Ithaca, NY 14853
Phone: (607) 255-5141
Fax: (607) 255-7193
E-mail: lawadmit@law.mail.cornell.edu
Web Site:
http://www.law.cornell.edu/admit/admit.htm

Characteristics of Entering Class 1997: Full-time students: 185. Minority: 26%. Women: 44%. Average Age: 24.

Academics: No evening program. No summer program offered.

Finances: Tuition: $22,100. Students receiving scholarships: 45%. Students receiving loans: 80%.

Admission Requirements: Application deadline: February 1. Admissions: fall term only.

Selectivity: Applications received: 3,400. Students enrolled: 185. Median undergraduate GPA: 3.56. Median LSAT: 165.

CUMBERLAND SCHOOL OF LAW

See Samford University.

CREIGHTON UNIVERSITY

2500 California Plaza
Omaha, NE 68178
Phone: (402) 280-2872
Fax: (402) 280-2244
E-mail: admit@culaw.creighton.edu
Web Site:
http://www.creighton.edu/culaw

Characteristics of Entering Class 1997:
Full-time students: 150. Part-time students: 6.

Directory of U.S. Law Schools

In-state: 40%. Minority: 14/11%. Women: 38%. Average Age: 23.
Academics: No evening program. No summer program offered.
Finances: Tuition: $14,936. Students receiving scholarships: 36%. Students receiving loans: 84%.
Admission Requirements: Application deadline: May 1. Admissions fall term only.
Selectivity: Applications received: 716. Students accepted: 523. Students enrolled: 156. Median undergraduate GPA: 3.04. Median LSAT: 149.

D

University of Dayton

School of Law
300 College Park
Dayton, OH 45469-2760
Phone: (937) 229-3555
Fax: (937) 229-2469
E-mail: lawinfo@udayton.edu
Web Site: http://www.udayton.edu/~law
Characteristics of Entering Class 1997: Full-time students: 178. In-state: 46%. Minority: 19%. Women: 45%. Average Age: 26.
Academics: No evening program. No summer program offered.
Finances: Tuition: $18,150. Students receiving scholarships: 30%. Students receiving loans: 85%.
Admission Requirements: Application deadline: May 1. Admissions fall term only.
Selectivity: Applications received: 1,350. Students accepted: 790. Students enrolled: 178. Median undergraduate GPA: 3.21. Median LSAT: 151.

University of Denver

College of Law
7039 E. 18th Avenue
Denver, CO 80220
Phone: (303) 871-6135
Fax: (303) 871-6100
E-mail: CTomlin@adm.law.du.edu
Web Site: http://www.law.du.edu
Characteristics of Entering Class 1997: Full-time students: 255. Part-time students: 78. In-state: 57%. Minority: 9/11%. Women: 55%. Average Age: 26.
Academics: Evening program. No summer program offered.
Finances: Tuition: $18,569. Students receiving scholarships: 27%. Students receiving loans: 85%.
Admission Requirements: Application deadline: May 1. Admissions: fall term only.
Selectivity: Applications received: 1,853. Students accepted: 1,210. Students enrolled: 333. Median undergraduate GPA: 3.14. Median LSAT: 154.

DePaul University

College of Law
25 East Jackson Boulevard
Chicago, IL 60604
Phone: (312) 362-8013
Fax: (312) 362-5280
E-mail: dshea@condv.depaul.edu
Web Site: http://www.law.depaul.edu
Characteristics of Entering Class 1997: Full-time students: 260. Part-time students: 80. In-state: 55%. Minority: 15/15%. Women: 51%. Average Age: 24.
Academics: Evening program. Summer program offered.
Finances: Tuition: $18,700. Students receiving scholarships: 20%. Students receiving loans: 85%.
Admission Requirements: Application deadline: April 1. Admissions: fall term only.
Selectivity: Applications received: 2,028. Students accepted: 1,383. Students enrolled: 340. Median undergraduate GPA: 3.12. Median LSAT: 154.

Detroit College of Law at Michigan State University

316 Law College Bldg.
E. Lansing, MI 48864
Phone: (517) 432-0222
Fax: (517) 432-0098
E-mail: pas@pilot.msu.edu
Web Site: http://www.dcl.edu
Characteristics of Entering Class 1997: Full-time students: 120. Part-time students: 27. Minority: 12.2/13%. Women: 41%. Average Age: 27.
Academics: Evening program. No summer program offered.
Finances: Tuition: $15,600.
Admission Requirements: Application deadline: April 15. Admissions: fall term only.
Selectivity: Applications received: 789. Students accepted: 463. Students enrolled: 147. Median undergraduate GPA: 307. Median LSAT: 152.

University of Detroit

Mercy School of Law
651 E. Jefferson Avenue
Detroit, MI 48226
Phone: (313) 596-9848
Fax: (313) 596-0280
E-mail: udmlawao@udmercy.edu
Web Site: http://www.udmercy.edu
Characteristics of Entering Class 1997: Full-time students: 92. Part-time students: 55. In-state: 91%. Minority: 20/13%. Women: 43%. Average Age: 27.
Academics: Evening program. Summer program offered.
Finances: Tuition: $17,600. Students receiving scholarships: 3%. Students receiving loans: 67%.
Admission Requirements: Application deadline: April 15. Admissions: fall term only.
Selectivity: Applications received: 685. Students accepted: 422. Students enrolled: 147. Median undergraduate GPA: 2.96. Median LSAT: 149.

LAW SCHOOLS

DICKINSON SCHOOL OF LAW

See Pennsylvania State University.

DISTRICT OF COLUMBIA SCHOOL OF LAW

4250 Connecticut Avenue, N.W.
Washington, DC 20008
Phone: (202) 274-7341
School did not submit data.

DRAKE UNIVERSITY

Law School
2507 University Avenue
Des Moines, IA 50311
Phone: (800) 443-7253
Fax: (515) 271-1990
E-mail: lawadmit@drake.edu
Web Site: http://www.drake.edu
Characteristics of Entering Class 1997: Full-time students: 121. Part-time students: 3. In-state: 54%. Minority: 11/11%. Women: 46%. Average Age: 25.
Academics: No evening program. No summer program offered.
Finances: Tuition: $16,330. Students receiving scholarships: 68%. Students receiving loans: 90%.
Admission Requirements: Application deadline: March 1. Admissions: fall term only.
Selectivity: Applications received: 887. Students accepted: 403. Students enrolled: 124. Median undergraduate GPA: 3.2. Median LSAT: 153.

DUKE UNIVERSITY

School of Law
Science Drive and Towerview Road
P.O. Box 90393
Durham, NC 27708
Phone: (919) 613-7200
Fax: (919) 613-7231
E-mail: admissions@law.duke.edu
Web Site: http://www.law.duke.edu
Characteristics of Entering Class 1997: Full-time students: 202. In-state: 8%. Minority: 19%. Women: 43%. Average Age: 24.
Academics: No evening program. No summer program offered.
Finances: Tuition: $23,350. Students receiving scholarships: 60%. Students receiving loans: 76%.
Admission Requirements: Application deadline: February 1. Admissions: fall term only.
Selectivity: Applications received: 3,152. Students enrolled: 205. Median undergraduate GPA: 3.6. Median LSAT: 166.

DUQUESNE UNIVERSITY

School of Law
217 Hanley Hall
900 Locust Street
Pittsburgh, PA 15282
Phone: (412) 396-6296
Fax: (412) 396-6283
E-mail: riccieduaz@cc.duq.edu
Characteristics of Entering Class 1997: Full-time students: 116. Part-time students: 89. In-state: 70%. Minority: 9/10%. Women: 45%. Average Age: 27.
Academics: Evening program. No summer program offered.
Finances: Tuition: $12,975. Students receiving scholarships: 20%. Students receiving loans: 80%.
Admission Requirements: Application deadline: April 1. Admissions fall term only.
Selectivity: Students enrolled: 205. Median undergraduate GPA: 3.25. Median LSAT: 156.

E

EMORY UNIVERSITY

School of Law
Gambrell Hall
Atlanta, GA 30322-2770
Phone: (404) 727-6802
Fax: (404) 727-2477
E-mail: lcadray@law.emory.edu
Web Site: http://www.law.emory.edu
Characteristics of Entering Class 1997: Full-time students: 207. In-state: 21%. Minority: 27/56%. Women: 51%. Average Age: 22.
Academics: No evening program. No summer program offered.
Finances: Tuition: $22,500. Students receiving scholarships: 35%. Students receiving loans: 99%.
Admission Requirements: Application deadline: March 1. Admissions: fall term only.
Selectivity: Applications received: 2,940. Students accepted: 1,069. Students enrolled: 207. Median undergraduate GPA: 3.47. Median LSAT: 161.

F

FLORIDA STATE UNIVERSITY

College of Law
425 W. Jefferson
Tallahassee, FL 32306-1034
Phone: (850) 644-3787
Fax: (850) 644-7284
E-mail: admissions@law.fsu.edu
Web Site: http://www.law.fsu.edu
Characteristics of Entering Class 1997: Full-time students: 221. In-state: 89%. Minority: 26%. Women: 43%. Average Age: 26.

Directory of U.S. Law Schools

Academics: No evening program. No summer program offered.
Finances: In-State Tuition: $4,240. Out-of-State Tuition: $13,465.
Admission Requirements: Application deadline: February 15. Admissions: fall term only.
Selectivity: Students accepted: 643. Students enrolled: 221. Median undergraduate GPA: 3.31. Median LSAT: 156.

UNIVERSITY OF FLORIDA

College of Law
P.O. Box 117622
Gainesville, FL 32611-7622
Phone: (352) 392-2087
Fax: (352) 392-8727
E-mail: patrick@law.ufl.edu
Web Site: http://www.law.ufl.edu
Characteristics of Entering Class 1997: Full-time students: 202. In-state: 90%. Minority: 23/24%. Women: 42%. Average Age: 24.
Academics: No evening program. No summer program offered.
Finances: In-State Tuition: $4,180. Out-of-State Tuition: $13,404. Students receiving scholarships: 9%. Students receiving loans: 85%.
Admission Requirements: Application deadline: February 1. Midyear admission allowed.
Selectivity: Applications received: 1,750. Students accepted: 485. Students enrolled: 202. Median undergraduate GPA: 3.58. Median LSAT: 159.

FORDHAM UNIVERSITY

School of Law
140 W. 62nd Street
New York, NY 10023
Phone: (212) 636-6810
Characteristics of Entering Class 1997: Full-time students: 316. Part-time students: 119. In-state: 59%. Minority: 24/26%. Women: 43%. Average Age: 24.
Academics: Evening program. No summer program offered.

Finances: Tuition: $21,520.
Admission Requirements: Application deadline: March 1. Admissions: fall term only.
Selectivity: Applications received: 4,223. Students accepted: 1,283. Students enrolled: 435. Median undergraduate GPA: 3.4. Median LSAT: 162.

FRANKLIN PIERCE LAW CENTER

2 White Street
Concord, NH 03301
Phone: (603) 228-9217
Fax: (603) 228-1074
E-mail: admissions@fplc.edu
Web Site: http://www.fplc.edu
Characteristics of Entering Class 1997: Full-time students: 132. Part-time students: 5. In-state: 20%. Minority: 23/17%. Women: 34%. Average Age: 30.
Academics: No evening program. No summer program offered.
Finances: Tuition: $15,832. Students receiving scholarships: 50%. Students receiving loans: 82%.
Admission Requirements: Application deadline: May 1. Admissions fall term only.
Selectivity: Applications received: 799. Students accepted: 546. Students enrolled: 137. Median undergraduate GPA: 2.9. Median LSAT: 151.

G

GEORGE MASON UNIVERSITY

School of Law
3401 North Fairfax Drive
Arlington, VA 22201-4498
Phone: (703) 993-8010
Fax: (703) 993-8088
E-mail: lawadmis@gmu.edu
Web Site: http://www.gmu.edu/departments/law

Characteristics of Entering Class 1997: Full-time students: 136. Part-time students: 77. In-state: 75%. Minority: 13%. Women: 43%. Average Age: 26.
Academics: Evening program. No summer program offered.
Finances: In-State Tuition: $7,448. Out-of-State Tuition: $17,990.
Admission Requirements: Application deadline: March 1. Admissions: fall term only.
Selectivity: Applications received: 1,641. Students accepted: 658. Students enrolled: 213. Median undergraduate GPA: 3.09. Median LSAT: 157.

GEORGETOWN UNIVERSITY

Law Center
600 New Jersey Avenue, N.W.
Washington, DC 20001
Phone: (202) 662-9015
Fax: (202) 662-9436
E-mail: admis@law.georgetown.edu
Web Site: http://www.georgetown.edu/lc
Characteristics of Entering Class 1997: Full-time students: 510. Part-time students: 125. Minority: 28%. Women: 51%. Average Age: 23.
Academics: Evening program. No summer program offered.
Finances: Tuition: $23,000. Students receiving scholarships: 33%. Students receiving loans: 82%.
Admission Requirements: Application deadline: February 1. Admissions: fall term only.
Selectivity: Applications received: 7,104. Students accepted: 2,100. Students enrolled: 635. Median undergraduate GPA: 3.5. Median LSAT: 166.

LAW SCHOOLS

George Washington University

Law School
2003 G Street, N.W.
Washington, DC 20052
Phone: (202) 994-7230
Fax: (202) 994-3597
E-mail: jd@admit.nlc.gwu.edu
Web Site: http://www.law.gwu.edu
**Characteristics of Entering Class
1997:** Full-time students: 377. Part-time students: 59. In-state: 3%. Minority: 28%. Women: 41%. Average Age: 24.
Academics: Evening program. No summer program offered.
Finances: Tuition: $22,035. Students receiving scholarships: 41%. Students receiving loans: 73%.
Admission Requirements: Application deadline: March 1. Admissions: fall term only.
Selectivity: Applications received: 6,592. Students accepted: 2,037. Students enrolled: 436. Median undergraduate GPA: 3.42. Median LSAT: 162.

University of Georgia

School of Law
Harold Hirsch Hall
Athens, GA 30602-6012
Phone: (706) 542-7060
Fax: (706) 542-5556
Web Site: http://www.lawsch.uga.edu
**Characteristics of Entering Class
1997:** Full-time students: 233. In-state: 79%. Minority: 9%. Women: 46%. Average Age: 24.
Academics: No evening program. Summer program offered.
Finances: In-State Tuition: $3,757. Out-of-State Tuition: $12,357. Students receiving scholarships: 20%. Students receiving loans: 70%.
Admission Requirements: Application deadline: March 1. Admissions: fall term only.
Selectivity: Applications received: 1,859. Students accepted: 482. Students enrolled: 233. Median undergraduate GPA: 3.55. Median LSAT: 161.

Georgia State University

College of Law
P.O. Box 4049
Atlanta, GA 30303
Phone: (404) 651-2048
Fax: (404) 651-1244
E-mail: admissions@gsulaw.gsu.edu
Web Site: http://www.gsulaw.gsu.edu
**Characteristics of Entering Class
1997:** Full-time students: 121. Part-time students: 79. In-state: 87%. Minority: 17/26%. Women: 49%. Average Age: 28.
Academics: Evening program. No summer program offered.
Finances: In-State Tuition: $3,748. Out-of-State Tuition: $11,844. Students receiving scholarships: 6%. Students receiving loans: 55%.
Admission Requirements: Application deadline: March 1. Admissions: fall term only.
Selectivity: Applications received: 1,870. Students accepted: 464. Students enrolled: 200. Median undergraduate GPA: 3.25. Median LSAT: 157.

Golden Gate University

School of Law
536 Mission Street
San Francisco, CA 94105
Phone: (415) 442-6630
Fax: (415) 442-6609
E-mail: lawadmit@ggu.edu
Web Site: http://www.ggu.edu/law
**Characteristics of Entering Class
1997:** Full-time students: 138. Part-time students: 40. Minority: 32%. Women: 58%.
Academics: Evening program. No summer program offered.
Finances: Tuition: $19,089.
Admission Requirements: Application deadline: April 15. Midyear admission allowed.
Selectivity: Applications received: 1,781. Students accepted: 1,056. Students enrolled: 178. Median undergraduate GPA: 2.97. Median LSAT: 149.

Gonzaga University

School of Law
704 E. Sharp
Spokane, WA 99202
Phone: (509) 324-5532
Fax: (509) 324-5710
E-mail: admissions@lawschool.gonzaga.edu
Web Site: http://www.law.gonzaga.edu
**Characteristics of Entering Class
1997:** Full-time students: 171. In-state: 57%. Minority: 18/15%. Women: 44%. Average Age: 28.
Academics: No evening program. Summer program offered.
Finances: Tuition: $16,950. Students receiving scholarships: 26%. Students receiving loans: 88%.
Admission Requirements: Application deadline: March 15. Admissions: fall term only.
Selectivity: Applications received: 1,005. Students accepted: 752. Students enrolled: 171. Median undergraduate GPA: 3.05. Median LSAT: 151.

H

Hamline University

School of Law
1536 Hewitt Avenue
St. Paul, MN 55104-1284
Phone: (800) 388-3688
Fax: (612) 523-2461
E-mail: lawadm@gw.hamline.edu
Web Site: http://www.hamline.edu
**Characteristics of Entering Class
1997:** Full-time students: 140. Part-time students: 2. In-state: 54%. Minority: 11%. Women: 51%. Average Age: 25.

Academics: No evening program. Summer program offered.
Finances: Tuition: $15,500. Students receiving scholarships: 17%. Students receiving loans: 90%.
Admission Requirements: Application deadline: May 15. Admissions: fall term only.
Selectivity: Applications received: 993. Students accepted: 522. Students enrolled: 142. Median undergraduate GPA: 3.24. Median LSAT: 153.

HARVARD UNIVERSITY

Law School
1563 Massachusetts Avenue
Cambridge, MA 02138
Phone: (617) 495-3109
E-mail: jdadmiss@law.harvard
Web Site: http://www.law.harvard.edu
Characteristics of Entering Class 1997: Full-time students: 556. Minority: 25/27%. Women: 43%. Average Age: 24.
Academics: No evening program. No summer program offered.
Finances: Tuition: $22,800. Students receiving scholarships: 40%. Students receiving loans: 80%.
Admission Requirements: Application deadline: February 2. Admissions: fall term only.
Selectivity: Applications received: 5,962. Students accepted: 843. Students enrolled: 556.

UNIVERSITY OF HAWAII—MANOA

School of Law
2515 Dole Street
Honolulu, HI 96822
Phone: (808) 956-7966
Fax: (808) 956-3813
E-mail: lawadm@hawaii.edu
Characteristics of Entering Class 1997: Full-time students: 77. In-state: 80%. Minority: 69%. Women: 44%. Average Age: 27.

Academics: No evening program. No summer program offered.
Finances: Tuition: $13,440.
Admission Requirements: Application deadline: March 1. Admissions: fall term only.
Selectivity: Applications received: 431. Students accepted: 158. Students enrolled: 77. Median undergraduate GPA: 3.25. Median LSAT: 157.

HOFSTRA UNIVERSITY

School of Law
121 Hofstra University
Hempstead, NY 11550
Phone: (516) 463-5916
Fax: (516) 463-6091
E-mail: lawale@hofstra.edu
Web Site: http://www.hofstra.edu
Characteristics of Entering Class 1997: Full-time students: 291. In-state: 87%. Minority: 19/18%. Women: 50%. Average Age: 24.
Academics: No evening program. No summer program offered.
Finances: Tuition: $20,780. Students receiving scholarships: 53%. Students receiving loans: 72%.
Admission Requirements: Application deadline: April 15. Admissions: fall term only.
Selectivity: Students enrolled: 291. Median undergraduate GPA: 3.3. Median LSAT: 155.

UNIVERSITY OF HOUSTON

Law Center
4800 Calhoun, Suite 30 TU-II
Houston, TX 77204-6391
Phone: (713) 743-2280
Fax: (713) 743-2194
E-mail: scrichardson@uh.edu
Web Site: http://www.law.uh.edu
Characteristics of Entering Class 1997: Full-time students: 257. Part-time students: 52. In-state: 79%. Minority: 22/20%. Women: 40%. Average Age: 26.

Academics: Evening program. No summer program offered.
Admission Requirements: Application deadline: February 1. Admissions: fall term only.
Selectivity: Applications received: 2,600. Students accepted: 853. Students enrolled: 309. Median undergraduate GPA: 3.28. Median LSAT: 160.

HOWARD UNIVERSITY

School of Law
2900 Van Ness Street, N.W.
Washington, DC 20008
Phone: (202) 806-8069
Fax: (202) 806-8162
E-mail: mmartin@law.howard.edu
Web Site: http://www.law.howard.edu
Characteristics of Entering Class 1997: Minority: 93/91%. Women: 57%. Average Age: 25.
Academics: No evening program. No summer program offered.
Finances: Tuition: $12,500. Students receiving scholarships: 51%. Students receiving loans: 75%.
Admission Requirements: Application deadline: April 30. Admissions: fall term only.
Selectivity: Applications received: 1,078. Students accepted: 391. Students enrolled: 140. Median undergraduate GPA: 2.98. Median LSAT: 151.

I

UNIVERSITY OF IDAHO

6th and Rayburn
Moscow, ID 83843
Phone: (208) 885-6423
Fax: (208) 885-7609
E-mail: barbaras@uidaho.edu
Web Site: http://www.uidaho.edu/law

LAW SCHOOLS

Characteristics of Entering Class 1997: Full-time students: 130. In-state: 62%. Minority: 6/12%. Women: 27%. Average Age: 25.
Academics: No evening program. No summer program offered.
Finances: Students receiving scholarships: 35%. Students receiving loans: 98%.
Admission Requirements: Application deadline: February 1. Admissions: fall term only.
Selectivity: Applications received: 428. Students accepted: 296. Students enrolled: 130. Median undergraduate GPA: 3.17. Median LSAT: 151.

UNIVERSITY OF ILLINOIS

College of Law
Room 201, 504 E. Pennsylvania Avenue
Champaign, IL 61820
Phone: (217) 244-6415
Fax: (217) 244-1478
E-mail: pbcolema@law.uiuc.edu
Web Site: http://www.law.uiuc.edu
Characteristics of Entering Class 1997: Full-time students: 200. In-state: 78%. Minority: 28/30%. Women: 42%. Average Age: 24.
Academics: No evening program. No summer program offered.
Finances: In-State Tuition: $6,538. Out-of-State Tuition: $16,610. Students receiving scholarships: 45%. Students receiving loans: none.
Admission Requirements: Application deadline: March 15. Admissions: fall term only.
Selectivity: Applications received: 1,635. Students accepted: 558. Students enrolled: 200. Median undergraduate GPA: 3.48. Median LSAT: 161.

ILLINOIS INSTITUTE OF TECHNOLOGY

Chicago–Kent College of Law
565 W. Adams
Chicago, IL 60661
Phone: (312) 906-5020
Fax: (312) 906-5274
E-mail: admitq@kentlaw.edu
Web Site: http://www.kentlaw.edu
Characteristics of Entering Class 1997: Full-time students: 282. Part-time students: 102. In-state: 67%. Minority: 21/16%. Women: 52%. Average Age: 24.
Academics: Evening program. No summer program offered.
Finances: Tuition: $19,850. Students receiving scholarships: 40%. Students receiving loans: 80%.
Admission Requirements: Application deadline: April 1. Admissions: fall term only.
Selectivity: Applications received: 1,958. Students accepted: 1,200. Students enrolled: 384. Median undergraduate GPA: 3.16. Median LSAT: 154.

INDIANA UNIVERSITY— BLOOMINGTON

School of Law
211 S. Indiana Avenue
Law Building, Room 230
Bloomington, IN 47405-1001
Phone: (812) 855-4765
Fax: (812) 855-0555
E-mail: lawadmis@indiana.edu
Web Site: http://www.law.indiana.edu
Characteristics of Entering Class 1997:
Full-time students: 203. Part-time students: 2. In-state: 50%. Minority: 16%. Women: 41%. Average Age: 24.
Academics: No evening program. No summer program offered.
Finances: In-State Tuition: $6,220. Out-of-State Tuition: $15,954. Students receiving scholarships: 49%. Students receiving loans: 70%.
Admission Requirements: Application deadline: rolling. Admissions: fall term only.
Selectivity: Applications received: 1,321. Students accepted: 547. Students enrolled: 205. Median undergraduate GPA: 3.35. Median LSAT: 160.

INDIANA UNIVERSITY— INDIANAPOLIS

School of Law
735 W. New York Street
Indianapolis, IN 46202
Phone: (317) 274-2459
Fax: (317) 274-3955
E-mail: kmiller@wpo.iupui.edu
Web Site: http://www.iulaw.indy.indiana.edu
Characteristics of Entering Class 1997: Full-time students: 186. Part-time students: 82. In-state: 10%. Minority: 14/15%. Women: 44%. Average Age: 28.
Academics: Evening program. Summer program offered.
Finances: In-State Tuition: $6,017. Out-of-State Tuition: $14,618. Students receiving scholarships: 15%. Students receiving loans: 42%.
Admission Requirements: Application deadline: March 1. Admissions: fall term only.
Selectivity: Applications received: 959. Students accepted: 505. Students enrolled: 268. Median undergraduate GPA: 3.2. Median LSAT: 156.

INTER AMERICAN UNIVERSITY

School of Law
PO Box 70351
San Juan, PR 00936-8351
Phone: (787) 751-1912
Fax: (787) 751-2975
Web Site: http://www.derecho.inter.edu
Characteristics of Entering Class 1997: Full-time students: 120. Part-time students: 104. In-state: 100%. Minority: 100%. Women: 55%. Average Age: 25.
Academics: Evening program. Summer program offered.

Finances: Tuition: $10,400. Students receiving scholarships: 82%. Students receiving loans: 82%.
Admission Requirements: Application deadline: March 31. Admissions: fall term only.
Selectivity: Applications received: 1,000. Students accepted: 340. Students enrolled: 225. Median undergraduate GPA: 3.15. Median LSAT: 141.

UNIVERSITY OF IOWA

College of Law
276 Boyd Law Building
Melrose at Byington Street
Iowa City, IA 52242
Phone: (319) 335-9142
Fax: (319) 335-9019
E-mail: law-admissions@uiowa.edu
Web Site: http://www.uiowa.edu/~/lawcoll
Characteristics of Entering Class 1997: Full-time students: 231. In-state: 63%. Minority: 18%. Women: 40%. Average Age: 25.
Academics: No evening program. No summer program offered.
Finances: Students receiving scholarships: 37%. Students receiving loans: 90%.
Admission Requirements: Application deadline: March 1. Admissions: fall term only.
Selectivity: Applications received: 1,006. Students accepted: 470. Students enrolled: 231. Median undergraduate GPA: 3.49. Median LSAT: 159.

J

JOHN MARSHALL

School of Law
315 South Plymouth Court
Chicago, IL 60604
Phone: (312) 987-1406
Fax: (312) 427-5136
E-mail: 6alonzo@jmls.edu
Web Site: http://www.jmls.edu
Characteristics of Entering Class 1997: Full-time students: 170. Part-time students: 59. In-state: 72%. Minority: 18%. Women: 50%. Average Age: 26.
Academics: Evening program. Summer program offered.
Finances: Tuition: $17,700. Students receiving scholarships: 15%. Students receiving loans: 76%.
Admission Requirements: Application deadline: March 1. Midyear admission allowed.
Selectivity: Applications received: 1,503. Students accepted: 942. Students enrolled: 229. Median undergraduate GPA: 3.01. Median LSAT: 150.

K

UNIVERSITY OF KANSAS

School of Law
205 Green Hall
Lawrence, KS 66045
Phone: (785) 864-4378
Fax: (785) 864-5054
E-mail: admit@law.wpo.ukans.edu
Web Site: http://www.law.ukans.edu
Characteristics of Entering Class 1997: Full-time students: 181. In-state: 69%. Minority: 9%. Women: 40%. Average Age: 25.
Academics: No evening program. No summer program offered.
Finances: Students receiving scholarships: 33%. Students receiving loans: 78%.
Admission Requirements: Application deadline: March 15. Admissions: fall term only.
Selectivity: Applications received: 812. Students accepted: 402. Students enrolled: 181. Median undergraduate GPA: 3.37. Median LSAT: 157.

UNIVERSITY OF KENTUCKY

College of Law
209 Law Building
Lexington, KY 40506-0048
Phone: (606) 257-1678
Fax: (606) 323-1061
E-mail: dbakert@pop.uky.edu
Web Site: http://www.uky.edu/Law
Characteristics of Entering Class 1997: Full-time students: 142. In-state: 83%. Minority: 8/6%. Women: 43%. Average Age: 23.
Academics: No evening program. Summer program offered.
Finances: In-State Tuition: $4,620. Out-of-State Tuition: $12,460. Students receiving scholarships: 33%. Students receiving loans: 74%.
Admission Requirements: Application deadline: March 1. Admissions: fall term only.
Selectivity: Applications received: 746. Students accepted: 323. Students enrolled: 142. Median undergraduate GPA: 3.42. Median LSAT: 158.

LAW SCHOOLS

L

LEWIS AND CLARK COLLEGE

Northwestern School of Law
10015 SW Terwillger
Portland, OR 97219
Phone: (503) 768-6616
Fax: (503) 768-6671
E-mail: lawadmss@lclark.edu
Web Site: http://www.lclark.edu/law

Characteristics of Entering Class 1997: Full-time students: 179. Part-time students: 41. In-state: 23%. Minority: 9/17%. Women: 42%. Average Age: 25.
Academics: Evening program. No summer program offered.
Finances: Tuition: $17,395. Students receiving scholarships: 53%. Students receiving loans: 89%.
Admission Requirements: Application deadline: March 15. Admissions: fall term only.
Selectivity: Applications received: 1,687. Students accepted: 930. Students enrolled: 220. Median undergraduate GPA: 3.23. Median LSAT: 160.

UNIVERSITY OF LOUISVILLE

Louis D. Brandeis School of Law
Admissions Office
Louisville, KY 40291
Phone: (502) 852-6096
Fax: (502) 852-0862
E-mail: jltorb01@ulkyvm.louisville.edu
Web Site: http://www.louisville.edu/brandeislaw

Characteristics of Entering Class 1997: Full-time students: 92. Part-time students: 32. In-state: 80%. Minority: 20%. Women: 35%. Average Age: 25.
Academics: Evening program. Summer program offered.
Finances: In-State Tuition: $4,850. Out-of-State Tuition: $12,690. Students receiving scholarships: 25%. Students receiving loans: 69%.
Admission Requirements: Application deadline: February 15. Admissions: fall term only.
Selectivity: Applications received: 884. Students accepted: 303. Students enrolled: 124. Median undergraduate GPA: 3.2. Median LSAT: 157.

LOUISIANA STATE UNIVERSITY

Law Center
210 Law Center Building
Baton Rouge, LA 70803
Phone: (504) 388-8646
Fax: (504) 388-8202

Characteristics of Entering Class 1997: Full-time students: 244. In-state: 85%. Minority: 14/9%. Women: 44%. Average Age: 24.
Academics: No evening program. No summer program offered.
Finances: In-State Tuition: $3,936. Out-of-State Tuition: $8,923.
Admission Requirements: Application deadline: February 1. Admissions: fall term only.
Selectivity: Applications received: 922. Students enrolled: 244.

LOYOLA MARYMOUNT UNIVERSITY—LOS ANGELES

919 S. Albany Street
Los Angeles, CA 90015
Phone: (213) 736-1074
Fax: (213) 736-6523
E-mail: lawadmis@lmulaw.lmu.edu
Web Site: http://www.law.lmu.edu

Characteristics of Entering Class 1997: Full-time students: 365. Part-time students: 119. Minority: 42/40%. Women: 48%. Average Age: 24.
Academics: Evening program. No summer program offered.
Finances: Tuition: $20,474. Students receiving scholarships: 10%. Students receiving loans: 85%.
Admission Requirements: Application deadline: February 2. Admissions: fall term only.
Selectivity: Applications received: 2,783. Students accepted: 1,064. Students enrolled: 484. Median undergraduate GPA: 3.24. Median LSAT: 158.

LOYOLA UNIVERSITY—CHICAGO

School of Law
One E. Pearson, Rm. 430
Chicago, IL 60611
Phone: (312) 915-7170
Fax: (312) 915-7906
E-mail: law-admissions@uc.edu
Web Site: http://www.luc.edu/schools/law

Characteristics of Entering Class 1997: Full-time students: 169. Part-time students: 72. In-state: 61%. Minority: 19/19%. Women: 60%. Average Age: 26.
Academics: Evening program. No summer program offered.
Finances: Tuition: $20,746. Students receiving scholarships: 35%.
Admission Requirements: Application deadline: April 1. Admissions fall term only.
Selectivity: Applications received: 2,231. Students accepted: 861. Students enrolled: 241. Median undergraduate GPA: 3.33. Median LSAT: 158.

LOYOLA UNIVERSITY—NEW ORLEANS

School of Law
7214 St. Charles Avenue, Box 904
New Orleans, LA 70118
Phone: (504) 861-5575
Fax: (504) 861-5772
E-mail: ladmit@beta.loyno.edu
Web Site: http://www.loyno.edu

Directory of U.S. Law Schools

**Characteristics of Entering Class
1997:** Full-time students: 168. Part-time students: 42. Minority: 27/20%. Women: 41%. Average Age: 23.
Academics: Evening program. No summer program offered.
Finances: Tuition: $18,228.
Admission Requirements: Application deadline: None. Admissions: fall term only.
Selectivity: Applications received: 1,380. Students accepted: 706. Students enrolled: 210. Median undergraduate GPA: 2.96. Median LSAT: 152.

M

University of Maine

School of Law
246 Deering Avenue
Portland, ME 04102
Phone: (207) 780-4341
Fax: (207) 780-4239
E-mail: gauditz@usm.maine.edu
Web Site: http://www.law.usm.maine.edu
**Characteristics of Entering Class
1997:** Full-time students: 97. In-state: 61%. Minority: 5/5%. Women: 40%. Average Age: 27.
Academics: No evening program. No summer program offered.
Finances: In-State Tuition: $8,520. Out-of-State Tuition: $16,680. Students receiving scholarships: 30%. Students receiving loans: 95%.
Admission Requirements: Application deadline: February 15. Admissions: fall term only.
Selectivity: Applications received: 569. Students accepted: 287. Students enrolled: 97. Median undergraduate GPA: 3.31. Median LSAT: 155.

Marquette University

Law School
Office of Admissions
Sensenbrenner Hall, Box 1881
Milwaukee, WI 53201-1881
Phone: (414) 288-6767
Fax: (414) 288-5914
E-mail: law.admission@marquette.edu
Web Site: http://www.mu.edu/law
**Characteristics of Entering Class
1997:** Full-time students: 141. Part-time students: 46. In-state: 69%. Minority: 11%. Women: 40%. Average Age: 24.
Academics: Evening program. No summer program offered.
Finances: Tuition: $17,830. Students receiving scholarships: 21%. Students receiving loans: 98%.
Admission Requirements: Application deadline: April 1. Admissions: fall term only.
Selectivity: Applications received: 1,004. Students accepted: 445. Students enrolled: 187. Median undergraduate GPA: 3.08. Median LSAT: 155.

University of Maryland

School of Law
500 W. Baltimore Street
Baltimore, MD 21201-1786
Phone: (410) 706-3492
Fax: (410) 706-4045
E-mail: admissions@law.umaryland.edu
Web Site: http://www.law.maryland.edu
**Characteristics of Entering Class
1997:** Full-time students: 212. Part-time students: 62. In-state: 69%. Minority: 27/27%. Women: 55%. Average Age: 26.
Academics: Evening program. No summer program offered.
Finances: Students receiving scholarships: 49%. Students receiving loans: 78%.
Admission Requirements: Application deadline: March 1. Admissions: fall term only.
Selectivity: Applications received: 2,416. Students accepted: 931. Students enrolled: 274. Median undergraduate GPA: 3.35. Median LSAT: 156.

McGeorge School of Law

University of the Pacific
3200 Fifth Avenue
Sacramento, CA 95817
Phone: (916) 739-7105
Fax: (916) 739-7134
E-mail: admissionsmcgeorge@uop.edu
**Characteristics of Entering Class
1997:** Full-time students: 290. Part-time students: 94. In-state: 84%. Minority: 22/23%. Women: 46%. Average Age: 24.
Academics: Evening program. No summer program offered.
Finances: Tuition: $18,340. Students receiving scholarships: 20%. Students receiving loans: 89%.
Admission Requirements: Application deadline: May 1. Admissions: fall term only.
Selectivity: Applications received: 1,811. Students accepted: 1,240. Students enrolled: 384. Median undergraduate GPA: 3.02. Median LSAT: 152.

University of Memphis

School of Law
Campus Box 526 513
Memphis, TN 38152-6513
Phone: (901) 678-2073
Fax: (901) 678-5210
E-mail: oufmlaw@profnet.law.memphis.edu
Web Site:
http://www.people.memphis.edu/~law
**Characteristics of Entering Class
1997:** Full-time students: 188. Part-time students: 17. In-state: 84%. Minority: 13%. Women: 43%. Average Age: 26.
Academics: No evening program. Summer program offered.
Finances: Tuition: $10,292. Students receiving scholarships: 18%. Students receiving loans: 81%.
Admission Requirements: Application deadline: February 15. Admissions: fall term only.
Selectivity: Applications received: 835. Students accepted: 489. Students enrolled: 205. Median undergraduate GPA: 3.09. Median LSAT: 155.

LAW SCHOOLS

MERCER UNIVERSITY

School of Law
1021 Georgia Avenue
Macon, GA 31201
Phone: (912) 752-2605
Fax: (912) 752-2989
E-mail: weblaw@mercer.edu
Characteristics of Entering Class
1997: Full-time students: 151. In-state: 148%. Minority: 22%. Women: 51%. Average Age: 22.
Academics: No evening program. No summer program offered.
Finances: Tuition: $17,990. Students receiving scholarships: 39%. Students receiving loans: 186%.
Admission Requirements: Application deadline: March 15. Admissions: fall term only.
Selectivity: Applications received: 1,071. Students accepted: 483. Students enrolled: 151. Median undergraduate GPA: 3.17. Median LSAT: 154.

UNIVERSITY OF MIAMI

School of Law
1311 Miller Drive, Room 203
Coral Gables, FL 33124-8087
Phone: (305) 284-2523
Fax: (305) 284-3084
E-mail: admissions@law.miami.edu
Web Site: http://www.law.miami.edu
Characteristics of Entering Class
1997: Full-time students: 354. Part-time students: 128. In-state: 56%. Minority: 34/34%. Women: 44%. Average Age: 26.
Academics: Evening program. No summer program offered.
Finances: Tuition: $20,600. Students receiving scholarships: 27%. Students receiving loans: 87%.
Admission Requirements: Application deadline: March 9. Admissions: fall term only.
Selectivity: Applications received: 2,501. Students accepted: 1,586. Students enrolled: 482. Median undergraduate GPA: 3.2. Median LSAT: 154.

UNIVERSITY OF MICHIGAN

Law School
625 S. State Street
Ann Arbor, MI 48109-1215
Phone: (313) 764-0537
Fax: (313) 647-3218
E-mail: law.jd.admissions@umich.edu
Web Site: http://www.law.umich.edu
Characteristics of Entering Class
1997: Full-time students: 339. In-state: 30%. Minority: 22%. Women: 44%.
Academics: No evening program. No summer program offered.
Finances: In-State Tuition: $17,550. Out-of-State Tuition: $23,550.
Admission Requirements: Application deadline: February 15. Admissions: fall term only.
Selectivity: Applications received: 3,374. Students accepted: 1,164. Students enrolled: 339. Median undergraduate GPA: 3.5. Median LSAT: 167.

UNIVERSITY OF MINNESOTA

Law School
290 Law Center
229 19th Avenue South
Minneapolis, MN 55455
Phone: (612) 625-3487
Fax: (612) 626-1874
E-mail: byrdj001@tc.umn.edu
Web Site: http://www.umn.edu/law
Characteristics of Entering Class
1997: Full-time students: 244. In-state: 46%. Minority: 27/19%. Women: 46%. Average Age: 25.
Academics: No evening program. No summer program offered.
Finances: In-State Tuition: $8,660. Out-of-State Tuition: $14,702. Students receiving scholarships: 22%.
Admission Requirements: Application deadline: March 1. Admissions: fall term only.
Selectivity: Applications received: 1,513. Students accepted: 642. Students enrolled: 244. Median undergraduate GPA: 3.56. Median LSAT: 162.

MISSISSIPPI COLLEGE

School of Law
151 E. Griffith
Jackson, MS 39201
Phone: (601) 925-7150
Fax: (601) 925-7117
E-mail: pevans@mc.edu
Web Site: http://www.mc.edu/~ladhttp://www
Characteristics of Entering Class
1997: Full-time students: 142. In-state: 53%. Minority: 11/12%. Women: 40%. Average Age: 26.
Academics: No evening program. No summer program offered.
Finances: Tuition: $13,600. Students receiving scholarships: 18%. Students receiving loans: 90%.
Admission Requirements: Application deadline: May 1. Admissions: fall term only.
Selectivity: Applications received: 699. Students accepted: 483. Students enrolled: 142. Median undergraduate GPA: 3.04. Median LSAT: 148.

UNIVERSITY OF MISSISSIPPI

School of Law
Law Center, Room 310
University, MS 38677
Phone: (601) 232-6910
Fax: (601) 232-1289
E-mail: lawmiss@olemiss.edu
Web Site: http://www.olemiss.edu/depts/law_school/law-hom.html
Characteristics of Entering Class
1997: Full-time students: 170. In-state: 82%. Minority: 10/12%. Women: 38%. Average Age: 24.
Academics: No evening program. No summer program offered.
Finances: Students receiving scholarships: 17%. Students receiving loans: 75%.
Admission Requirements: Application deadline: March 1. Admissions: fall term only.

Directory of U.S. Law Schools

Selectivity: Applications received: 1,244. Students accepted: 441. Students enrolled: 170. Median undergraduate GPA: 3.29. Median LSAT: 153.

UNIVERSITY OF MISSOURI— COLUMBIA

School of Law
103 Hulston Hall
Columbia, MO 65211
Phone: (573) 882-6042
Fax: (573) 882-9625
E-mail: gregory@law.missouri.edu
Web Site: http://www.law.missouri.edu
Characteristics of Entering Class 1997: Full-time students: 192. In-state: 82%. Minority: 11/10%. Women: 42%. Average Age: 25.
Academics: No evening program. No summer program offered.
Finances: In-State Tuition: $8,555. Out-of-State Tuition: $16,588. Students receiving scholarships: 25%. Students receiving loans: 80%.
Admission Requirements: Application deadline: March 1 pref. Admissions: fall term only.
Selectivity: Applications received: 727. Students accepted: 413. Students enrolled: 192. Median undergraduate GPA: 3.49. Median LSAT: 157.

UNIVERSITY OF MISSOURI— KANSAS CITY

School of Law
5100 Rockhill Road
Kansas City, MO 64110-2499
Phone: (816) 235-1644
Fax: (816) 235-5276
E-mail: staplesc@smtpgate.umkc.edu
Web Site: http://www.law.umkc.edu
Characteristics of Entering Class 1997: Full-time students: 156. Part-time students: 15. In-state: 70%. Minority: 11/11%. Women: 43%. Average Age: 27.
Academics: No evening program. No summer program offered.

Finances: In-State Tuition: $8,548. Out-of-State Tuition: $16,581.
Admission Requirements: Application deadline: N/A. Admissions: fall term only.
Selectivity: Applications received: 778. Students accepted: 467. Students enrolled: 171. Median undergraduate GPA: 3.14. Median LSAT: 153.

UNIVERSITY OF MONTANA

School of Law
Maurice & Eddy
Missoula, MT 59812
Phone: (406) 243-4311
Fax: (406) 243-2576
E-mail: lawadmis@selway.umt.edu
Web Site: http://www.umt.edu/law/hompage.htm
Characteristics of Entering Class 1997: Full-time students: 82. In-state: 73%. Minority: 7%. Women: 48%. Average Age: 26.
Academics: No evening program. No summer program offered.
Finances: In-State Tuition: $6,262. Out-of-State Tuition: $11,264. Students receiving scholarships: 33%. Students receiving loans: 61%.
Admission Requirements: Application deadline: March 1. Admissions: fall term only.
Selectivity: Applications received: 413. Students accepted: 221. Students enrolled: 82. Median undergraduate GPA: 3.35. Median LSAT: 157.

N

UNIVERSITY OF NEBRASKA

College of Law
42nd & Fair Streets
Lincoln, NE 68583-0902
Phone: (402) 472-2161
Fax: (402) 472-5185
E-mail: lawadm@unlinfo.unl.edu
Web Site: http://www.unl.edu/lawcoll
Characteristics of Entering Class 1997: Full-time students: 139. Part-time students: 1. In-state: 77%. Minority: 11/10%. Women: 36%. Average Age: 23.
Academics: No evening program. No summer program offered.
Finances: In-State Tuition: $3,672. Out-of-State Tuition: $9,414. Students receiving scholarships: 66%. Students receiving loans: 80%.
Admission Requirements: Application deadline: March 1. Admissions: fall term only.
Selectivity: Applications received: 670. Students accepted: 351. Students enrolled: 140. Median undergraduate GPA: 3.48. Median LSAT: 154.

NEW ENGLAND SCHOOL OF LAW

154 Stuart Street
Boston, MA 02116
Phone: (617) 422-7210
Fax: (617) 422 7200
E-mail: admit@admin.nesl.edu
Web Site: http://www.nesl.edu
Characteristics of Entering Class 1997: Full-time students: 187. Part-time students: 99. In-state: 30%. Minority: 27/14%. Women: 52%. Average Age: 27.
Academics: Evening program. No summer program offered.

LAW SCHOOLS

Finances: Tuition: $14,300. Students receiving scholarships: 51%. Students receiving loans: 91%.
Admission Requirements: Application deadline: March 15, June 1. Admissions: fall term only.
Selectivity: Applications received: 2,218. Students accepted: 1,513. Students enrolled: 286. Median undergraduate GPA: 2.93. Median LSAT: 149.

University of New Mexico

School of Law
1117 Stanford N.E.
Albuquerque, NM 87131-1431
Phone: (505) 277-0958
Fax: (505) 277-9958
E-mail: gonzalesco@libra.unm.edu
Characteristics of Entering Class 1997: Full-time students: 118. In-state: 86%. Minority: 39/40%. Women: 57%. Average Age: 29.
Academics: No evening program. Summer program offered.
Finances: In-State Tuition: $3,612. Out-of-State Tuition: $12,116. Students receiving scholarships: 17%.
Admission Requirements: Application deadline: February 15. Admissions: fall term only.
Selectivity: Applications received: 734. Students accepted: 251. Students enrolled: 118. Median undergraduate GPA: 3.15. Median LSAT: 156.

New York Law School

57 Worth Street
New York, NY 10013-2960
Phone: (212) 431-2888
Fax: (212) 966-1522
E-mail: admissions@nyls.edu
Web Site: http://www.nyls.edu
Characteristics of Entering Class 1997: Full-time students: 332. Part-time students: 127. In-state: 56%. Minority: 25/24%. Women: 45%. Average Age: 27.
Academics: Evening program. No summer program offered.

Finances: Tuition: $20,770. Students receiving scholarships: 40%. Students receiving loans: 79%.
Admission Requirements: Application deadline: April 1. Admissions fall term only.
Selectivity: Applications received: 4,177. Students accepted: 1,989. Students enrolled: 459. Median undergraduate GPA: 3.02. Median LSAT: 151.

New York University

School of Law
110 West Third Street
New York, NY 10012
Phone: (212) 998-6060
Fax: (212) 995-9527
Web Site: http://www.nyu.edu./law/admissions
Characteristics of Entering Class 1997: Full-time students: 393. Minority: 21/23%. Women: 48%.
Academics: No evening program. No summer program offered.
Finances: Tuition: $24,740. Students receiving scholarships: 21%. Students receiving loans: 79%.
Admission Requirements: Application deadline: February 1. Admissions: fall term only.
Selectivity: Applications received: 6,185. Students enrolled: 393. Median undergraduate GPA: 3.67. Median LSAT: 168.

University of North Carolina

School of Law
Ridge Road
Chapel Hill, NC 27599-3380
Phone: (919) 962-5109
Fax: (919) 962-1170
E-mail: law-admission@unc.edu
Web Site: http://www.law.unc.edu
Characteristics of Entering Class 1997: Full-time students: 230. In-state: 75%. Minority: 19%. Women: 53%.
Academics: No evening program. No summer program offered.

Finances: In-State Tuition: $2,881. Out-of-State Tuition: $14,743. Students receiving scholarships: 18%.
Admission Requirements: Application deadline: February 1. Admissions: fall term only.
Selectivity: Applications received: 1,720. Students accepted: 582. Students enrolled: 230. Median undergraduate GPA: 3.5. Median LSAT: 160.

North Carolina Central University

School of Law
1512 S. Alston Avenue
Durham, NC 27707
Phone: (919) 560-6333
Web Site: http://www.nccu.edu./law
School did not submit data.

University of North Dakota

School of Law
P.O. Box 9003
Grand Forks, ND 58202
Phone: (701) 777-2104
Fax: (701) 777-2217
E-mail: mark.brickson@thor.law.und.nodak.edu
Web Site: http://www.law.und.nodak.edu
Characteristics of Entering Class 1997: Full-time students: 64. In-state: 45%. Minority: 03/05%. Women: 47%.
Academics: No evening program. No summer program offered.
Finances: In-State Tuition: $4,097. Out-of-State Tuition: $8,533. Students receiving scholarships: 35%. Students receiving loans: 89%.
Admission Requirements: Application deadline: April 1. Admissions: fall term only.
Selectivity: Applications received: 263. Students accepted: 157. Students enrolled: 64. Median undergraduate GPA: 3.28. Median LSAT: 151.

Directory of U.S. Law Schools

NORTHEASTERN UNIVERSITY

School of Law
400 Huntington Avenue
Boston, MA 02115
Phone: (617) 373-2395
Fax: (617) 373-8865
E-mail: admissions@slaw.neu.edu
Web Site: http://www.slaw.neu.edu
**Characteristics of Entering Class
1997:** Full-time students: 175. In-state: 39%. Minority: 26/26%. Women: 70%. Average Age: 25.
Academics: No evening program. No summer program offered.
Finances: Tuition: $21,300. Students receiving scholarships: 47%. Students receiving loans: 82%.
Admission Requirements: Application deadline: December 1, January 15, March 1. Admissions: fall term only.
Selectivity: Applications received: 2,167. Students accepted: 754. Students enrolled: 175. Median undergraduate GPA: 3.3. Median LSAT: 156.

NORTHERN ILLINOIS UNIVERSITY

College of Law
DeKalb, IL 60115
Phone: (815) 753-1420
Fax: (815) 753-4501
E-mail: internet:lawadm@niu.edu
Web Site: http://www.niu.edu/claw/lawhome.html
**Characteristics of Entering Class
1997:** Full-time students: 82. Part-time students: 5. In-state: 78%. Minority: 18%. Women: 33%. Average Age: 28.
Academics: No evening program. No summer program offered.
Finances: In-State Tuition: $5,038. Out-of-State Tuition: $10,076. Students receiving scholarships: 30%. Students receiving loans: 75%.
Admission Requirements: Application deadline: March 15-prior. Admissions: fall term only.

Selectivity: Applications received: 889. Students accepted: 338. Students enrolled: 87. Median undergraduate GPA: 3. Median LSAT: 155.

NORTHERN KENTUCKY UNIVERSITY

Salmon P. Chase College of Law
Nunn Hall, Rm. 529
Highland Height, KY 41099
Phone: (606) 572-5490
Fax: (606) 572-6081
E-mail: brayg@nku.edu
Web Site: http://www.nku.edu/~chase
**Characteristics of Entering Class
1997:** Full-time students: 64. Part-time students: 53. In-state: 62%. Minority: 7/7%. Women: 36%. Average Age: 29.
Academics: Evening program. No summer program offered.
Finances: In-State Tuition: $4,920. Out-of-State Tuition: $12,760. Students receiving scholarships: 25%. Students receiving loans: 53%.
Admission Requirements: Application deadline: May 15. Admissions: fall term only.
Selectivity: Applications received: 701. Students accepted: 272. Students enrolled: 117. Median undergraduate GPA: 3.18. Median LSAT: 154.

NORTHWESTERN UNIVERSITY

School of Law
357 East Chicago Avenue
Chicago, IL 60611
Phone: (312) 503-8465
Fax: (312) 503-0178
E-mail: nulawadm@harold.law.nwu.edu
Web Site: http://www.nuinfo.nwu.edu/lawschool
**Characteristics of Entering Class
1997:** Full-time students: 204. Minority: 29%. Women: 46%. Average Age: 24.
Academics: No evening program. No summer program offered.

Finances: Tuition: $22,638. Students receiving scholarships: 39%. Students receiving loans: 70%.
Admission Requirements: Application deadline: February 16. Admissions: fall term only.
Selectivity: Applications received: 3,536. Students enrolled: 204. Median undergraduate GPA: 3.52. Median LSAT: 165.

NOTRE DAME LAW SCHOOL

P.O. Box 959
Notre Dame, IN 46556-0959
Phone: (219) 631-6626
Fax: (219) 631-6371
E-mail: law.bulletin.1@nd.edu
Web Site: http://www.nd.edu/~ndlaw
**Characteristics of Entering Class
1997:** Full-time students: 180. In-state: 6%. Minority: 22%. Women: 35%.
Academics: No evening program. No summer program offered.
Finances: Tuition: $20,390.
Admission Requirements: Application deadline: March 1. Admissions: fall term only.
Selectivity: Applications received: 1,845. Students accepted: 514. Students enrolled: 180. Median undergraduate GPA: 3.44. Median LSAT: 163.

NOVA SOUTHEASTERN UNIVERSITY

Shepard Broad Law Center
3305 College Avenue
Lauderdale, FL 33314
Phone: (954) 262-6117
Fax: (954) 262-3844
E-mail: admission@usu.law.nova.edu
Web Site: http://www.nsulaw.nova.edu
**Characteristics of Entering Class
1997:** Full-time students: 256. Part-time students: 71. In-state: 74%. Minority: 27/25%. Women: 46%. Average Age: 28.

LAW SCHOOLS

Academics: Evening program. Summer program offered.
Finances: Tuition: $19,400. Students receiving scholarships: 18%. Students receiving loans: 85%.
Admission Requirements: Application deadline: February 1. Admissions: fall term only.
Selectivity: Applications received: 1,520. Students accepted: 809. Students enrolled: 327. Median undergraduate GPA: 2.88. Median LSAT: 147.

OHIO NORTHERN UNIVERSITY

College of Law
525 South Main Street
Ada, OH 45810
Phone: (419) 772-2211
Fax: (419) 772-1875
E-mail: g-justice@onu.edu
Web Site: http://www.law.onu.edu
Characteristics of Entering Class 1997: Full-time students: 129. In-state: 33%. Minority: 18/12%. Women: 32%. Average Age: 27.
Academics: No evening program. No summer program offered.
Finances: Tuition: $18,980. Students receiving scholarships: 27%. Students receiving loans: 82%.
Admission Requirements: Application deadline: rolling. Admissions: fall term only.
Selectivity: Applications received: 859. Students accepted: 656. Students enrolled: 129. Median undergraduate GPA: 2.96. Median LSAT: 147.

OHIO STATE UNIVERSITY

College of Law
55 West 12th Avenue, Room 104
Columbus, OH 43210
Phone: (614) 292-8810
Fax: (614) 292-1383
E-mail: Berry.78@osu.edu
  Rapoport.3@osu.edu
Web Site: http://www.acs.ohio-state.edu/units/law/index.htm
Characteristics of Entering Class 1997: Full-time students: 244. In-state: 74%. Minority: 20%. Women: 48%. Average Age: 24.
Academics: No evening program. No summer program offered.
Finances: In-State Tuition: $6,412. Out-of-State Tuition: $14,932. Students receiving scholarships: 60%. Students receiving loans: 75%.
Admission Requirements: Application deadline: March 15. Admissions: fall term only.
Selectivity: Applications received: 1,387. Students accepted: 582. Students enrolled: 244. Median undergraduate GPA: 3.5. Median LSAT: 157.

UNIVERSITY OF OKLAHOMA

College of Law
300 Timberdell Road
Norman, OK 73019
Phone: (405) 325-4726
Fax: (405) 325-6282
E-mail: srichard@hamilton.law.uoknor.edu
Web Site: http://www.uoknor.edu
Characteristics of Entering Class 1997: Full-time students: 167. In-state: 85%. Minority: 17%. Women: 43%. Average Age: 24.
Academics: No evening program. Summer program offered.
Finances: In-State Tuition: $3,600. Out-of-State Tuition: $11,238. Students receiving scholarships: 16%. Students receiving loans: 70%.
Admission Requirements: Application deadline: March 15. Admissions: fall term only.
Selectivity: Applications received: 704. Students accepted: 291. Students enrolled: 167. Median undergraduate GPA: 3.25. Median LSAT: 152.

OKLAHOMA CITY UNIVERSITY

School of Law
P.O. Box 61310
Oklahoma City, OK 73146-1310
Phone: (405) 521-5354
Fax: (405) 521-5814
E-mail: lawadmit@lec.okcu.edu
Web Site: http://www.okcu.edu
Characteristics of Entering Class 1997: Full-time students: 149. Part-time students: 41. In-state: 49%. Minority: 15%. Women: 39%. Average Age: 27.
Academics: Evening program. Summer program offered.
Finances: Tuition: $14,725. Students receiving scholarships: 5%.
Admission Requirements: Application deadline: August 1. Admissions: fall term only.
Selectivity: Applications received: 893. Students accepted: 615. Students enrolled: 190. Median undergraduate GPA: 2.86. Median LSAT: 149.

UNIVERSITY OF OREGON

School of Law
1221 University of Oregon
Eugene, OR 97403-1221
Phone: (541) 346-3846
Fax: (541) 346-1564
E-mail: admissions@law.uoregon.edu
Web Site: http://www.law.uoregon.edu
Characteristics of Entering Class 1997: Full-time students: 194. In-state: 57%. Minority: 11%. Women: 48%. Average Age: 25.
Academics: No evening program. Summer program offered.

Finances: In-State Tuition: $10,050. Out-of-State Tuition: $13,700. Students receiving scholarships: 26%.
Admission Requirements: Application deadline: April 1. Admissions: fall term only.
Selectivity: Applications received: 1,046. Students accepted: 602. Students enrolled: 194. Median undergraduate GPA: 3.35. Median LSAT: 156.

P

PACE UNIVERSITY

School of Law
78 N. Broadway
White Plains, NY 10603
Phone: (914) 422-4210
Fax: (914) 422-4248
Web Site: http://www.law.pace.edu
Characteristics of Entering Class 1997: Full-time students: 170. Part-time students: 98. Minority: 25%. Women: 52%. Average Age: 28.
Academics: Evening program. Summer program offered.
Finances: In-State Tuition: $20,560. Out-of-State Tuition: $14,540.
Admission Requirements: Application deadline: February 15. Admissions: fall term only.
Selectivity: Applications received: 1,840. Students accepted: 798. Students enrolled: 268. Median undergraduate GPA: 3.1. Median LSAT: 151.

UNIVERSITY OF THE PACIFIC

See McGeorge School of Law

PENNSYLVANIA STATE UNIVERSITY

Dickinson School of Law
150 S. College St.
Carlisle, PA 17013
Phone: (717) 240-5207
Fax: (717) 243-4366
E-mail: dsladmit@psu.edu
Web Site: http://www.dsl.edu
Characteristics of Entering Class 1997: Full-time students: 176. In-state: 69%. Minority: 8/14%. Women: 41%. Average Age: 25.
Academics: No evening program. No summer program offered.
Finances: Tuition: $14,500. Students receiving scholarships: 35%. Students receiving loans: 80%.
Admission Requirements: Application deadline: March 15. Admissions: fall term only.
Selectivity: Applications received: 1,054. Students accepted: 650. Students enrolled: 176. Median undergraduate GPA: 3.2. Median LSAT: 154.

UNIVERSITY OF PENNSYLVANIA

Law School
3400 Chestnut Street
Philadelphia, PA 19004
Phone: (215) 898-7400
Fax: (215) 573-2025
E-mail: admissions@0452.law.upenn.edu
Web Site: http://www.law.upenn.edu
Characteristics of Entering Class 1997: Full-time students: 230. In-state: 16%. Minority: 23/26%. Women: 43%. Average Age: 24.
Academics: No evening program. No summer program offered.
Finances: Tuition: $22,960. Students receiving scholarships: 44%. Students receiving loans: 74%.
Admission Requirements: Application deadline: March 1. Admissions: fall term only.
Selectivity: Applications received: 3,844. Students accepted: 1,141. Students enrolled: 230. Median undergraduate GPA: 3.58. Median LSAT: 165.

PEPPERDINE UNIVERSITY

24255 Pacific Coast Hwy.
Malibu, CA 90263
Phone: (310) 456-4631
Fax: (310) 317-7668
E-mail: aoladmis@pepperdine.edu
Web Site: http://www.law.pepperdine.edu
Characteristics of Entering Class 1997: Full-time students: 244. In-state: 55%. Minority: 13%. Women: 48%. Average Age: 23.
Academics: No evening program. No summer program offered.
Finances: Tuition: $21,850.
Admission Requirements: Application deadline: March 1. Admissions: fall term only.
Selectivity: Applications received: 2,265. Students accepted: 1,046. Students enrolled: 244. Median undergraduate GPA: 3.26. Median LSAT: 157.

UNIVERSITY OF PITTSBURGH

School of Law
3900 Forbes Avenue
Pittsburgh, PA 15260
Phone: (412) 648-1415
Fax: (412) 648-2647
E-mail: admissions@law.pitt.edu
Web Site: http://www.law.pitt.edu
Characteristics of Entering Class 1997: Full-time students: 222. In-state: 64%. Minority: 9%. Women: 42%. Average Age: 24.
Academics: No evening program. No summer program offered.
Finances: Students receiving scholarships: 30%. Students receiving loans: 85%.
Admission Requirements: Application deadline: March 1. Admissions: fall term only.

LAW SCHOOLS

Selectivity: Applications received: 1,184. Students accepted: 801. Students enrolled: 222. Median undergraduate GPA: 3.15. Median LSAT: 154.

PONTIFICAL CATHOLIC UNIVERSITY OF PUERTO RICO

School of Law
2250 Avenue Las Americas, Suite 633
Ponce, PR 00731-6382
Phone: (787) 841-2000
Fax: (787) 841-4620
Characteristics of Entering Class 1997: Full-time students: 110. Part-time students: 58. In-state: 100%. Women: 49%. Average Age: 26.
Academics: Evening program. Summer program offered.
Finances: Tuition: $8,000. Students receiving scholarships: 7%.
Admission Requirements: Application deadline: April 15. Admissions fall term only.
Selectivity: Applications received: 489. Students accepted: 212. Students enrolled: 168. Median undergraduate GPA: 3.08. Median LSAT: 137.

UNIVERSITY OF PUERTO RICO

School of Law
PO Box 23349
San Juan, PR 00931
Phone: (787) 764-1655
Fax: (787) 764-4601
E-mail: none
Characteristics of Entering Class 1997: Full-time students: 101. Part-time students: 50. In-state: 1%. Minority: 0%. Women: 59%. Average Age: 24.
Academics: Evening program. Summer program offered.
Finances: In-State Tuition: $2,850. Out-of-State Tuition: $3,500. Students receiving loans: 5%.
Admission Requirements: Application deadline: February 16. Admissions: fall term only.

Selectivity: Applications received: 825. Students accepted: 177. Students enrolled: 151. Median undergraduate GPA: 3.5. Median LSAT: 147.

Q

QUINNIPIAC COLLEGE

School of Law
275 Mt. Carmel Avenue
Hamden, CT 06518
Phone: (203) 287-3400
Fax: (203) 287-3339
E-mail: ladm@quinnipiac.edu
Web Site: http://www.quinnipiac.edu/law.html
Characteristics of Entering Class 1997: Full-time students: 197. Part-time students: 60. In-state: 56%. Minority: 14/12%. Women: 39%. Average Age: 27.
Academics: Evening program. Summer program offered.
Finances: Tuition: $18,888. Students receiving scholarships: 33%. Students receiving loans: 87%.
Admission Requirements: Application deadline: rolling. Midyear admission allowed.
Selectivity: Applications received: 1,965. Students accepted: 1,085. Students enrolled: 257. Median undergraduate GPA: 2.8. Median LSAT: 149.

R

REGENT UNIVERSITY

School of Law
1000 Regent University Drive
Virginia Beach, VA 23464
Phone: (757) 579-4584
Fax: (757) 579-4595
E-mail: lawschool@regent.edu
Web Site: http://www.regent.edu/acad/schlaw
Characteristics of Entering Class 1997: Full-time students: 143. In-state: 27%. Minority: 12/9%. Women: 37%. Average Age: 27.
Academics: Evening program. Summer program offered.
Finances: Tuition: $15,345. Students receiving scholarships: 82%. Students receiving loans: 81%.
Admission Requirements: Application deadline: April 1. Admissions: fall term only.
Selectivity: Applications received: 419. Students accepted: 237. Students enrolled: 143. Median undergraduate GPA: 3.04. Median LSAT: 151.

UNIVERSITY OF RICHMOND

TC Williams School of Law
Richmond, VA 23173
Phone: (804) 289-8189
Fax: (804) 287-6516
E-mail: mrahman@richmond.edu
Web Site: http://www.law.richmond.edu
Characteristics of Entering Class 1997: Full-time students: 166. In-state: 58%. Minority: 19/24%. Women: 41%. Average Age: 25.
Academics: No evening program. Summer program offered.
Finances: Tuition: $18,170.
Admission Requirements: Application deadline: February 1. Admissions: fall term only.

Directory of U.S. Law Schools

Selectivity: Applications received: 1,314. Students accepted: 550. Students enrolled: 166. Median undergraduate GPA: 3.08. Median LSAT: 158.

ROGER WILLIAMS UNIVERSITY

School of Law
Ten Metacom Avenue
Bristol, RI 02809
Phone: (401) 254-4555
Fax: (401) 254-4516
E-mail: ll@rwulaw.rwu.edu
Web Site: http://www.rwu.edu
Characteristics of Entering Class 1997: Full-time students: 99. Part-time students: 51. Minority: 13/10%. Women: 45%. Average Age: 27.
Academics: Evening program. Summer program offered.
Finances: Tuition: $18,030. Students receiving scholarships: 10%. Students receiving loans: 75%.
Admission Requirements: Application deadline: May 15. Admissions: fall term only.
Selectivity: Applications received: 706. Students accepted: 425. Students enrolled: 150. Median undergraduate GPA: 3.02. Median LSAT: 148.

RUTGERS UNIVERSITY— CAMDEN

School of Law
406 Penn Street, 3rd Floor
Camden, NJ 08102
Phone: (609) 225-6102
Fax: (609) 225-6537
E-mail: maureeno@crab.rutgers.edu
Web Site: http://www.camlaw.rutgers.edu
Characteristics of Entering Class 1997: Full-time students: 191. Part-time students: 45. In-state: 67%. Minority: 16/20%. Women: 47%. Average Age: 26.
Academics: Evening program. No summer program offered.

Finances: In-State Tuition: $9,046. Out-of-State Tuition: $13,272. Students receiving scholarships: 12%. Students receiving loans: 80%.
Admission Requirements: Application deadline: March 1. Admissions fall term only.
Selectivity: Applications received: 1,500. Students accepted: 754. Students enrolled: 236. Median undergraduate GPA: 3.22. Median LSAT: 153.

RUTGERS UNIVERSITY— NEWARK

School of Law
15 Washington Street
Newark, NJ 07102
Phone: (973) 353-5380
Fax: (973) 353-1445
E-mail: geddis@andromeda.rutgers.edu
Web Site: http://www.info.rutgers.edu/rusln/rulnindx.html
Characteristics of Entering Class 1997: Full-time students: 155. Part-time students: 55. In-state: 80%. Minority: 37/39%. Women: 48%. Average Age: 27.
Academics: Evening program. No summer program offered.
Finances: In-State Tuition: $9,046. Out-of-State Tuition: $13,272. Students receiving scholarships: 11%. Students receiving loans: 71%.
Admission Requirements: Application deadline: March 15. Admissions: fall term only.
Selectivity: Applications received: 2,327. Students accepted: 758. Students enrolled: 210. Median undergraduate GPA: 3.26. Median LSAT: 157.

S

ST. JOHN'S UNIVERSITY

School of Law
8000 Utopia Parkway
Jamaica, NY 11439
Phone: (718) 990-6611
Fax: (718) 591-1855
E-mail: admisns@sjulaw/stjohns.edu
Web Site: http://www.stjohns.edu/law
Characteristics of Entering Class 1997: Full-time students: 202. Part-time students: 70. In-state: 84%. Minority: 26%. Women: 42%. Average Age: 23.
Academics: Evening program. No summer program offered.
Finances: Tuition: $21,000. Students receiving scholarships: 26%.
Admission Requirements: Application deadline: March 15. Midyear admission allowed.
Selectivity: Applications received: 2,398. Students accepted: 1,084. Students enrolled: 272. Median undergraduate GPA: 3. Median LSAT: 155.

SAINT LOUIS UNIVERSITY

School of Law
3700 Lindell Blvd.
St. Louis, MO 63108
Phone: (314) 977-2800
Fax: (314) 977-3966
E-mail: Admissions@lawlib.slu.edu
Web Site: http://www.lawlib.slu.edu/hometext.htm
Characteristics of Entering Class 1997: Full-time students: 182. Part-time students: 72. In-state: 54%. Minority: 18/18%. Women: 49%. Average Age: 25.
Academics: Evening program. Summer program offered.
Finances: Tuition: $18,150. Students receiving scholarships: 50%. Students receiving loans: 85%.

LAW SCHOOLS

Admission Requirements: Application deadline: March 15. Admissions: fall term only.
Selectivity: Applications received: 1,067. Students accepted: 675. Students enrolled: 254. Median undergraduate GPA: 3.26. Median LSAT: 154.

St. Mary's University

School of Law
One Camino Santa Maria
San Antonio, TX 78228-8601
Phone: (210) 436-3523
Fax: (210) 431-4202
E-mail: meryc @ law.stmarytx.edu
Characteristics of Entering Class 1997: Full-time students: 272. In-state: 85%. Minority: 41%. Women: 43%. Average Age: 26.
Academics: No evening program. Summer program offered.
Finances: Tuition: $16,213. Students receiving scholarships: 40%. Students receiving loans: 90%.
Admission Requirements: Application deadline: March 1. Admissions: fall term only.
Selectivity: Applications received: 1,270. Students accepted: 733. Students enrolled: 272. Median undergraduate GPA: 2.81. Median LSAT: 150.

St. Thomas University

School of Law
16400 NW 32nd Avenue
Miami, FL 33054
Phone: (305) 623-2310
Fax: (305) 623-2357
E-mail: admitme@law.stu.edu
Web Site: http://www.stu.edu
Characteristics of Entering Class 1997: Full-time students: 202. In-state: 51%. Minority: 33/31%. Women: 44%. Average Age: 28.
Academics: No evening program. No summer program offered.

Finances: Tuition: $18,900. Students receiving scholarships: 40%. Students receiving loans: 92%.
Admission Requirements: Application deadline: April 30. Admissions: fall term only.
Selectivity: Applications received: 1,502. Students accepted: 771. Students enrolled: 202. Median undergraduate GPA: 2.98. Median LSAT: 150.

Samford University

Cumberland School of Law
800 Lakeshore Drive
Birmingham, AL 35229
Phone: (800) 888-7213
Fax: (205) 870-2673
E-mail: lawadmissions@samford.edu
Web Site: http://www.samford.edu/schools/law.html
Characteristics of Entering Class 1997: Full-time students: 212. In-state: 38%. Minority: 6/8%. Women: 34%. Average Age: 24.
Academics: No evening program. No summer program offered.
Finances: Tuition: $17,700. Students receiving scholarships: 26%. Students receiving loans: 80%.
Admission Requirements: Application deadline: February 28. Admissions: fall term only.
Selectivity: Applications received: 1,003. Students accepted: 580. Students enrolled: 212. Median undergraduate GPA: 3.02. Median LSAT: 151.

University of San Diego

School of Law
5998 Alcala Park
San Diego, CA 92110
Phone: (619) 260-4528
Fax: (619) 260-2218
E-mail: jdinfo@asusd.edu
Web Site: http://www.acusd.edu/~usdlaw

Characteristics of Entering Class 1997: Full-time students: 246. Part-time students: 80. Minority: 23%. Women: 43%. Average Age: 24.
Academics: Evening program. No summer program offered.
Finances: Tuition: $19,980. Students receiving scholarships: 30%. Students receiving loans: 80%.
Admission Requirements: Application deadline: February 1. Admissions: fall term only.
Selectivity: Applications received: 2,773. Students enrolled: 326. Median undergraduate GPA: 3.07. Median LSAT: 160.

University of San Francisco

School of Law
2130 Fulton Street
San Francisco, CA 94117
Phone: (415) 422-6586
Fax: (415) 422-6433
Web Site: http://www.usfca.edu/law
Characteristics of Entering Class 1997: Full-time students: 172. Part-time students: 46. In-state: 70%. Minority: 31%. Women: 53%. Average Age: 26.
Academics: Evening program. No summer program offered.
Finances: Tuition: $19,940. Students receiving scholarships: 37%. Students receiving loans: 78%.
Admission Requirements: Application deadline: April 1. Admissions fall term only.
Selectivity: Applications received: 2,525. Students accepted: 1,038. Students enrolled: 218. Median undergraduate GPA: 3.08. Median LSAT: 156.

Directory of U.S. Law Schools

SANTA CLARA UNIVERSITY

School of Law
500 El Camino Real
Santa Clara, CA 95053
Phone: (408) 554-4800
Fax: (408) 554-7897
E-mail: lawadmission@scu.edu
Web Site: http://www.scu.edu/law
**Characteristics of Entering Class
1997:** Full-time students: 242. Part-time students: 56. In-state: 22%. Minority: 30%. Women: 47%. Average Age: 26.
Academics: Evening program. No summer program offered.
Finances: Tuition: $19,990.
Admission Requirements: Application deadline: March 1. Admissions: fall term only.
Selectivity: Applications received: 2,559. Students enrolled: 298. Median undergraduate GPA: 3.22. Median LSAT: 156.

SEATTLE UNIVERSITY

School of Law
950 Broadway Plaza
Tacoma, WA 98402
Phone: (253) 591-2252
Fax: (253) 591-6313
E-mail: lawadmis@seattleu.edu
Web Site: http://www.law.seattleu.edu
**Characteristics of Entering Class
1997:** Full-time students: 210. Part-time students: 52. In-state: 74%. Minority: 29/23%. Women: 49%. Average Age: 31.
Academics: Evening program. No summer program offered.
Finances: Tuition: $17,040. Students receiving scholarships: 35%. Students receiving loans: 82%.
Admission Requirements: Application deadline: April 1. Admissions fall term only.
Selectivity: Applications received: 1,218. Students accepted: 748. Students enrolled: 261. Median undergraduate GPA: 3.28. Median LSAT: 155.

SETON HALL UNIVERSITY

School of Law
One Newark Center
Newark, NJ 07102
Phone: (973) 642-8747
Fax: (973) 642-8876
E-mail: http://www.shu.edu/law
Web Site: http://www.shu.edu/law
**Characteristics of Entering Class
1997:** Full-time students: 321. Part-time students: 64. In-state: 71%. Minority: 17%. Women: 38%. Average Age: 25.
Academics: Evening program. No summer program offered.
Finances: Tuition: $19,200.
Admission Requirements: Application deadline: April 1. Admissions: fall term only.
Selectivity: Applications received: 2,402. Students accepted: 1,134. Students enrolled: 385. Median undergraduate GPA: 3.09. Median LSAT: 154.

UNIVERSITY OF SOUTH CAROLINA

School of Law
Corner of Greene and Main
Columbia, SC 29208
Phone: (803) 777-6605
Fax: (803) 777-7751
E-mail: usclaw@law.law.sc.edu
Web Site: http://www.usclaw.sc.edu
**Characteristics of Entering Class
1997:** Full-time students: 242. In-state: 84%. Minority: 9%. Women: 45%. Average Age: 25.
Academics: No evening program. No summer program offered.
Finances: In-State Tuition: $6,864. Out-of-State Tuition: $13,606. Students receiving scholarships: 30%. Students receiving loans: 85%.
Admission Requirements: Application deadline: February 15. Admissions: fall term only.
Selectivity: Applications received: 1,163. Students accepted: 461. Students enrolled: 242. Median undergraduate GPA: 3.23. Median LSAT: 156.

UNIVERSITY OF SOUTH DAKOTA

School of Law
414 E. Clark
Vermillion, SD 57069-2390
Phone: (605) 677-5443
Fax: (605) 677-5417
E-mail: henri@jurist.law.usd.edu
Web Site: http://www.usd.edu/law
**Characteristics of Entering Class
1997:** Full-time students: 88. In-state: 73%. Minority: 5%. Women: 43%. Average Age: 27.
Academics: No evening program. Summer program offered.
Finances: In-State Tuition: $2,970. Out-of-State Tuition: $8,610. Students receiving scholarships: 14%.
Admission Requirements: Application deadline: March 1 pref. Admissions: fall term only.
Selectivity: Applications received: 321. Students accepted: 172. Students enrolled: 88. Median undergraduate GPA: 3.15. Median LSAT: 152.

UNIVERSITY OF SOUTHERN CALIFORNIA

Law School
University Park
Los Angeles, CA 90089-0071
Phone: (213) 740-7331
Fax: (213) 740-5502
E-mail: admissions@law.usc.edu
Web Site: http://www.usc.edu/dept/law
**Characteristics of Entering Class
1997:** Full-time students: 200. In-state: 60%. Minority: 40%. Women: 45%. Average Age: 25.
Academics: No evening program. No summer program offered.
Finances: Tuition: $23,464. Students receiving scholarships: 33%. Students receiving loans: 80%.
Admission Requirements: Application deadline: February 1. Admissions: fall term only.

KAPLAN 223

LAW SCHOOLS

Selectivity: Applications received: 3,300. Students accepted: 850. Students enrolled: 200. Median undergraduate GPA: 3.5. Median LSAT: 164.

Southern Illinois University—Carbondale

School of Law
Carbondale, IL 62901-6804
Phone: (618) 453-8767
Fax: (618) 453-8769
E-mail: lawadmit@siu.edu
Web Site: http://www.siu.edu/~lawsch
Characteristics of Entering Class 1997: Full-time students: 120. Part-time students: 1. In-state: 75%. Minority: 10%. Women: 31%. Average Age: 26.
Academics: No evening program. No summer program offered.
Finances: Students receiving scholarships: 22%.
Admission Requirements: Application deadline: March 1. Admissions: fall term only.
Selectivity: Applications received: 681. Students accepted: 219. Students enrolled: 121. Median undergraduate GPA: 3.12. Median LSAT: 153.

Southern Methodist University

School of Law
6501 Athens Street
P.O. Box 750110
Dallas, TX 75275-0110
Phone: (214) 768-2550
Fax: (214) 768-2549
E-mail: lswitzer@mail.smu.edu
Web Site: http://www.smu.edu\~law
Characteristics of Entering Class 1997: Full-time students: 235. Part-time students: 2. In-state: 60%. Minority: 13/19%. Women: 43%. Average Age: 25.
Academics: No evening program. No summer program offered.

Finances: Tuition: $20,794. Students receiving scholarships: 40%.
Admission Requirements: Application deadline: February 1. Admissions: fall term only.
Selectivity: Applications received: 1,698. Students accepted: 661. Students enrolled: 237. Median undergraduate GPA: 3.18. Median LSAT: 157.

Southern University

Law Center
P.O. Box 9294
Baton Rouge, LA 70813
Phone: (504) 771-5340
E-mail: Simmons@iAmerica.Net
School did not submit data.

South Texas College of Law

1303 San Jacinto
Houston, TX 77002
Phone: (713) 646-1810
Fax: (713) 646-2929
E-mail: acramer@stcl.edu
Web Site: http://www.stcl.edu
Characteristics of Entering Class 1997: Full-time students: 258. Part-time students: 95. In-state: 85%. Minority: 18%. Women: 46%. Average Age: 26.
Academics: Evening program. No summer program offered.
Finances: Tuition: $14,100. Students receiving scholarships: 20%. Students receiving loans: 80%.
Admission Requirements: Application deadline: March 1. Midyear admission allowed.
Selectivity: Applications received: 1,436. Students accepted: 932. Students enrolled: 353. Median undergraduate GPA: 2.95. Median LSAT: 151.

Southwestern University

School of Law
675 S. Westmoreland Avenue
Los Angeles, CA 90005-3992
Phone: (213) 738-6717
Fax: (213) 383-1688
E-mail: admissions@swlaw.edu
Web Site: http://www.swlaw.edu
Characteristics of Entering Class 1997: Full-time students: 260. Part-time students: 77. In-state: 85%. Minority: 38/36%. Women: 49%. Average Age: 27.
Academics: Evening program. Summer program offered.
Finances: Tuition: $19,950. Students receiving scholarships: 25%. Students receiving loans: 79%.
Admission Requirements: Application deadline: June 30. Admissions: fall term only.
Selectivity: Applications received: 2,193. Students accepted: 1,133. Students enrolled: 337.

Stanford University

Law School
Office of Admissions, Stanford Law School
Stanford, CA 94305-8610
Phone: (650) 723-4985
Fax: (650) 723-0838
E-mail: law.admissions@forsythe.stanford.edu
Web Site: http://www-leland.stanford.edu/group/law
Characteristics of Entering Class 1997: Full-time students: 178. Minority: 30%. Women: 40%. Average Age: 25.
Academics: No evening program. No summer program offered.
Finances: Tuition: $24,166. Students receiving scholarships: 35%. Students receiving loans: 75%.
Admission Requirements: Application deadline: February 1. Admissions: fall term only.
Selectivity: Applications received: 3,611. Students accepted: 500. Students enrolled: 178. Median undergraduate GPA: 3.79. Median LSAT: 167.

Stetson University

College of Law
1401 61st Street South
St. Petersburg, FL 33707
Phone: (813) 562-7802
Fax: (813) 343-0136
E-mail: lawadmit@hermes.law.stetson.edu
Web Site: http://www.law.stetson.edu
Characteristics of Entering Class 1997: Full-time students: 220. In-state: 75%. Minority: 19%. Women: 49%. Average Age: 26.
Academics: No evening program. No summer program offered.
Finances: Students receiving scholarships: 20%. Students receiving loans: 88%.
Admission Requirements: Application deadline: March 1. Midyear admission allowed.
Selectivity: Applications received: 1,702. Students accepted: 726. Students enrolled: 220. Median undergraduate GPA: 3.2. Median LSAT: 152.

Suffolk University

Law School
41 Temple Street
Boston, MA 02114
Phone: (617) 573-8144
Fax: (617) 573-8706
E-mail: lawadm@admin.suffolk.edu
Web Site: http://www.suffolk.edu/law
Characteristics of Entering Class 1997: Full-time students: 351. Part-time students: 187. In-state: 65%. Minority: 14%. Women: 50%. Average Age: 26.
Academics: Evening program. No summer program offered.
Finances: Students receiving scholarships: 30%. Students receiving loans: 80%.
Admission Requirements: Application deadline: March 2. Admissions: fall term only.
Selectivity: Applications received: 1,933. Students accepted: 1,375. Students enrolled: 538. Median undergraduate GPA: 3.1. Median LSAT: 150.

Syracuse University

College of Law
Office of the Dean, Suite 230
Syracuse, NY 13244-1030
Phone: (315) 443-2540
Fax: (315) 443-4213
E-mail: ficarra@law.syr.edu
Web Site: http://www.law.syr.edu
Characteristics of Entering Class 1997: Full-time students: 247. Part-time students: 6. In-state: 45%. Minority: 22%. Women: 39%. Average Age: 25.
Academics: No evening program. Summer program offered.
Finances: Tuition: $20,600. Students receiving scholarships: 61%. Students receiving loans: 83%.
Admission Requirements: Application deadline: April 1. Admissions: fall term only.
Selectivity: Applications received: 1,715. Students accepted: 1,124. Students enrolled: 253. Median undergraduate GPA: 3.2. Median LSAT: 151.

T

Temple University

School of Law
1719 N. Broad Street
Philadelphia, PA 19122
Phone: (215) 204-8925
Fax: (215) 204-1185
E-mail: law@astro.ocis.temple.edu
Web Site: http://www.temple.edu/lawschool
Characteristics of Entering Class 1997: Full-time students: 287. Part-time students: 83. In-state: 71%. Minority: 27/28%. Women: 49%. Average Age: 26.
Academics: Evening program. No summer program offered.
Finances: In-State Tuition: $8,590. Out-of-State Tuition: $15,104. Students receiving scholarships: 53.3%. Students receiving loans: 71%.
Admission Requirements: Application deadline: March 1. Admissions: fall term only.
Selectivity: Applications received: 2,712. Students accepted: 1,065. Students enrolled: 370. Median undergraduate GPA: 3.2. Median LSAT: 155.

University of Tennessee

College of Law
1505 W. Cumberland Avenue
Knoxville, TN 37996-1816
Phone: (423) 974-4131
Fax: (423) 974-1572
E-mail: lawadmit@libra.law.utk.edu
Web Site: http://www.law.utk.edu
Characteristics of Entering Class 1997: Full-time students: 182. In-state: 84%. Minority: 9/11%. Women: 48%. Average Age: 25.
Academics: No evening program. No summer program offered.
Finances: In-State Tuition: $4,204. Out-of-State Tuition: $10,496. Students receiving scholarships: 23%. Students receiving loans: 72%.
Admission Requirements: Application deadline: February 1. Admissions: fall term only.
Selectivity: Applications received: 1,144. Students accepted: 390. Students enrolled: 182. Median undergraduate GPA: 3.54. Median LSAT: 156.

University of Texas

School of Law
727 E. Dean Keeton St
Austin, TX 78705
Phone: (512) 471-6201
Fax: (512) 471-6988
E-mail: admissions@mail-law.utexas.edu
Web Site: http://www.utexas.edu/law
Characteristics of Entering Class 1997: Full-time students: 468. In-state: 80%. Minority: 16/22%. Women: 45%. Average Age: 25.
Academics: No evening program. No summer program offered.

LAW SCHOOLS

Finances: In-State Tuition: $6,750. Out-of-State Tuition: $14,000. Students receiving scholarships: 78%. Students receiving loans: 78%.
Admission Requirements: Application deadline: February 1. Admissions: fall term only.
Selectivity: Applications received: 3,487. Students accepted: 1,092. Students enrolled: 468. Median undergraduate GPA: 3.56. Median LSAT: 162.

TEXAS SOUTHERN UNIVERSITY

Thurgood Marshall School of Law
3100 Cleburne
Houston, TX 77004
Phone: (713) 313-1004
Fax: (713) 313-1049
E-mail: chanks@tsulaw.edu
Web Site: http://www.tsulaw.edu
Characteristics of Entering Class 1997: Full-time students: 260. In-state: 67%. Minority: 84/80%. Women: 47%. Average Age: 27.
Academics: No evening program. Summer program offered.
Finances: In-State Tuition: $3,960. Out-of-State Tuition: $7,860. Students receiving scholarships: 15%. Students receiving loans: 90%.
Admission Requirements: Application deadline: April 1. Admissions: fall term only.
Selectivity: Applications received: 1,165. Students accepted: 548. Students enrolled: 260. Median undergraduate GPA: 2.6. Median LSAT: 143.

TEXAS TECH UNIVERSITY

School of Law
Box 40004
Lubbock, TX 79409
Phone: (806) 742-3985
Fax: (806) 742-1629
E-mail: xydaw@ttacs.ttu.edu
Web Site: http://www.law.ttu.edu

Characteristics of Entering Class 1997: Full-time students: 205. In-state: 89%. Minority: 12%. Women: 49%. Average Age: 25.
Academics: No evening program. No summer program offered.
Finances: Students receiving scholarships: 35%. Students receiving loans: 74%.
Admission Requirements: Application deadline: February 1. Admissions: fall term only.
Selectivity: Applications received: 1,165. Students accepted: 547. Students enrolled: 205. Median undergraduate GPA: 3.42. Median LSAT: 155.

TEXAS WESLYAN UNIVERSITY

School of Law
2535 East Grauwyler
Irving, TX 75061
Phone: (972) 579-5700
Web-Site: http://www.txweslyan.edu
School did not submit data.

THOMAS M. COOLEY LAW SCHOOL

217 South Capitol Avenue
P.O. 13038
Lansing, MI 48901
Phone: (517) 371-5140
Fax: (517) 334-5718
E-mail: greggs@mlc.lib.mi.us
Characteristics of Entering Class 1997: Full-time students: 209. Part-time students: 553. In-state: 32%. Minority: 28/18%. Women: 38%. Average Age: 26.
Academics: Evening program. No summer program offered.
Finances: Tuition: $15,075. Students receiving scholarships: 11%. Students receiving loans: 80%.
Admission Requirements: Application deadline: rolling. Midyear admission allowed.

Selectivity: Applications received: 2,118. Students accepted: 1,610. Students enrolled: 762. Median undergraduate GPA: 2.82. Median LSAT: 144.

UNIVERSITY OF TOLEDO

College of Law
2801 West Bancroft Street
Toledo, OH 43537
Phone: (419) 530-4131
Fax: (419) 530-4526
E-mail: law0046@uoft01.utoledo.edu
Web Site: http://www.utoledo.edu/law
Characteristics of Entering Class 1997: Full-time students: 152. Part-time students: 40. In-state: 77%. Minority: 13/10%. Women: 44%. Average Age: 25.
Academics: Evening program. No summer program offered.
Finances: In-State Tuition: $6,969. Out-of-State Tuition: $13,406. Students receiving scholarships: 30%. Students receiving loans: 75%.
Admission Requirements: Application deadline: March 15. Admissions: fall term only.
Selectivity: Applications received: 712. Students accepted: 460. Students enrolled: 192. Median undergraduate GPA: 3.1. Median LSAT: 151.

TOURO COLLEGE

Jacob D. Fuchsberg Law Center
300 Nassau Road
Huntington, NY 11743
Phone: (516) 421-2244
Fax: (516) 421-2675
E-mail: admissions@tourolaw.edu
Web Site: http://www.tourolaw.edu
Characteristics of Entering Class 1997: Full-time students: 131. Part-time students: 103. In-state: 85%. Minority: 22/26%. Women: 46%. Average Age: 30.
Academics: Evening program. No summer program offered.
Finances: Tuition: $19,150. Students receiving scholarships: 40%. Students receiving loans: 92%.

Directory of U.S. Law Schools

Admission Requirements: Application deadline: rolling. Admissions fall term only.
Selectivity: Applications received: 1,434. Students accepted: 744. Students enrolled: 234.

TULANE UNIVERSITY

Law School
Weinmann Hall, Law Admission
New Orleans, LA 70118
Phone: (504) 865-5930
Fax: (504) 865-6710
E-mail: admissions@law.tulane.edu
Web Site: http://www.law.tulane.edu
Characteristics of Entering Class 1997: Full-time students: 315. In-state: 20%. Minority: 26/2%. Women: 47%. Average Age: 24.
Academics: No evening program. No summer program offered.
Finances: Tuition: $21,364. Students receiving scholarships: 40%. Students receiving loans: 77%.
Admission Requirements: Application deadline: N/A. Admissions: fall term only.
Selectivity: Applications received: 2,640. Students accepted: 1,400. Students enrolled: 305. Median undergraduate GPA: 3.27. Median LSAT: 159.

U

UNIVERSITY OF UTAH

College of Law
332 South 1400 East Front
Salt Lake City, UT 84112
Phone: (801) 581-7479
Fax: (801) 581-6897
E-mail: laura.nicklas@law.utah.edu
Web Site: http://www.law.utah.edu
Characteristics of Entering Class Full-time students: 128. In-state: 77%. Minority: 15%. Women: 40%. Average Age: 26.
Academics: No evening program. No summer program offered.
Finances: In-State Tuition: $4,685. Out-of-State Tuition: $10,503. Students receiving scholarships: 43%. Students receiving loans: 80%.
Admission Requirements: Application deadline: February 1. Admissions: fall term only.
Selectivity: Applications received: 717. Students accepted: 298. Students enrolled: 126. Median undergraduate GPA: 3.51. Median LSAT: 159.

V

VALPARAISO UNIVERSITY

School of Law
Wesemann Hall
Valparaiso, IN 46383-6493
Phone: (219) 465-7829
Fax: (219) 465-7808
E-mail: hspahn@wesemann.law.valpo.edu
Web Site: http://www.valpo.edu/law
Characteristics of Entering Class 1997: Full-time students: 119. Part-time students: 7. In-state: 54%. Minority: 23/19%. Women: 46%. Average Age: 26.
Academics: No evening program. No summer program offered.
Finances: Students receiving scholarships: 46%. Students receiving loans: 90%.
Admission Requirements: Application deadline: April 15. Admissions: fall term only.
Selectivity: Applications received: 674. Students accepted: 401. Students enrolled: 126. Median undergraduate GPA: 3.05. Median LSAT: 150.

VANDERBILT UNIVERSITY

School of Law
Admissions Office
Nashville, TN 37240
Phone: (615) 322-6452
Fax: (615) 322-6631
E-mail: admissions@law.vanderbilt.edu
Web Site: http://www.vanderbilt.edu/Law
Characteristics of Entering Class 1997: Full-time students: 187. In-state: 15%. Minority: 20%. Women: 41%. Average Age: 25.
Academics: No evening program. No summer program offered.
Finances: Students receiving scholarships: 40%. Students receiving loans: 80%.
Admission Requirements: Application deadline: February 1. Admissions fall term only.
Selectivity: Applications received: 2,230. Students accepted: 746. Students enrolled: 187. Median undergraduate GPA: 3.63. Median LSAT: 163.

VERMONT LAW SCHOOL

Chelsea Street
South Royalton, VT 05068-0096
Phone: (888) APP-YVLS
Fax: (802) 763-7071
E-mail: admiss@vermontlaw.edu
Web Site: http://www.vermontlaw.edu
Characteristics of Entering Class 1997: Full-time students: 146. In-state: 7%. Minority: 8/9%. Women: 51%. Average Age: 26.
Academics: No evening program. No summer program offered.
Finances: Tuition: $18,490. Students receiving scholarships: 35%. Students receiving loans: 85%.
Admission Requirements: Application deadline: February 15. Midyear admission allowed.
Selectivity: Applications received: 927. Students accepted: 597. Students enrolled: 146. Median undergraduate GPA: 3.1. Median LSAT: 154.

LAW SCHOOLS

Villanova University

School of Law
299 N. Spring Mill Road
Villanova, PA 19085
Phone: (610) 519-7010
Fax: (610) 519-6472
E-mail: pallozzi@law.vill.edu
Web Site: http://www.vls.law.vill.edu
Characteristics of Entering Class 1997: Full-time students: 242. In-state: 53%. Minority: 22%. Women: 53%. Average Age: 23.
Academics: No evening program. No summer program offered.
Finances: Tuition: $18,750. Students receiving scholarships: 4%. Students receiving loans: 70%.
Admission Requirements: Application deadline: January 31. Admissions: fall term only.
Selectivity: Applications received: 1,282. Students accepted: 714. Students enrolled: 242. Median undergraduate GPA: 3.42. Median LSAT: 158.

University of Virginia

School of Law
580 Massie Road
Charlottesville, VA 22903-1789
Phone: (804) 924-4676
E-mail: lawadmit@uva.pcmail.virginia.edu
Web Site: http://www.law.virginia.edu
Characteristics of Entering Class 1997: Full-time students: 362. Minority: 13/15%. Women: 39%. Average Age: 24.
Academics: No evening program. No summer program offered.
Finances: In-State Tuition: $13,954. Out-of-State Tuition: $19,870. Students receiving scholarships: 34%. Students receiving loans: 74%.
Admission Requirements: Application deadline: January 15. Admissions: fall term only.
Selectivity: Applications received: 3,091. Students accepted: 938. Students enrolled: 362. Median undergraduate GPA: 3.64. Median LSAT: 166.

W

Wake Forest University

Law School
P.O. Box 7206, Reynolda Station
Winston-Salem, NC 27109
Phone: (910) 759-5437
Fax: (910) 759-4632
E-mail: mnuttelaw.wfu.edu
Web Site: http://www.law.wfu.edu
Characteristics of Entering Class 1997: Full-time students: 164. Minority: 11/10%. Women: 38%. Average Age: 24.
Academics: No evening program. No summer program offered.
Finances: Tuition: $19,500. Students receiving scholarships: 20%. Students receiving loans: 78%.
Admission Requirements: Application deadline: March 15. Admissions: fall term only.
Selectivity: Applications received: 1,218. Students accepted: 518. Students enrolled: 164. Median undergraduate GPA: 3.27. Median LSAT: 160.

Washburn University

School of Law
1700 College
Topeka, KS 66621
Phone: (785) 231-1185
Fax: (785) 232-8087
E-mail: admissions@washburnlaw.edu
Web Site: http://www.washburnlaw.edu
Characteristics of Entering Class 1997: Full-time students: 148. In-state: 62%. Minority: 13/11%. Women: 45%. Average Age: 27.
Academics: No evening program. No summer program offered.
Finances: In-State Tuition: $6,583. Out-of-State Tuition: $9,773. Students receiving scholarships: 27%. Students receiving loans: 80%.
Admission Requirements: Application deadline: March 15. Midyear admission allowed.
Selectivity: Applications received: 649. Students accepted: 389. Students enrolled: 148. Median undergraduate GPA: 3.15. Median LSAT: 152.

University of Washington

School of Law
1100 N.E. Campus Pkwy.
Seattle, WA 98105-6617
Phone: (206) 543-4078
Fax: (206) 543-5671
E-mail: admit@law.washington.edu
Web Site: http://www.law.washington.edu
Characteristics of Entering Class 1997: Full-time students: 166. In-state: 78%. Minority: 31%. Women: 52%. Average Age: 25.
Academics: No evening program. No summer program offered.
Finances: In-State Tuition: $5,388. Out-of-State Tuition: $13,293. Students receiving scholarships: 60%. Students receiving loans: 70%.
Admission Requirements: Application deadline: January 15. Admissions: fall term only.
Selectivity: Applications received: 1,759. Students accepted: 469. Students enrolled: 166. Median undergraduate GPA: 3.56. Median LSAT: 162.

Washington and Lee University

School of Law
Lewis Hall
Lexington, VA 24450
Phone: (540) 463-8504
Fax: (540) 463-8586
E-mail: lawadm@wlu.edu
Web Site: http://www.wlu.edu

Directory of U.S. Law Schools

Characteristics of Entering Class
1997: Full-time students: 128. In-state: 16%. Minority: 7%. Women: 42%. Average Age: 24.
Academics: No evening program. No summer program offered.
Finances: Tuition: $16,990. Students receiving scholarships: 60%. Students receiving loans: 90%.
Admission Requirements: Application deadline: February 1. Admissions: fall term only.
Selectivity: Applications received: 1,389. Students accepted: 500. Students enrolled: 128. Median undergraduate GPA: 3.41. Median LSAT: 165.

Washington University

School of Law
Box 1120, One Brookings Drive
St. Louis, MO 63130
Phone: (314) 935-4525
Fax: (314) 935-6959
E-mail: admiss@wulaw.wustl.edu
Web Site: http://www.ls.wustl.edu
Characteristics of Entering Class
1997: Full-time students: 197. In-state: 37%. Minority: 23%. Women: 47%. Average Age: 25.
Academics: No evening program. No summer program offered.
Finances: Tuition: $21,675. Students receiving scholarships: 60%. Students receiving loans: 75%.
Admission Requirements: Application deadline: March 1. Admissions: fall term only.
Selectivity: Applications received: 1,357. Students accepted: 758. Students enrolled: 197. Median undergraduate GPA: 3.4. Median LSAT: 160.

Wayne State University

Law School
468 W. Ferry
Detroit, MI 48202
Phone: (313) 577-3937
Fax: (313) 577-6000
Web Site: http://www.law.wayne.edu
Characteristics of Entering Class
1997: Full-time students: 187. Part-time students: 73. In-state: 98%. Minority: 18%. Women: 43%. Average Age: 26.
Academics: Evening program. Summer program offered.
Finances: In-State Tuition: $7,038. Out-of-State Tuition: $14,778. Students receiving loans: 66%.
Admission Requirements: Application deadline: March 15. Admissions: fall term only.
Selectivity: Applications received: 1,030. Students accepted: 542. Students enrolled: 260. Median undergraduate GPA: 3.27. Median LSAT: 154.

Western New England College

School of Law
1215 Wilbraham Rd.
Springfield, MA 01119
Phone: (413) 782-6665
Fax: (800) 782-6665
E-mail: lawadmis@wnec.edu
Web Site: http://www.law.wnec.edu
Characteristics of Entering Class
1997: Full-time students: 131. Part-time students: 71. In-state: 35%. Minority: 11/10%. Women: 46%. Average Age: 26.
Academics: Evening program. No summer program offered.
Finances: Tuition: $16,750. Students receiving scholarships: 41%. Students receiving loans: 95%.
Admission Requirements: Application deadline: None. Admissions: fall term only.
Selectivity: Applications received: 1,375. Students accepted: 925. Students enrolled: 202. Median undergraduate GPA: 3. Median LSAT: 148.

West Virginia University

School of Law
P.O. Box 6130
Morgantown, WV 26506
Phone: (304) 293-5304
Fax: (304) 293-6891
E-mail: lawaply@wvu.edu
Web Site: http://www.wvu.edu/~law
Characteristics of Entering Class
1997: Full-time students: 144. Part-time students: 4. In-state: 89%. Minority: 7/5%. Women: 44%. Average Age: 27.
Academics: No evening program. No summer program offered.
Finances: In-State Tuition: $5,062. Out-of-State Tuition: $12,104.
Admission Requirements: Application deadline: March 1. Admissions: fall term only.
Selectivity: Applications received: 511. Students accepted: 228. Students enrolled: 147. Median undergraduate GPA: 3.33. Median LSAT: 153.

Whittier Law School

3333 Harbor Blvd.
Costa Mesa, CA 92626
Phone: (714) 444-4141
Fax: (714) 444-0250
Characteristics of Entering Class
1997: Full-time students: 164. Part-time students: 90. In-state: 76%. Minority: 43/37%. Women: 46%. Average Age: 26.
Academics: Evening program. Summer program offered.
Finances: Tuition: $19,980. Students receiving scholarships: 43%. Students receiving loans: 87%.
Admission Requirements: Application deadline: March 15. Midyear admission allowed.
Selectivity: Applications received: 1,743. Students accepted: 1,045. Students enrolled: 254.

LAW SCHOOLS

WIDENER UNIVERSITY

School of Law
4601 Concord Pike
P.O. Box 7474
Wilmington, DE 19803
Phone: (302) 477-2162
3800 Vartan Way
P.O. Box 69381
Harrisburg, PA 17106
Phone: (717) 541-3903
Web Site:
http://www.widener.edu/law/law.html
Characteristics of Entering Class 1997: Full-time students: 347. Part-time students: 167. Minority: 9/8%. Women: 45%. Average Age: 25.
Academics: Evening program. Summer program offered.
Finances: Tuition: $17,770. Students receiving scholarships: 11%. Students receiving loans: 80%.
Admission Requirements: Application deadline: May 15. Admissions: fall term only.
Selectivity: Applications received: 1,963. Students accepted: 1,423. Students enrolled: 514. Median undergraduate GPA: 2.95. Median LSAT: 148.

WILLAMETTE UNIVERSITY

College of Law
900 State Street
Salem, OR 97301
Phone: (503) 370-6282
Fax: (503) 370-6375
E-mail: law-admission@willamette.edu
Web Site: http://www.willamette.edu
Characteristics of Entering Class 1997: Full-time students: 158. Part-time students: 2. In-state: 40%. Minority: 8/11%. Women: 48%. Average Age: 27.
Academics: No evening program. No summer program offered.
Finances: Tuition: $17,050. Students receiving scholarships: 7%. Students receiving loans: 90%.

Admission Requirements: Application deadline: March 15. Admissions: fall term only.
Selectivity: Applications received: 778. Students accepted: 574. Students enrolled: 160. Median undergraduate GPA: 3.24. Median LSAT: 154.

COLLEGE OF WILLIAM AND MARY

School of Law
South Henry Street
Williamsburg, VA 23185
Phone: (757) 221-3785
Fax: (757) 221-3261
E-mail: lawadm@facstaff.wm.edu
Web Site: http://www.wm.edu/law
Characteristics of Entering Class 1997: Full-time students: 171. In-state: 61%. Minority: 19/22%. Women: 43%. Average Age: 25.
Academics: No evening program. No summer program offered.
Finances: Students receiving scholarships: 37%. Students receiving loans: 78%.
Admission Requirements: Application deadline: March 1. Admissions: fall term only.
Selectivity: Applications received: 2,330. Students accepted: 688. Students enrolled: 171. Median undergraduate GPA: 3.3. Median LSAT: 162.

WILLIAM MITCHELL COLLEGE OF LAW

875 Summit Avenue
St. Paul, MN 55105
Phone: (888) WMCL-LAW
Characteristics of Entering Class 1997: Full-time students: 205. Part-time students: 130. In-state: 76%. Minority: 13/12%. Women: 35%. Average Age: 29
Academics: Evening program. Summer program offered.
Finances: Tuition: $16,250. Students receiving scholarships: 45%. Students receiving loans: 85%.

Admission Requirements: Application deadline: July 1. Admissions fall term only.
Selectivity: Applications received: 938. Students accepted: 695. Students enrolled: 335. Median undergraduate GPA: 3.11. Median LSAT: 152.

UNIVERSITY OF WISCONSIN

Law School
975 Bascom Mall
Madison, WI 53706
Phone: (608) 262-8559
Fax: (608) 262-5485
Characteristics of Entering Class 1997: In-state: 160%. Minority: 18/23%. Women: 44%. Average Age: 26.
Academics: Evening program. No summer program offered.
Finances: In-State Tuition: $5,710. Out-of-State Tuition: $15,442.
Admission Requirements: Application deadline: February 1. Admissions: fall term only.
Selectivity: Applications received: 1,550. Students accepted: 520. Students enrolled: 225. Median undergraduate GPA: 3.52. Median LSAT: 158.

UNIVERSITY OF WYOMING

College of Law
P O Box 3035
Laramie, WY 82071-3035
Phone: (307) 766-6416
Fax: (307) 766-6417
E-mail: candid@uwyo.edu
Web Site: http://www.uwyo.edu
Characteristics of Entering Class 1997: Full-time students: 82. In-state: 68%. Minority: 2/3%. Women: 45%. Average Age: 27.
Academics: No evening program. No summer program offered.
Finances: Students receiving scholarships: 30%. Students receiving loans: 80%.
Admission Requirements: Application deadline: April 1. Admissions fall term only.

Selectivity: Applications received: 441. Students accepted: 267. Students enrolled: 82. Median undergraduate GPA: 3.24. Median LSAT: 154.

Y

YALE UNIVERSITY

Law School
127 Wall Street, P. O. Box 208329
New Haven, CT 06520-8329
Phone: (203) 432-4995
E-mail: admissions@mail.law.yale.edu
Web Site: http://www.law.yale.edu
Characteristics of Entering Class 1997: Full-time students: 188. Minority: 31%. Women: 42%. Average Age: 23.
Academics: No evening program. No summer program offered.
Finances: Tuition: $23,940. Students receiving scholarships: 35%. Students receiving loans: 75%.
Admission Requirements: Application deadline: February 15. Admissions: fall term only.
Selectivity: Applications received: 3,576. Students accepted: 306. Students enrolled: 188. Median undergraduate GPA: 3.88. Median LSAT: 172.

YESHIVA UNIVERSITY

See Benjamin N. Cardozo School of Law.

Academic Specialties

In this section, you'll find information on law schools that reported offering special programs in the academic specialties listed below. We've provided the most complete information available to us, but keep in mind that a school's absence from a particular list may simply mean that the school did not give a full report of their offerings. Check with the law schools themselves for complete details on their programs.

Arts/Communications/Entertainment Law 235

Civil Rights Law 236

Constitutional Law 237

Corporate Law 239

Energy Law 242

Environmental/Natural Resources Law 243

Health/Medicine Law 245

Insurance Law 247

International/Comparative Law 247

LAW SCHOOLS

Patent Law 250

Public Interest Law 251

Tax Law 254

Women's Rights Law 256

Academic Specialties

ARTS, COMMUNICATION, ENTERTAINMENT LAW

Boston College Law School
Newton, MA

Boston University School of Law
Boston, MA

University of California
School of Law
Berkeley, CA

University of California
School of Law
Davis, CA

University of California
School of Law
Los Angeles, CA

Catholic University of America
Columbus School of Law
Washington, DC

Columbia University School of Law
New York, NY

DePaul University College of Law
Chicago, IL

University of Detroit Mercy
School of Law
Detroit, MI

Dickinson School of Law
Pennsylvania State University
Carlisle, PA

Drake University Law School
Des Moines, IA

Fordham University School of Law
New York, NY

Georgetown University Law Center
Washington, DC

Golden Gate University
School of Law
San Francisco, CA

Harvard University Law School
Cambridge, MA

Hofstra University School of Law
Hempstead, NY

Howard University School of Law
Washington, DC

Illinois Institute of Technology
Chicago-Kent College of Law
Chicago, IL

Indiana University School of Law
Bloomington, IN

John Marshall School of Law
Chicago, IL

Loyola Marymount Loyola
Law School
Los Angeles, CA

University of Miami School of Law
Coral Gables, FL

New York Law School
New York, NY

New York University
School of Law
New York, NY

Oregon-University of Oregon
School of Law
Eugene, OR

Pepperdine University
School of Law
Malibu, CA

Seton Hall University
School of Law
Newark, NJ

University of Southern California
Law Center
Los Angeles, CA

Southwestern University
School of Law
Los Angeles, CA

St. John's University
School of Law
Jamaica, NY

St. Mary's University
School of Law
San Antonio, TX

Suffolk University Law School
Boston, MA

Syracuse University
College of Law
Syracuse, NY

Texas Southern University
Thurgood Marshall School of Law
Houston, TX

Valparaiso University
School of Law
Valparaiso, IN

Vanderbilt University
School of Law
Nashville, TN

Vermont School of Law
South Royalton, VT

Villanova University School of Law
Villanova, PA

Whittier Law School
Los Angeles, CA

Yeshiva University
Benjamin N. Cardozo School of Law
New York, NY

LAW SCHOOLS

CIVIL RIGHTS LAW

Albany Law School
Albany, NY

Boston College Law School
Newton, MA

Boston University School of Law
Boston, MA

Brooklyn Law School
Brooklyn, NY

University of California
School of Law
Davis, CA

University of California
School of Law
Los Angeles, CA

Catholic University of America
Columbus School of Law
Washington, DC

City University of New York
School of Law
Flushing, NY

Cleveland State University
Cleveland-Marshall College of Law
Cleveland, Oh

Columbia University School of Law
New York, NY

University of Connecticut
School of Law
Hartford, CT

Cornell University Law School
Ithaca, NY

DePaul University College of Law
Chicago, IL

Drake University Law School
Des Moines, IA

Emory University School of Law
Atlanta, GA

Fordham University School of Law
New York, NY

George Washington University
Law School
Washington, DC

Georgetown University Law Center
Washington, DC

Georgia State University
College of Law
Atlanta, GA

Harvard University Law School
Cambridge, MA

Howard University School of Law
Washington, DC

Indiana University School of Law
Bloomington, IN

University of Kansas
School of Law
Lawrence, KS

Louisiana State University
Law Center
Baton Rouge, LA

Loyola University School of Law
Chicago, IL

University of Miami School of Law
Coral Gables, FL

University of Michigan Law School
Ann Arbor, MI

University of Minnesota
Law School
Minneapolis, MN

New York Law School
New York, NY

New York University
School of Law
New York, NY

University of North Carolina
School of Law
Chapel Hill, NC

University of Notre Dame
Notre Dame Law School
Notre Dame, IN

Nova Southeastern University
Shepard Broad Law Center
Fort Lauderdale, FL

Ohio State University
College of Law
Columbus, OH

Pace University School of Law
White Plains, NY

University of Pittsburgh
School of Law
Pittsburgh, PA

Quinnipiac College School of Law
Hamden, CT

Rutgers University School of Law
Newark, NJ

Samford University
Cumberland School of Law
Birmingham, AL

University of San Francisco
School of Law
San Francisco, CA

Seton Hall University
School of Law
Newark, NJ

Academic Specialties

University of Southern California
Law Center
Los Angeles, CA

Southern University Law Center
Baton Rouge, LA

Southwestern University
School of Law
Los Angeles, CA

St. John's University School of Law
Jamaica, NY

St. Mary's University
School of Law
San Antonio, TX

Suffolk University Law School
Boston, MA

Syracuse University
College of Law
Syracuse, NY

Temple University School of Law
Philadelphia, PA

Touro College
Jacob D. Fuchsberg Law Center
Huntington, NY

University of the Pacific
McGeorge School of Law
Sacramento, CA

Valparaiso University
School of Law
Valparaiso, IN

University of Virginia
School of Law
Charlottesville, VA

University of Washington
School of Law
Seattle, WA

Wayne State University
Law School
Detroit, MI

Yale University
Yale Law School
New Haven, CT

CONSTITUTIONAL LAW

University of Alabama
School of Law
Tuscaloosa, AL

Albany Law School
Albany, NY

Arizona State University
College of Law
Tempe, AZ

University of Arizona
College of Law
Tucson, AZ

Boston College Law School
Newton, MA

Boston University School of Law
Boston, MA

Brigham Young University
Law School
Provo, UT

Brooklyn Law School
Brooklyn, NY

California Western
School of Law
San Diego, CA

University of California
School of Law
Berkeley, CA

University of California
School of Law
Davis, CA

University of California
School of Law
Los Angeles, CA

Case Western Reserve University
School of Law
Cleveland, OH

Catholic University of America
Columbus School of Law
Washington, DC

City University of New York
School of Law
Flushing, NY

Cleveland State University
Cleveland-Marshall College of Law
Cleveland, Oh

College of William and Mary
School of Law
Williamsburg, VA

University of Colorado
School of Law
Boulder, CO

Columbia University School of Law
New York, NY

University of Connecticut
School of Law
Hartford, CT

Cornell University Law School
Ithaca, NY

Creighton University School of Law
Omaha, NE

Drake University Law School
Des Moines, IA

KAPLAN 237

LAW SCHOOLS

Duke University School of Law
Durham, NC

Emory University School of Law
Atlanta, GA

University of Florida
College of Law
Gainesville, FL

Fordham University School of Law
New York, NY

George Washington University
Law School
Washington, DC

Georgetown University Law Center
Washington, DC

Georgia State University
College of Law
Atlanta, GA

University of Georgia
School of Law
Athens, GA

Golden Gate University
School of Law
San Francisco, CA

Harvard University Law School
Cambridge, MA

Hofstra University School of Law
Hempstead, NY

University of Houston Law Center
Houston, TX

Howard University School of Law
Washington, DC

Illinois Institute of Technology
Chicago-Kent College of Law
Chicago, IL

Indiana University School of Law
Bloomington, IN

University of Kansas
School of Law
Lawrence, KS

University of Kentucky
College of Law
Lexington, KY

Louisiana State University
Law Center
Baton Rouge, LA

Loyola Marymount Loyola
Law School
Los Angeles, CA

Loyola University School of Law
Chicago, IL

University of Miami School of Law
Coral Gables, FL

University of Michigan Law School
Ann Arbor, MI

University of Minnesota
Law School
Minneapolis, MN

University of Missouri
School of Law
Kansas City, MO

New York Law School
New York, NY

New York University
School of Law
New York, NY

University of North Carolina
School of Law
Chapel Hill, NC

University of Notre Dame
Notre Dame Law School
Notre Dame, IN

Nova Southeastern University
Shepard Broad Law Center
Fort Lauderdale, FL

Ohio State University
College of Law
Columbus, OH

University of Oklahoma
College of Law
Norman, OK

University of Oregon
School of Law
Eugene, OR

Pace University School of Law
White Plains, NY

University of Pennsylvania
Law School
Philadelphia, PA

University of Pittsburgh
School of Law
Pittsburgh, PA

Regent University School of Law
Virginia Beach, VA

University of Richmond
T. C. Williams School of Law
Richmond, VA

Rutgers University School of Law
Camden, NJ

Rutgers University School of Law
Newark, NJ

Samford University
Cumberland School of Law
Birmingham, AL

Academic Specialties

University of San Francisco
School of Law
San Francisco, CA

Seton Hall University
School of Law
Newark, NJ

University of South Carolina
School of Law
Columbia, SC

University of Southern California
Law Center
Los Angeles, CA

Southwestern University
School of Law
Los Angeles, CA

St. John's University School of Law
Jamaica, NY

St. Mary's University
School of Law
San Antonio, TX

Stanford University Law School
Stanford, CA

Suffolk University Law School
Boston, MA

Syracuse University
College of Law
Syracuse, NY

Temple University School of Law
Philadelphia, PA

University of Texas School of Law
Austin, TX

University of Toledo
College of Law
Toledo, OH

University of Utah College of Law
Salt Lake City, UT

Valparaiso University
School of Law
Valparaiso, IN

Vermont Law School
South Royalton, VT

University of Virginia
School of Law
Charlottesville, VA

University of Washington
School of Law
Seattle, WA

Wayne State University
Law School
Detroit, MI

Yale University
Yale Law School
New Haven, CT

Yeshiva University
Benjamin N. Cardozo School of Law
New York, NY

Corporate Law

Albany Law School
Albany, NY

University of Akron School of Law
Akron, OH

University of Alabama
School of Law
Tuscaloosa, AL

University of Arizona
College of Law
Tucson, AZ

University of Baltimore
School of Law
Baltimore, MD

Baylor University Law School
Waco, TX

Boston College Law School
Newton, MA

Boston University School of Law
Boston, MA

Brigham Young University
Law School
Provo, UT

Brooklyn Law School
Brooklyn, NY

California Western School of Law
San Diego, CA

University of California
School of Law
Berkeley, CA

University of California
School of Law
Davis, CA

University of California
School of Law
Los Angeles, CA

Case Western Reserve University
School of Law
Cleveland, OH

Catholic University of America
Columbus School of Law
Washington, DC

University of Cincinnati
College of Law
Cincinnati, OH

University of Colorado
School of Law
Boulder, CO

Columbia University School of Law
New York, NY

KAPLAN 239

LAW SCHOOLS

University of Connecticut
School of Law
Hartford, CT

Cornell University Law School
Ithaca, NY

Creighton University School of Law
Omaha, NE

University of Dayton
School of Law
Dayton, OH

University of Denver
College of Law
Denver, CO

DePaul University College of Law
Chicago, IL

University of Detroit Mercy
School of Law
Detroit, MI

Dickinson School of Law
Carlisle, PA

Drake University Law School
Des Moines, IA

Duke University School of Law
Durham, NC

Duquesne University
School of Law
Pittsburgh, PA

Emory University School of Law
Atlanta, GA

University of Florida
College of Law
Gainesville, FL

Fordham University School of Law
New York, NY

Franklin Pierce Law Center
Concord, NH

George Mason University
School of Law
Arlington, VA

George Washington University
Law School
Washington, DC

Georgetown University Law Center
Washington, DC

Georgia State University
College of Law
Atlanta, GA

Golden Gate University
School of Law
San Francisco, CA

Gonzaga University School of Law
Spokane, WA

Harvard University Law School
Cambridge, MA

Hofstra University School of Law
Hempstead, NY

University of Houston Law Center
Houston, TX

Illinois Institute of Technology
Chicago-Kent College of Law
Chicago, IL

University of Illinois
College of Law
Champaign, IL

Indiana University School of Law
Bloomington, IN

Indiana University School of Law
Indianapolis, IN

University of Kansas
School of Law
Lawrence, KS

University of Kentucky
College of Law
Lexington, KY

Lewis & Clark
Northwestern School of Law
Portland, OR

University of Nebraska
College of Law
Lincoln, NE

Louisiana State University
Law Center
Baton Rouge, LA

University of Louisville
School of Law
Louisville, KY

Loyola Marymount Loyola
Law School
Los Angeles, CA

Loyola University School of Law
Chicago, IL

University of Maryland
School of Law
Baltimore, MD

University of Miami School of Law
Coral Gables, FL

University of Michigan Law School
Ann Arbor, MI

University of Minnesota
Law School
Minneapolis, MN

University of Mississippi
School of Law
University, MS

240 KAPLAN

Academic Specialties

University of Missouri
School of Law
Columbia, MO

University of Missouri
School of Law
Kansas City, MO

New York University
School of Law
New York, NY

University of North Carolina
School of Law
Chapel Hill, NC

Northern Illinois University
College of Law
DeKalb, IL

University of Notre Dame
Notre Dame Law School
Notre Dame, IN

Nova Southeastern University
Shepard Broad Law Center
Fort Lauderdale, FL

Ohio State University
College of Law
Columbus, OH

Oklahoma City University
School of Law
Oklahoma City, OK

University of Oklahoma
College of Law
Norman, OK

University of Oregon
School of Law
Eugene, OR

Pace University School of Law
White Plains, NY

University of the Pacific
McGeorge School of Law
Sacramento, CA

University of Pennsylvania
Law School
Philadelphia, PA

Pepperdine University
School of Law
Malibu, CA

University of Pittsburgh
School of Law
Pittsburgh, PA

Quinnipiac College School of Law
Hamden, CT

University of Richmond
T. C. Williams School of Law
Richmond, VA

Rutgers University School of Law
Camden, NJ

Rutgers University School of Law
Newark, NJ

Samford University
Cumberland School of Law
Birmingham, AL

University of San Diego
School of Law
San Diego, CA

University of San Francisco
School of Law
San Francisco, CA

Santa Clara University
School of Law
Santa Clara, CA

Seattle University School of Law
Tacoma, WA

Seton Hall University
School of Law
Newark, NJ

University of South Carolina
School of Law
Columbia, SC

University of South Dakota
School of Law
Vermillion, SD

South Texas College of Law
Houston, TX

University of Southern California
Law Center
Los Angeles, CA

Southern Methodist University
School of Law
Dallas, TX

Southwestern University
School of Law
Los Angeles, CA

St. John's University School of Law
Jamaica, NY

St. Mary's University
School of Law
San Antonio, TX

St. Thomas University
School of Law
Miami, FL

Stetson University College of Law
St. Petersburg, FL

Suffolk University Law School
Boston, MA

Syracuse University
College of Law
Syracuse, NY

KAPLAN 241

LAW SCHOOLS

Temple University School of Law
Philadelphia, PA

University of Texas School of Law
Austin, TX

University of Toledo
College of Law
Toledo, OH

Touro College
Jacob D. Fuchsberg Law Center
Huntington, NY

Valparaiso University
School of Law
Valparaiso, IN

Vanderbilt University
School of Law
Nashville, TN

Vermont Law School
South Royalton, VT

Villanova University School of Law
Villanova, PA

University of Virginia
School of Law
Charlottesville, VA

Wake Forest University
School of Law
Winston-Salem, NC

Washington and Lee University
School of Law
Lexington, VA

Washington University
School of Law
St. Louis, MO

University of Washington
School of Law
Seattle, WA

Wayne State University
Law School
Detroit, MI

Widener University School of Law
Wilmington, DE

William Mitchell College of Law
Saint Paul, MN

University of Wisconsin
Law School
Madison, WI

University of Wyoming
College of Law
Laramie, WY

Yale University
Yale Law School
New Haven, CT

Yeshiva University
Benjamin N. Cardozo School of Law
New York, NY

ENERGY LAW

University of Denver
College of Law
Denver, CO

University of Houston Law Center
Houston, TX

Illinois Institute of Technology
Chicago-Kent College of Law
Chicago, IL

Indiana University School of Law
Bloomington, IN

University of Kansas
School of Law
Lawrence, KS

University of Kentucky
College of Law
Lexington, KY

Lewis & Clark College
Northwestern School of Law
Portland, OR

Loyola University School of Law
New Orleans, LA

University of Oklahoma
College of Law
Norman, OK

University of Oregon
School of Law
Eugene, OR

St. John's University School of Law
Jamaica, NY

St. Mary's University
School of Law
San Antonio, TX

Suffolk University Law School
Boston, MA

University of Tulsa College of Law
Tulsa, OK

University of Utah College of Law
Salt Lake City, UT

University of Washington
School of Law
Seattle, WA

Washburn University
School of Law
Topeka, KS

Widener University School of Law
Wilmington, DE

Academic Specialties

ENVIRONMENTAL/ NATURAL RESOURCES LAW

University of Alabama
School of Law
Tuscaloosa, AL

Albany Law School
Albany, NY

Arizona State University
College of Law
Tempe, AZ

University of Baltimore
School of Law
Baltimore, MD

Boston College Law School
Newton, MA

Boston University
School of Law
Boston, MA

Brigham Young University
Law School
Provo, UT

California Western School of Law
San Diego, CA

University of California
School of Law
Davis, CA

University of California
School of Law
Los Angeles, CA

Case Western Reserve University
School of Law
Cleveland, OH

University of Cincinnati
College of Law
Cincinnati, OH

City University of New York
School of Law
Flushing, NY

Cleveland State University
Cleveland-Marshall College of Law
Cleveland, OH

College of William and Mary
School of Law
Williamsburg, VA

University of Colorado
School of Law
Boulder, CO

Cornell University Law School
Ithaca, NY

University of Denver
College of Law
Denver, CO

University of Detroit Mercy
School of Law
Detroit, MI

Drake University Law School
Des Moines, IA

Duke University School of Law
Durham, NC

Duquesne University
School of Law
Pittsburgh, PA

Emory University School of Law
Atlanta, GA

Florida State University
College of Law
Tallahassee, FL

University of Florida
College of Law
Gainesville, FL

George Washington University
Law School
Washington, DC

Golden Gate University
School of Law
San Francisco, CA

Gonzaga University School of Law
Spokane, WA

Harvard University Law School
Cambridge, MA

University of Hawaii
William S. Richardson School of Law
Honolulu, HI

Hofstra University School of Law
Hempstead, NY

University of Houston Law Center
Houston, TX

Illinois Institute of Technology
Chicago-Kent College of Law
Chicago, IL

University of Illinois
College of Law
Champaign, IL

Indiana University School of Law
Bloomington, IN

Indiana University School of Law
Indianapolis, IN

University of Kansas
School of Law
Lawrence, KS

University of Kentucky
College of Law
Lexington, KY

Lewis & Clark College
Northwestern School of Law
Portland, OR

LAW SCHOOLS

Louisiana State University
Law Center
Baton Rouge, LA

University of Louisville
School of Law
Louisville, KY

Loyola Marymount Loyola
Law School
Los Angeles, CA

Loyola University School of Law
New Orleans, LA

University of Maine School of Law
Portland, OR

University of Maryland
School of Law
Baltimore, MD

University of Michigan Law School
Ann Arbor, MI

University of Minnesota
Law School
Minneapolis, MN

University of Missouri
School of Law
Columbia, MO

University of Missouri
School of Law
Kansas City, MO

University of Montana
School of Law
Missoula, MT

University of Nebraska
College of Law
Lincoln, NE

New England School of Law
Boston, MA

University of New Mexico
School of Law
Albuquerque, NM

New York University
School of Law
New York, NY

Northern Kentucky University
Salmon P. Chase College of Law
Highland Heights KY

Ohio Northern University
College of Law
Ada, OH

Ohio State University
College of Law
Columbus, OH

University of Oklahoma
College of Law
Norman, OK

University of Oregon
School of Law
Eugene, OR

Pace University School of Law
White Plains, NY

University of the Pacific
McGeorge School of Law
Sacramento, CA

Pepperdine University
School of Law
Malibu, CA

University of Pittsburgh
School of Law
Pittsburgh, PA

Roger Williams University
School of Law
Bristol, RI

Rutgers University School of Law
Camden, NJ

Rutgers University School of Law
Newark, NJ

St. John's University School of Law
Jamaica, NY

St. Mary's University
School of Law
San Antonio, TX

Samford University
Cumberland School of Law
Birmingham, AL

University of San Diego
School of Law
San Diego, CA

Santa Clara University
School of Law
Santa Clara, CA

Seattle University School of Law
Tacoma, WA

Seton Hall University
School of Law
Newark, NJ

University of South Carolina
School of Law
Columbia, SC

University of South Dakota
School of Law
Vermillion, SD

University of Southern California
Law Center
Los Angeles, CA

Southern Illinois University
School of Law
Carbondale, IL

Southern Methodist University
School of Law
Dallas, TX

244 KAPLAN

Academic Specialties

Southwestern University
School of Law
Los Angeles, CA

Stanford University Law School
Stanford, CA

State University of New York
School of Law
Buffalo, New York

Stetson University College of Law
St. Petersburg, FL

Suffolk University Law School
Boston, MA

Suffolk University Law School
Boston, MA

Syracuse University
College of Law
Syracuse, NY

Temple University School of Law
Philadelphia, PA

Texas Tech University
School of Law
Lubbock, TX

University of Texas School of Law
Austin, TX

Thomas M. Cooley Law School
Lansing, MI

University of Toledo
College of Law
Toledo, OH

Tulane University Law School
New Orleans, LA

University of Tulsa College of Law
Tulsa, OK

University of Utah College of Law
Salt Lake City, UT

Valparaiso University
School of Law
Valparaiso, IN

Vermont Law School
South Royalton, VT

Villanova University School of Law
Villanova, PA

Washburn University
School of Law
Topeka, KS

Washington University
School of Law
St. Louis, MO

University of Washington
School of Law
Seattle, WA

Widener University School of Law
Wilmington, DE

Widener University School of Law
Wilmington, DE

Willamette University
College of Law
Salem, OR

University of Wisconsin
Law School
Madison, WI

University of Wyoming
College of Law
Laramie, WY

Yale University
Yale Law School
New Haven, CT

HEALTH/MEDICINE LAW

Albany Law School
Albany, NY

Arizona State University
College of Law
Tempe, AZ

Baylor University Law School
Waco, TX

Boston University School of Law
Boston, MA

California Western University
School of Law
San Diego, CA

University of California
School of Law
Los Angeles, CA

Capital University Law School
Columbus, OH

Case Western Reserve University
School of Law
Cleveland, OH

City University of New York
School of Law
Flushing, NY

Cleveland State University
Cleveland-Marshall College of Law
Cleveland, Oh

DePaul University College of Law
Chicago, IL

University of Detroit Mercy
School of Law
Detroit, MI

Dickinson School of Law
Pennsylvania State University
Carlisle, PA

KAPLAN 245

LAW SCHOOLS

Duquesne University
School of Law
Pittsburgh, PA

Franklin Pierce Law Center
Concord, NH

Georgetown University Law Center
Washington, DC

University of Houston Law Center
Houston, TX

Illinois Institute of Technology
Chicago-Kent College of Law
Chicago, IL

Indiana University School of Law
Bloomington, IN

Indiana University School of Law
Indianapolis, IN

University of Kansas
School of Law
Lawrence, KS

Loyola University School of Law
Chicago, IL

University of Maryland
School of Law
Baltimore, MD

Mercer University School of Law
Macon, GA

University of Michigan Law School
Ann Arbor, MI

University of Minnesota
Law School
Minneapolis, MN

Ohio Northern University
College of Law
Ada, OH

Oklahoma City University
School of Law
Oklahoma City, OK

Pace University School of Law
White Plains, NY

University of Pittsburgh
School of Law
Pittsburgh, PA

Quinnipiac College School of Law
Hamden, CT

Rutgers University School of Law
Newark, NJ

Saint Louis University
School of Law
St. Louis, MO

Samford University
Cumberland School of Law
Birmingham, AL

Seattle University School of Law
Tacoma, WA

Seton Hall University
School of Law
Newark, NJ

University of South Dakota
School of Law
Vermillion, SD

Southern Illinois University
School of Law
Carbondale, IL

Southern Methodist University
School of Law
Dallas, TX

Southwestern University
School of Law
Los Angeles, CA

St. Mary's University
School of Law
San Antonio, TX

Stetson University College of Law
St. Petersburg, FL

Suffolk University Law School
Boston, MA

Temple University School of Law
Philadelphia, PA

University of Toledo
College of Law
Toledo, OH

University of Tulsa College of Law
Tulsa, OK

University of Utah College of Law
Salt Lake City, UT

Valparaiso University
School of Law
Valparaiso, IN

Wake Forest University
School of Law
Winston-Salem, NC

Washburn University
School of Law
Topeka, KS

University of Washington
School of Law
Seattle, WA

Whittier Law School
Los Angeles, CA

Widener University School of Law
Wilmington, DE

University of Wisconsin
Law School
Madison, WI

Academic Specialties

Yale University
Yale Law School
New Haven, CT

INSURANCE LAW

University of California
School of Law
Los Angeles, CA

University of Connecticut
School of Law
Hartford, CT

University of Kansas
School of Law
Lawrence, KS

Louisiana State University
Law Center
Baton Rouge, LA

Loyola Marymount Loyola
Law School
Los Angeles, CA

Marquette University Law School
Milwaukee, WI

University of Michigan Law School
Ann Arbor, MI

University of Minnesota
Law School
Minneapolis, MN

Oklahoma City University
School of Law
Oklahoma City, OK

University of Richmond
T. C. Williams School of Law
Richmond, VA

Rutgers University School of Law
Newark, NJ

St. John's University School of Law
Jamaica, NY

St. Mary's University
School of Law
San Antonio, TX

Samford University
Cumberland School of Law
Birmingham, AL

Stetson University College of Law
St. Petersburg, FL

Suffolk University Law School
Boston, MA

University of Virginia
School of Law
Charlottesville, VA

Yale University
Yale Law School
New Haven, CT

INTERNATIONAL/ COMPARATIVE LAW

University of Alabama
School of Law
Tuscaloosa, AL

Albany Law School
Albany, NY

American University
Washington College of Law
Washington, DC

University of Arizona
College of Law
Tucson, AZ

University of Baltimore
School of Law
Baltimore, MD

Boston College Law School
Newton, MA

Boston University School of Law
Boston, MA

Brigham Young University
Law School
Provo, UT

Brooklyn Law School
Brooklyn, NY

California Western School of Law
San Diego, CA

University of California
School of Law
Davis, CA

University of California
Hastings College of Law
San Francisco, CA

University of California
School of Law
Los Angeles, CA

Capital University Law School
Columbus, OH

Case Western Reserve University
School of Law
Cleveland, OH

Catholic University of America
Columbus School of Law
Washington, DC

City University of New York
School of Law
Flushing, NY

Cleveland State University
Cleveland-Marshall College of Law
Cleveland, Oh

LAW SCHOOLS

College of William and Mary
School of Law
Williamsburg, VA

Columbia University School of Law
New York, NY

University of Connecticut
School of Law
Hartford, CT

Cornell University Law School
Ithaca, NY

University of Denver
College of Law
Denver, CO

DePaul University College of Law
Chicago, IL

Detroit College of Law
at Michigan State University
East Lansing, MI

University of Detroit Mercy
School of Law
Detroit, MI

Dickinson School of Law
Pennsylvania State University
Carlisle, PA

Duke University School of Law
Durham, NC

Emory University School of Law
Atlanta, GA

Florida State University
College of Law
Tallahassee, FL

University of Florida
College of Law
Gainesville, FL

Franklin Pierce Law Center
Concord, NH

George Mason University
School of Law
Arlington, VA

Georgetown University Law Center
Washington, DC

Georgia State University
College of Law
Atlanta, GA

University of Georgia
School of Law
Athens, GA

Golden Gate University
School of Law
San Francisco, CA

Harvard University Law School
Cambridge, MA

University of Hawaii
School of Law
Honolulu, HI

Hofstra University School of Law
Hempstead, NY

University of Houston Law Center
Houston, TX

Howard University School of Law
Washington, DC

Illinois Institute of Technology
Chicago-Kent College of Law
Chicago, IL

University of Illinois
College of Law
Champaign, IL

Indiana University School of Law
Bloomington, IN

Indiana University School of Law
Indianapolis, IN

University of Iowa College of Law
Iowa City, IA

John Marshall School of Law
Chicago, IL

University of Kansas
School of Law
Lawrence, KS

University of Kentucky
College of Law
Lexington, KY

Lewis & Clark Northwestern
School of Law
Portland, OR

Louisiana State University
Law Center
Baton Rouge, LA

University of Louisville
School of Law
Louisville, KY

Loyola Marymount Loyola
Law School
Los Angeles, CA

Loyola University School of Law
Chicago, IL

Loyola University School of Law
New Orleans, LA

University of Maryland
School of Law
Baltimore, MD

Mercer University School of Law
Macon, GA

University of Miami School of Law
Coral Gables, FL

University of Michigan Law School
Ann Arbor, MI

Academic Specialties

University of Minnesota
Law School
Minneapolis, MN

New England School of Law
Boston, MA

New York Law School
New York, NY

New York University
School of Law
New York, NY

University of North Carolina
School of Law
Chapel Hill, NC

Northern Illinois University
College of Law
DeKalb, IL

University of Notre Dame
Notre Dame Law School
Notre Dame, IN

Ohio Northern University
College of Law
Ada, OH

Ohio State University
College of Law
Columbus, OH

Oklahoma City University
School of Law
Oklahoma City, OK

University of Oklahoma
College of Law
Norman, OK

University of Oregon
School of Law
Eugene, OR

Pace University School of Law
White Plains, NY

University of Pennsylvania
Law School
Philadelphia, PA

Pepperdine University
School of Law
Malibu, CA

University of Pittsburgh
School of Law
Pittsburgh, PA

Quinnipiac College School of Law
Hamden, CT

University of Richmond
T. C. Williams School of Law
Richmond, VA

Rutgers University School of Law
Camden, NJ

Rutgers University School of Law
Newark, NJ

St. John's University School of Law
Jamaica, NY

St. Louis University
School of Law
St. Louis, MO

St. Mary's University
School of Law
San Antonio, TX

Samford University
Cumberland School of Law
Birmingham, AL

University of San Diego
School of Law
San Diego, CA

University of San Francisco
School of Law
San Francisco, CA

Santa Clara University
School of Law
Santa Clara, CA

Seattle University School of Law
Tacoma, WA

Seton Hall University
School of Law
Newark, NJ

South Texas College of Law
Houston, TX

University of Southern California
Law Center
Los Angeles, CA

Southern Illinois University
School of Law
Carbondale, IL

Southern Methodist University
School of Law
Dallas, TX

Southwestern University
School of Law
Los Angeles, CA

Stanford University Law School
Stanford, CA

Stetson University College of Law
St. Petersburg, FL

Suffolk University Law School
Boston, MA

Syracuse University
College of Law
Syracuse, NY

Temple University School of Law
Philadelphia, PA

University of Texas School of Law
Austin, TX

KAPLAN 249

LAW SCHOOLS

University of Toledo
College of Law
Toledo, OH

Touro College
Jacob D. Fuchsberg Law Center
Huntington, NY

Tulane University Law School
New Orleans, LA

University of Tulsa College of Law
Tulsa, OK

University of Utah College of Law
Salt Lake City, UT

Valparaiso University
School of Law
Valparaiso, IN

Vanderbilt University
School of Law
Nashville, TN

Vermont Law School
South Royalton, VT

Villanova University School of Law
Villanova, PA

University of Virginia
School of Law
Charlottesville, VA

Wake Forest University
School of Law
Winston-Salem, NC

Washington and Lee University
School of Law
Lexington, VA

Washington University
School of Law
St. Louis, MO

University of Washington
School of Law
Seattle, WA

Wayne State University
Law School
Detroit, MI

Whittier Law School
Los Angeles, CA

Willamette University
College of Law
Salem, OR

William Mitchell
College of Law
St. Paul, MN

University of Wisconsin
Law School
Madison, WI

Yeshiva University
Benjamin N. Cardozo School of Law
New York, NY

PATENT LAW

University of Alabama
School of Law
Tuscaloosa, AL

Arizona State University
College of Law
Tempe, AZ

University of Baltimore
School of Law
Baltimore, MD

Boston University School of Law
Boston, MA

California Western School of Law
San Diego, CA

University of California
School of Law
Los Angeles, CA

Catholic University of America
Columbus School of Law
Washington, DC

Columbia University School of Law
New York, NY

University of Dayton
School of Law
Dayton, OH

DePaul University College of Law
Chicago, IL

University of Detroit Mercy
School of Law
Detroit, MI

Drake University Law School
Des Moines, IA

Duquesne University
School of Law
Pittsburgh, PA

Franklin Pierce Law Center
Concord, NH

George Mason University
School of Law
Arlington, VA

George Washington University
Law School
Washington, DC

Georgia State University
College of Law
Atlanta, GA

Golden Gate University
School of Law
San Francisco, CA

Academic Specialties

Hofstra University School of Law
Hempstead, NY

Illinois Institute of Technology
Chicago-Kent College of Law
Chicago, IL

Indiana University School of Law
Bloomington, IN

John Marshall School of Law
Chicago, IL

University of Kansas
School of Law
Lawrence, KS

Louisiana State University
Law Center
Baton Rouge, LA

Loyola Marymount Loyola
Law School
Los Angeles, CA

Marquette University Law School
Milwaukee, WI

University of Maryland
School of Law
Baltimore, MD

University of Minnesota
Law School
Minneapolis, MN

New York University
School of Law
New York, NY

University of Oregon
School of Law
Eugene, OR

University of Pittsburgh
School of Law
Pittsburgh, PA

Rutgers University School of Law
Newark, NJ

St. John's University School of Law
Jamaica, NY

St. Mary's University
School of Law
San Antonio, TX

University of San Francisco
School of Law
San Francisco, CA

Santa Clara University
School of Law
Santa Clara, CA

Seton Hall University
School of Law
Newark, NJ

University of Southern California
Law Center
Los Angeles, CA

Southwestern University
School of Law
Los Angeles, CA

Suffolk University Law School
Boston, MA

Syracuse University
College of Law
Syracuse, NY

University of Texas School of Law
Austin, TX

University of Toledo
College of Law
Toledo, OH

Valparaiso University
School of Law
Valparaiso, IN

University of Washington
School of Law
Seattle, WA

Wayne State University
Law School
Detroit, MI

William Mitchell College of Law
Saint Paul, MN

Yeshiva University
Benjamin N. Cardozo School of Law
New York, NY

Public Interest Law

University of Alabama
School of Law
Tuscaloosa, AL

American University
Washington College of Law
Washington, DC

University of Baltimore
School of Law
Baltimore, MD

Boston College Law School
Newton, MA

Boston University
School of Law
Boston, MA

Brooklyn Law School
Brooklyn, NY

University of California
Hastings College of Law
San Francisco, CA

University of California
School of Law
Davis, CA

LAW SCHOOLS

University of California
School of Law
Los Angeles, CA

Catholic University of America
Columbus School of Law
Washington, DC

City University of New York
School of Law
Flushing, NY

Cleveland State University
Cleveland-Marshall College of Law
Cleveland, Oh

College of William and Mary
School of Law
Williamsburg, VA

University of Connecticut
School of Law
Hartford, CT

Cornell University Law School
Ithaca, NY

University of Denver
College of Law
Denver, CO

DePaul University College of Law
Chicago, IL

University of Detroit Mercy
School of Law
Detroit, MI

Drake University Law School
Des Moines, IA

Emory University School of Law
Atlanta, GA

University of Florida
College of Law
Gainesville, FL

Franklin Pierce Law Center
Concord, NH

George Washington University
Law School
Washington, DC

Georgetown University Law Center
Washington, DC

Georgia State University
College of Law
Atlanta, GA

University of Georgia
School of Law
Athens, GA

Golden Gate University
School of Law
San Francisco, CA

Gonzaga University School of Law
Spokane, WA

Hamline University School of Law
St. Paul, MN

Harvard University Law School
Cambridge, MA

Hofstra University School of Law
Hempstead, NY

Howard University School of Law
Washington, DC

Illinois Institute of Technology
Chicago-Kent College of Law
Chicago, IL

University of Illinois
College of Law
Champaign, IL

Indiana University School of Law
Bloomington, IN

Indiana University School of Law
Indianapolis, IN

University of Kansas
School of Law
Lawrence, KS

Lewis & Clark College
Northwestern School of Law
Portland, OR

University of Louisville
School of Law
Louisville, KY

Loyola Marymount Loyola
Law School
Los Angeles, CA

Loyola University School of Law
Chicago, IL

Loyola University School of Law
New Orleans, LA

University of Maryland
School of Law
Baltimore, MD

Mercer University School of Law
Macon, GA

University of Miami School of Law
Coral Gables, FL

University of Michigan Law School
Ann Arbor, MI

University of Minnesota
Law School
Minneapolis, MN

University of Mississippi
School of Law
University, MS

New York University
School of Law
New York, NY

Academic Specialties

University of North Carolina
School of Law
Chapel Hill, NC

Northern Illinois University
DeKalb, IL

University of Notre Dame
Notre Dame Law School
Notre Dame, IN

Ohio Northern University
College of Law
Ada, OH

University of Oregon
School of Law
Eugene, OR

Pace University School of Law
White Plains, NY

University of Pennsylvania
Law School
Philadelphia, PA

Pepperdine University
School of Law
Malibu, CA

Quinnipiac College School of Law
Hamden, CT

Regent University School of Law
Virginia Beach, VA

Roger Williams University
School of Law
Bristol, RI

Rutgers University School of Law
Camden, NJ

Rutgers University School of Law
Newark, NJ

St. John's University School of Law
Jamaica, NY

St. Mary's University
School of Law
San Antonio, TX

St. Thomas University
School of Law
Miami, FL

University of San Diego
School of Law
San Diego, CA

University of San Francisco
School of Law
San Francisco, CA

Santa Clara University
School of Law
Santa Clara, CA

Seattle University School of Law
Tacoma, WA

Seton Hall University
School of Law
Newark, NJ

University of South Carolina
School of Law
Columbia, SC

University of Southern California
Law Center
Los Angeles, CA

Southwestern University
School of Law
Los Angeles, CA

Stanford University Law School
Stanford, CA

State University of New York
School of Law
Buffalo, NY

Stetson University College of Law
St. Petersburg, FL

Suffolk University Law School
Boston, MA

Syracuse University
College of Law
Syracuse, NY

Temple University School of Law
Philadelphia, PA

University of Tennessee
College of Law
Knoxville, TN

University of Texas School of Law
Austin, TX

University of Toledo
College of Law
Toledo, OH

Touro College
Jacob D. Fuchsberg Law Center
Huntington, NY

University of Utah College of Law
Salt Lake City, UT

Valparaiso University
School of Law
Valparaiso, IN

Vermont Law School
South Royalton, VT

University of Virginia
School of Law
Charlottesville, VA

University of Washington
School of Law
Seattle, WA

Wayne State University
Law School
Detroit, MI

LAW SCHOOLS

West Virginia University
College of Law
Morgantown, WV

Widener University School of Law
Wilmington, DE

University of Wisconsin
Law School
Madison, WI

Yale Law School
New Haven, CT

Yeshiva University
Benjamin N. Cardozo School of Law
New York, NY

TAX LAW

University of Akron School of Law
Akron, OH

University of Alabama
School of Law
Tuscaloosa, AL

Albany Law School
Albany, NY

American University
Washington College of Law
Washington, DC

University of Arizona
College of Law
Tucson, AZ

University of Baltimore
School of Law
Baltimore, MD

Boston College Law School
Newton, MA

Boston University
School of Law
Boston, MA

Brigham Young University
Law School
Provo, UT

Brooklyn Law School
Brooklyn, NY

California Western School of Law
San Diego, CA

University of California
Hastings College of Law
San Francisco, CA

University of California
School of Law
Los Angeles, CA

Capital University Law School
Columbus, OH

Case Western Reserve University
School of Law
Cleveland, OH

Catholic University of America
Columbus School of Law
Washington, DC

Cleveland State University
Cleveland–Marshall College of Law
Cleveland, Oh

University of Colorado
School of Law
Boulder, CO

University of Connecticut
School of Law
Hartford, CT

Cornell University Law School
Ithaca, NY

Creighton University School of Law
Omaha, NE

University of Dayton
School of Law
Dayton, OH

University of Denver
College of Law
Denver, CO

DePaul University College of Law
Chicago, IL

Detroit College of Law
at Michigan State University
East Lansing, MI

University of Detroit Mercy
School of Law
Detroit, MI

Drake University Law School
Des Moines, IA

Emory University School of Law
Atlanta, GA

University of Florida
College of Law
Gainesville, FL

George Washington University
Law School
Washington, DC

Georgetown University
Law Center
Washington, DC

Georgia State University
College of Law
Atlanta, GA

Golden Gate University
School of Law
San Francisco, CA

Academic Specialties

Gonzaga University School of Law
Spokane, WA

Harvard University Law School
Cambridge, MA

Hofstra University School of Law
Hempstead, NY

University of Houston
Law Center
Houston, TX

Illinois Institute of Technology
Chicago-Kent College of Law
Chicago, IL

University of Illinois
College of Law
Champaign, IL

Indiana University School of Law
Bloomington, IN

Indiana University School of Law
Indianapolis, IN

John Marshall School of Law
Chicago, IL

University of Kansas
School of Law
Lawrence, KS

University of Kentucky
College of Law
Lexington, KY

Lewis & Clark Northwestern
School of Law
Portland, OR

Louisiana State University
Law Center
Baton Rouge, LA

University of Louisville
School of Law
Louisville, KY

Loyola Marymount Loyola
Law School
Los Angeles, CA

Loyola University School of Law
Chicago, IL

Loyola University School of Law
New Orleans, LA

University of Maryland
School of Law
Baltimore, MD

University of Miami School of Law
Coral Gables, FL

University of Michigan Law School
Ann Arbor, MI

University of Minnesota
Law School
Minneapolis, MN

University of Mississippi
School of Law
University, MS

University of Missouri
School of Law
Columbia, MO

University of Missouri
School of Law
Kansas City, MO

University of Montana
School of Law
Missoula, MT

University of Nebraska
College of Law
Lincoln, NE

New England School of Law
Boston, MA

New York University
School of Law
New York, NY

University of North Carolina
School of Law
Chapel Hill, NC

Nova Southeastern University
Shepard Broad Law Center
Fort Lauderdale, FL

Ohio Northern University
College of Law
Ada, OH

Ohio State University
College of Law
Columbus, OH

University of Oklahoma
College of Law
Norman, OK

University of Oregon
School of Law
Eugene, OR

University of Pennsylvania
Law School
Philadelphia, PA

Pepperdine University
School of Law
Malibu, CA

University of Pittsburgh
School of Law
Pittsburgh, PA

Quinnipiac College School of Law
Hamden, CT

Roger Williams University
School of Law
Bristol, RI

Rutgers University School of Law
Camden, NJ

LAW SCHOOLS

Rutgers University School of Law
Newark, NJ

St. John's University School of Law
Jamaica, NY

St. Mary's University
School of Law
San Antonio, TX

St. Thomas University
School of Law
Miami, FL

Samford University
Cumberland School of Law
Birmingham, AL

University of San Diego
School of Law
San Diego, CA

University of San Francisco
School of Law
San Francisco, CA

Seattle University School of Law
Tacoma, WA

University of South Carolina
School of Law
Columbia, SC

University of Southern California
Law Center
Los Angeles, CA

Southern Methodist University
School of Law
Dallas, TX

Southwestern University
School of Law
Los Angeles, CA

State University of New York
School of Law
Buffalo, NY

Stetson University College of Law
St. Petersburg, FL

Suffolk University Law School
Boston, MA

Syracuse University
College of Law
Syracuse, NY

Temple University School of Law
Philadelphia, PA

Texas Southern University
Thurgood Marshall School of Law
Houston, TX

University of Texas School of Law
Austin, TX

University of Toledo
College of Law
Toledo, OH

Valparaiso University
School of Law
Valparaiso, IN

Vermont Law School
South Royalton, VT

Villanova University School of Law
Villanova, PA

University of Virginia
School of Law
Charlottesville, VA

Wake Forest University
School of Law
Winston-Salem, NC

Washburn University
School of Law
Topeka, KS

Washington University
School of Law
St. Louis, MO

University of Washington
School of Law
Seattle, WA

Wayne State University
Law School
Detroit, MI

West Virginia University
College of Law
Morgantown, WV

Widener University School of Law
Harrisburg, PA

Willamette University
College of Law
Salem, OR

University of Wisconsin
Law School
Madison, WI

Yale University
Yale Law School
New Haven, CT

Yeshiva University
Benjamin N. Cardozo School of Law
New York, NY

WOMEN'S RIGHTS LAW

American University
Washington College of Law
Washington, DC

Boston University School of Law
Boston, MA

Brigham Young University
Law School
Provo, UT

Brooklyn Law School
Brooklyn, NY

Academic Specialties

California Western School of Law
San Diego, CA

University of California
School of Law
Davis, CA

University of California
School of Law
Los Angeles, CA

City University of New York
School of Law
Flushing, NY

Columbia University School of Law
New York, NY

University of Connecticut
School of Law
Hartford, CT

Cornell University Law School
Ithaca, NY

University of Denver
College of Law
Denver, CO

DePaul University College of Law
Chicago, IL

Georgetown University
Law Center
Washington, DC

Golden Gate University
School of Law
San Francisco, CA

Harvard University Law School
Cambridge, MA

Indiana University School of Law
Bloomington, IN

University of Michigan Law School
Ann Arbor, MI

University of Minnesota
Law School
Minneapolis, MN

University of Oregon
School of Law
Eugene, OR

University of Pittsburgh
School of Law
Pittsburgh, PA

Roger Williams University
School of Law
Bristol, RI

Rutgers University School of Law
Newark, NJ

Seton Hall University
School of Law
Newark, NJ

University of Southern California
Law Center
Los Angeles, CA

Southwestern University
School of Law
Los Angeles, CA

St. John's University School of Law
Jamaica, NY

St. Mary's University
School of Law
San Antonio, TX

Suffolk University Law School
Boston, MA

Valparaiso University
School of Law
Valparaiso, IN

Vermont Law School
South Royalton, VT

University of Wisconsin
Law School
Madison, WI

Yale University
Yale Law School
New Haven, CT

Joint Degree Programs

In this section, you'll find information on schools offering joint degree programs that provide a master's degree in business administration, public administration, and several other popular fields in addition to the law degree. We've provided the most complete information available to us, but keep in mind that a school's absence from a particular list may simply mean that the school did not give a full report of their offerings. Check with the law schools themselves for complete details on their programs.

J.D.-M.A.Communication/
Journalism Joint Degree Programs 261

J.D.-M.A. International Affairs/Relations/
Studies Joint Degree Programs 261

J.D.-M.B.A. Joint Degree Programs 261

J.D.-M.Div. Joint Degree Programs 264

J.D.-M.L.S./M.S. Library and Information Science
Joint Degree Programs 264

J.D.-M.P.A. Joint Degree Programs 264

SELECTING A SCHOOL

J.D.-M.S. Environmental Studies/
Environmental Management Joint Degree Programs 265

J.D.-M.S.W. Joint Degree Programs 265

Joint Degree Programs

J.D.-M.A. COMMUNICATION/JOURNALISM JOINT DEGREE PROGRAMS

Boston University School of Law
Boston, MA

Columbia University School of Law
New York, NY

Drake University School of Law
Des Moines, IA

Loyola University School of Law
New Orleans, LA

Regent University School of Law
Virginia Beach, VA

University of California
School of Law
Berkeley, CA

University of Florida
College of Law
Gainesville, FL

J.D.-M.A. INTERNATIONAL AFFAIRS/RELATIONS/STUDIES JOINT DEGREE PROGRAMS

American University
Washington College of Law
Washington, DC

Boston University School of Law
Boston, MA

University of California
School of Law
Berkeley, CA

University of Chicago
School of Law
Chicago, IL

Columbia University School of Law
New York, NY

University of Denver
College of Law
Denver, CO

Florida State University
College of Law
Tallahassee, FL

George Washington University
Law School
Washington, DC

Marquette University
Law School
Milwaukee, WI

University of Pittsburgh
School of Law
Pittsburgh, PA

University of San Diego
School of Law
San Diego, CA

St. Mary's University
School of Law
San Antonio, TX

J.D.-M.B.A. JOINT DEGREE PROGRAMS

University of Akron School of Law
Akron, OH

University of Alabama
School of Law
Tuscaloosa, AL

Albany Law School
Albany, NY

American University Washington
College of Law
Washington, DC

Arizona State University
College of Law
Tempe, AZ

University of Arizona
Tucson, AZ

University of Arkansas
School of Law
Fayetteville, AR

University of Arkansas
School of Law
Little Rock, AR

University of Baltimore
School of Law
Baltimore, MD

Baylor University Law School
Waco, TX

Boston College Law School
Newton, MA

Boston University School of Law
Boston, MA

Brigham Young University
Law School
Provo, UT

Brooklyn Law School
Brooklyn, NY

University of California
School of Law
Davis, CA

University of California
Hastings College of Law
San Francisco, CA

Capital University Law School
Columbus, OH

Case Western Reserve University
School of Law
Cleveland, OH

LAW SCHOOLS

University of Cincinnati
College of Law
Cincinnati, OH

University of Colorado
School of Law
Boulder, CO

Columbia University School of Law
New York, NY

University of Connecticut
School of Law
Hartford, CT

Cornell University Law School
Ithaca, NY

Creighton University School of Law
Omaha, NE

University of Dayton
School of Law
Dayton, OH

DePaul University College of Law
Chicago, IL

University of Detroit Mercy
School of Law
Detroit, MI

Drake University Law School
Des Moines, IA

Duke University School of Law
Durham, NC

Duquesne University
School of Law
Pittsburgh, PA

Emory University School of Law
Atlanta, GA

Florida State University
College of Law
Tallahassee, FL

University of Florida
College of Law
Gainesville, FL

Fordham University School of Law
New York, NY

George Washington University
Law School
Washington, DC

Georgia State University
College of Law
Atlanta, GA

University of Georgia
School of Law
Athens, GA

Gonzaga University School of Law
Spokane, WA

Hamline University School of Law
St. Paul, MN

Harvard University Law School
Cambridge, MA

University of Hawaii
William S. Richardson School of Law
Honolulu, HI

Hofstra University School of Law
Hempstead, NY

University of Houston Law Center
Houston, TX

Howard University School of Law
Washington, DC

Illinois Institute of Technology
Chicago Kent College of Law
Chicago, IL

University of Illinois
College of Law
Champaign, IL

Indiana University School of Law
Bloomington, IN

Indiana University School of Law
Indianapolis, IN

University of Iowa College of Law
Iowa City, IA

John Marshall School of Law
Chicago, IL

University of Kansas
School of Law
Lawrence, KS

University of Kentucky
College of Law
Lexington, KY

University of Louisville
School of Law
Louisville, KY

Loyola Marymount Loyola
Law School
Los Angeles, CA

Loyola University School of Law
Chicago, IL

Loyola University School of Law
New Orleans, LA

Marquette University Law School
Milwaukee, WI

University of Memphis
School of Law
Memphis, TN

Mercer University School of Law
Macon, GA

University of Miami School of Law
Coral Gables, FL

University of Michigan Law School
Ann Arbor, MI

Joint Degree Programs

University of Minnesota
Law School
Minneapolis, MN

University of Mississippi
School of Law
University, MS

University of Missouri
School of Law
Columbia, MO

University of Missouri
School of Law
Kansas City, MO

University of Nebraska
College of Law
Lincoln, NE

New York Law School
New York, NY

New York University
School of Law
New York, NY

University of North Carolina
School of Law
Chapel Hill, NC

Northern Illinois University
College of Law
DeKalb, IL

Northern Kentucky University
Salmon P. Chase College of Law
Highland Heights, KY

University of Notre Dame
Notre Dame Law School
Notre Dame, IN

Nova Southeastern University
Shepard Broad Law Center
Fort Lauderdale, FL

Ohio State University
College of Law
Columbus, OH

Oklahoma City University
School of Law
Oklahoma City, OK

University of Oregon
School of Law
Eugene, OR

Pace University School of Law
White Plains, NY

University of Pennsylvania
Law School
Philadelphia, PA

Pepperdine University
School of Law
Malibu, CA

University of Pittsburgh
School of Law
Pittsburgh, PA

Pontifical Catholic-
University of Puerto Rico School of Law
Ponce, PR

University of Puerto Rico
School of Law
San Juan, PR

Quinnipiac College School of Law
Hamden, CT

Regent University School of Law
Virginia Beach, VA

University of the Pacific
McGeorge School of Law
Sacramento, CA

University of Richmond
T. C. Williams School of Law
Richmond, VA

Rutgers University School of Law
Newark, NJ

St. John's University School of Law
Jamaica, NY

St. Louis University
School of Law
St. Louis, MO

Samford University
Cumberland School of Law
Birmingham, AL

University of San Diego
School of Law
San Diego, CA

University of San Francisco
School of Law
San Francisco, CA

Santa Clara University
School of Law
Santa Clara, CA

Seton Hall University
School of Law
Newark, NJ

University of South Carolina
School of Law
Columbia, SC

University of South Dakota
School of Law
Vermillion, SD

Southern Illinois University
School of Law
Carbondale, IL

Southern Methodist University
School of Law
Dallas, TX

Stanford University Law School
Stanford, CA

State University of New York
School of Law
Buffalo, NY

Stetson University College of Law
St. Petersburg, FL

KAPLAN 263

LAW SCHOOLS

Suffolk University Law School
Boston, MA

Syracuse University
College of Law
Syracuse, NY

Temple University School of Law
Philadelphia, PA

University of Tennessee
College of Law
Knoxville, TN

Texas Tech University
School of Law
Lubbock, TX

University of Texas School of Law
Austin, TX

University of Toledo
College of Law
Toledo, OH

Touro College
Jacob D. Fuchsberg Law Center
Huntington, NY

Tulane University Law School
New Orleans, LA

University of Tulsa College of Law
Tulsa, OK

University of the Pacific
McGeorge School of Law
Sacramento, CA

University of Utah College of Law
Salt Lake City, UT

Vanderbilt University
School of Law
Nashville, TN

Villanova University School of Law
Villanova, PA

Wake Forest University
School of Law
Winston-Salem, NC

Washington University
School of Law
St. Louis, MO

Wayne State University
Law School
Detroit, MI

West Virginia University
College of Law
Morgantown, WV

Widener University School of Law
Wilmington, DE

University of Wyoming
College of Law
Laramie, WY

J.D.-M.DIV. JOINT DEGREE PROGRAMS

Duquesne University
School of Law
Pittsburgh, PA

Emory University School of Law
Atlanta, GA

University of Louisville
School of Law
Louisville, KY

Samford University
Cumberland School of Law
Birmingham, AL

Vanderbilt University
School of Law
Nashville, TN

Yale University
Yale Law School
New Haven, CT

J.D.-M.L.S./M.S. LIBRARY AND INFORMATION SCIENCE JOINT DEGREE PROGRAMS

Brooklyn Law School
Brooklyn, NY

Catholic University of America
Columbus School of Law
Washington, DC

Indiana School of Law
Bloomington, IN

J.D.-M.P.A. JOINT DEGREE PROGRAM

University of Akron College of Law
Akron, OH

Albany Law School
Albany, NY

University of Arizona
Tucson, AZ

University of Baltimore
School of Law
Baltimore, MD

Brigham Young University
Law School
Provo, UT

Brooklyn Law School
Brooklyn, NY

Cleveland State University
Cleveland-Marshall College of Law
Cleveland, OH

University of Colorado
School of Law
Boulder, CO

Joint Degree Programs

Columbia University School of Law
New York, NY

University of Connecticut
School of Law
Hartford, CT

Drake University Law School
Des Moines, IA

Florida State University
College of Law
Tallahassee, FL

Georgia State University
College of Law
Atlanta, GA

Indiana University School of Law
Bloomington, IN

Indiana University School of Law
Indianapolis, IN

John Marshall School of Law
Chicago, IL

University of Kansas
School of Law
Lawrence, KS

University of Kentucky
College of Law
Lexington, KY

Louisiana State University
Law Center
Baton Rouge, LA

Loyola University School of Law
New Orleans, LA

University of Minnesota
Law School
Minneapolis, MN

University of Montana
School of Law
Missoula, MT

University of Nebraska
College of Law
Lincoln, NE

New York University
School of Law
New York, NY

University of North Carolina
School of Law
Chapel Hill, NC

Ohio State University
College of Law
Columbus, OH

Pace University School of Law
White Plains, NY

University of Pittsburgh
School of Law
Pittsburgh, PA

St. Louis University
School of Law
St. Louis, MO

Samford University
Cumberland School of Law
Birmingham, AL

University of South Carolina
School of Law
Columbia, SC

University of South Dakota
School of Law
Vermillion, SD

Southern Illinois University
School of Law
Carbondale, IL

Suffolk University Law School
Boston, MA

Syracuse University
College of Law
Syracuse, NY

University of Tennessee
College of Law
Knoxville, TN

Texas Tech University
School of Law
Lubbock, TX

University of Texas School of Law
Austin, TX

University of Utah College of Law
Salt Lake City, UT

West Virginia University
College of Law
Morgantown, WV

University of Wyoming
College of Law
Laramie, WY

Yale University Yale Law School
New Haven, CT

J.D.-M.S. ENVIRONMENTAL STUDIES/ENVIRONMENTAL MANAGEMENT JOINT DEGREE PROGRAMS

Duke University School of Law
Durham, NC

Duquesne University
School of Law
Pittsburgh, PA

University of Hawaii
School of Law
Honolulu, HI

Illinois Institute of Chicago
Kent College of Law
Chicago, IL

Indiana University School of Law
Bloomington, IN

LAW SCHOOLS

University of Maryland
School of Law
Baltimore, MD

University of Oklahoma
College of Law
Norman, OK

University of Oregon
School of Law
Eugene, OR

Pace University School of Law
White Plains, NY

Samford University
Cumberland School of Law
Birmingham, AL

Vermont Law School
South Royalton, VT

Washington University
School of Law
St. Louis, MO

University of Wisconsin
Law School
Madison, WI

Yale University Yale Law School
New Haven, CT

J.D.-M.S.W.
JOINT DEGREE PROGRAMS

Boston College Law School
Newton, MA

California Western School of Law
San Diego, CA

University of California
School of Law
Berkeley, CA

Case Western Reserve University
School of Law
Cleveland, OH

Catholic University of America
Columbus School of Law
Washington, DC

Columbia University School of Law
New York, NY

University of Denver
College of Law
Denver, CO

Drake University School of Law
Des Moines, IA

Florida State University
College of Law
Tallahassee, FL

Fordham University School of Law
New York, NY

University of Hawaii
School of Law
Honolulu, HI

University of Kansas
School of Law
Lawrence, KS

Loyola University School of Law
Chicago, IL

University of Maryland
School of Law
Baltimore, MD

New York University School of Law
New York, NY

University of Pennsylvania
Law School
Philadelphia, PA

University of Richmond
T.C. Williams School of Law
Richmond, VA

St. Louis University
School of Law
St. Louis, MO

State University of New York
Buffalo, NY

Washington University
School of Law
St. Louis, MO

Geographic Location

ALABAMA

University of Alabama
Samford University

ARIZONA

University of Arizona
Arizona State University

ARKANSAS

University of Arkansas—Fayetteville
University of Arkansas—Little Rock

CALIFORNIA

University of California—Berkeley
University of California—Davis
University of California—Hastings
University of California—Los Angeles
California Western University
Golden Gate University
Loyola Marymount University
McGeorge School of Law
Pepperdine University
San Diego University
Santa Clara University
University of Southern California
Southwestern University
Stanford University
University of San Francisco
Whittier College

COLORADO

University of Colorado
University of Denver

CONNECTICUT

University of Connecticut
Quinnipiac College
Yale University

DELAWARE

Widener University

DISTRICT OF COLUMBIA

American University
Catholic University of America
District of Columbia School of Law
Georgetown University
George Washington University
Howard University

FLORIDA

Florida State University
University of Florida
Stetson University
Nova Southeastern University
St. Thomas University
Miami University

GEORGIA

Emory University
University of Georgia
Georgia State University
Mercer University

LAW SCHOOLS

Hawaii

University of Hawaii

Idaho

University of Idaho

Illinois

University of Chicago
DePaul University
University of Illinois
Illinois Institute of Technology
John Marshall
Loyola University—Chicago
Northern Illinois University
Northwestern University
Southern Illinois University

Indiana

University of Indiana—Bloomington
University of Indiana—Indianapolis
Notre Dame University
Valparaiso University

Iowa

University of Iowa
Drake University

Kansas

University of Kansas
Washburn University

Kentucky

University of Kentucky
University of Louisville
Northern Kentucky University

Louisiana

Louisiana State University
Loyola University—New Orleans
Southern University
Tulane University

Maine

University of Maine

Maryland

University of Baltimore
University of Maryland

Massachusetts

Boston College
Boston University
Harvard University
New England School of Law
Northeastern University
Suffolk University
Western New England College

Michigan

Detroit College of Law
University of Detroit Mercy
University of Michigan
Thomas M. Cooley
Wayne State University

Minnesota

Hamline University
University of Minnesota
William Mitchell College of Law

Mississippi

University of Mississippi
Mississippi College

Missouri

University of Missouri—Columbia
University of Missouri—Kansas City
Saint Louis University
Washington University

Montana

University of Montana

Nebraska

Creighton University
University of Nebraska

New Hampshire

Franklin Pierce

New Jersey

Rutgers University—Newark
Rutgers University—Camden
Seton Hall University

New Mexico

University of New Mexico

New York

Albany Law School
Brooklyn Law School
City University of New York
Columbia University
Cornell University
Fordham University
Hofstra University
New York Law School
New York University
Pace University
St. John's University
SUNY—Buffalo
Syracuse University

Touro College
Yeshiva University

NORTH CAROLINA

Campbell University
Duke University
North Carolina Central
University of North Carolina
Wake Forest University

NORTH DAKOTA

University of North Dakota

OHIO

University of Akron
Capital University
Case Western Reserve
Cincinnati
Cleveland State
Dayton University
Ohio Northern University
Ohio State
University of Toledo

OKLAHOMA

Oklahoma City University
University of Oklahoma
University of Tulsa

OREGON

Lewis and Clark College
University of Oregon
Willamette University

PENNSYLVANIA

Duquesne University
Pennsylvania State (Dickinson)
University of Pennsylvania
Pittsburgh University

Temple University
Villanova University
Widener University

RHODE ISLAND

Roger Williams University

SOUTH CAROLINA

University of South Carolina

SOUTH DAKOTA

University of South Dakota

TENNESSEE

University of Tennessee
University of Memphis
Vanderbilt University

TEXAS

Baylor University
University of Houston
South Texas College
Southern Methodist University
St. Mary's University
University of Texas
Texas Southern University
Texas Tech
Texas Wesleyan

UTAH

University of Utah
Brigham Young University

VERMONT

Vermont Law School

VIRGINIA

George Mason University
Regent University
University of Richmond
University of Virginia
Washington and Lee University
College of William and Mary

WASHINGTON

Gonzaga University
University of Seattle
University of Washington

WEST VIRGINIA

University of West Virginia

WISCONSIN

Marquette University
University of Wisconsin

WYOMING

University of Wyoming

PUERTO RICO

Inter American University of Puerto Rico
Pontifical Catholic University of Puerto Rico
University of Puerto Rico

Appendix

Appendix

LSAT Sampler

The LSAT, or Law School Admission Test, is a half-day standardized test required for admission to all schools that are members of the Law School Admission Council, an organization also known as Law Services.

The LSAT is designed to measure skills that are considered essential for success in law school: comprehending complex written material with accuracy and insight; analyzing arguments and drawing reliable conclusions; organizing and managing information; and writing persuasively.

Content and Structure

The LSAT consists of five 35-minute sections (totalling 175 minutes) of multiple-choice questions, a break of 10–15 minutes, and a 30-minute writing sample. A typical LSAT can last five hours or more because of administrative necessities before and after the test. Here's how the test format works:

Section	# of Questions	Time
Logical Reasoning	24–26	35 minutes
Logical Reasoning	24–26	35 minutes
Reading Comprehension	27–28	35 minutes
Logic Games	24	35 minutes
"Experimental"	24–28	30 minutes
Writing Sample	—	30 minutes

APPENDIX

The experimental section is unscored and allows the test makers to test questions that they may use on future tests. It will look exactly like a scored section of the same question type, so when you're taking the LSAT, *don't spend time trying to figure out which section is experimental.*

Scoring

The scoring scale for the multiple-choice sections of the LSAT runs from 120–180; 120 is the lowest possible score and 180 the highest. Your score on this 120–180 scale is based on your raw score, the total number of questions that you get right. All questions are weighted equally. Your scaled score also corresponds to a percentile ranking, which allows law schools to compare scores from various LSAT administrations.

If you get about half of the questions on your LSAT right (about 50), you'll score in approximately the 30th percentile. After getting 50 questions right, if you get only one more question right every ten minutes during the exam, you'll jump to the 60th percentile (about 64 questions right). And get this: On most LSATs you can get as many as 28 questions wrong and score above the 80th percentile, and as many as 21 wrong and score above the 90th percentile.

The writing sample is not scored. However, a copy of your essay is sent to every law school to which you apply.

Here's a quick, important tip. Since there's no penalty for wrong answers on the LSAT, select an answer choice for every question.

The Sample Questions

To introduce you to the LSAT, we've included samples of every type of multiple-choice question* that appears on the LSAT: Logical Reasoning, Logic Games, and Reading Comprehension. We've also included a Writing Sample topic. Answers to the multiple-choice questions are on page 280. If you'd like to take a full-length practice test and receive a score, visit any Kaplan center.

Good Luck!

Instructions for Kaplan LSAT sample questions © Law School Admission Council, Inc. Reprinted by permission.

LOGICAL REASONING

Directions: *The questions in this section are based on the reasoning contained in brief statements or passages. For some questions, more than one of the choices could conceivably answer the question. However, you are to choose the* best *answer; that is, the response that most accurately and completely answers the question. You should not make assumptions that are by commonsense standards implausible, superfluous, or incompatible with the passage. After you have chosen the best answer, blacken the corresponding space on your answer sheet.*

1. One morning, George Petersen of Petersen's Garage watches as a 1995 Da Volo station wagon is towed onto his lot. Because he knows that nearly 90 percent of the 1995 Da Volo station wagons brought to his garage for work in the past were brought in because of malfunctioning power windows, he reasons that there is an almost 9 to 1 chance that the car he saw this morning has also been brought in to correct its faulty power windows.

   Which one of the following employs flawed reasoning most similar to that employed by George Petersen?

   (A) Mayor Lieberman was reelected by a majority of almost 75 percent. Since Janine Davis voted in that mayoral election, the chances are almost 3 to 1 that she voted for Mayor Lieberman.
   (B) Each week nine out of ten best-selling paperback books at The Reader's Nook are works of fiction. Since Nash's history of World War II was among the ten best-selling paperback books at The Reader's Nook this week, the chances are 9 to 1 that it is a work of fiction.
   (C) Ninety percent of those who attempt to get into Myrmidon Military Academy are turned down. Since the previous ten candidates to the academy were not accepted, Vladimir's application will almost certainly be approved.
   (D) Only one out of 50 applications to bypass zoning regulations and establish a new business in the Gedford residential district is accepted. Since only 12 such applications were made last month, there is virtually no chance that any of them will be accepted.
   (E) Nearly 95 percent of last year's Borough High School graduating class went on to some type of further schooling. Since only a little more than 5 percent of that graduating class took longer than the usual four years to graduate, it is probable that everyone who did graduate within four years went on to further schooling.

       Ⓐ Ⓑ Ⓒ Ⓓ Ⓔ

Questions 2–3

Bruce: Almost a century ago, country X annexed its neighbor's western province, clearly an unjust act. It is the obligation of country X to return the province to its former possessors, even if doing so would involve great sacrifice on the part of those citizens of country X who are currently living within that province.

Linda: A nation's paramount responsibility is the well being of its own citizens. Country X should make the sacrifice of returning the province only if it can be sure that such an act will provide some tangible benefit to the citizens of country X. The issue of whether the original annexation was just is a secondary consideration.

2. Linda's reply to Bruce most closely conforms to which one of the following principles?

   (A) A nation is obliged to make sacrifices only in order to fulfill its paramount responsibility.
   (B) Historical wrongs can properly be redressed only when all interested parties agree that a wrong has been committed.
   (C) No national sacrifice is too great, provided that it is undertaken in order to ensure the future well being of the nation.
   (D) The views of the entire nation should be consulted before the nation takes an action that involves considerable sacrifice from any part of the nation.
   (E) A nation is obliged to redress historical injustices only when such redress would involve minimal sacrifice from that nation.

       Ⓐ Ⓑ Ⓒ Ⓓ Ⓔ

3. Bruce and Linda are committed to holding opposing points of view in answer to which one of the following questions?

   (A) Can the original annexation of the neighboring nation's western province accurately be characterized as an unjust act?
   (B) Would the return of the annexed province to its original possessors involve appreciable sacrifice on the part of the citizens of country X?
   (C) Would the return of the annexed province to its original possessors confer any benefit on the citizens of country X?
   (D) Should the citizens of country X who are currently living in the annexed province be consulted in deciding whether or not to return the province to its original possessors?
   (E) Does country X have the obligation to redress an historic injustice at the risk of providing no benefit to its own citizens?

       Ⓐ Ⓑ Ⓒ Ⓓ Ⓔ

APPENDIX

4. Biologists attached a radio transmitter to one of a number of wolves that had been released earlier in the White River Wilderness Area as part of a relocation project. The biologists hoped to use this wolf to track the movements of the whole pack. Wolves usually range over a wide area in search of prey, and frequently follow the migrations of their prey animals. The biologists were surprised to find that this particular wolf never moved more than five miles away from the location in which it was first tagged.

   Which one of the following, if true, would by itself most help to explain the behavior of the wolf tagged by the biologists?

   (A) The area in which the wolf was released was rocky and mountainous, in contrast to the flat, heavily wooded area from which it was taken.
   (B) The wolf had been tagged and released by the biologists only three miles away from a sheep ranch that provided a large, stable population of prey animals.
   (C) The White River Wilderness Area had supported a population of wolves in past years, but they had been hunted to extinction.
   (D) Although the wolves in the White River Wilderness Area were under government protection, their numbers had been sharply reduced, within a few years of their release, by illegal hunting.
   (E) The wolf captured and tagged by the biologists had split off from the main pack whose movements the biologists had hoped to study, and its movements did not represent those of the main pack.

   Ⓐ Ⓑ Ⓒ Ⓓ Ⓔ

5. Video arcades, legally defined as video parlors having at least five video games, require a special city license and, in primarily residential areas such as Eastview, a zoning variance. The owners of the Video Zone, popular with Eastview teenagers, have maintained that their establishment requires neither an arcade license nor a zoning variance, because it is really a retail outlet.

   Which one of the following is an assumption on which the argument of the Video Zone's owners is based?

   (A) The existing Eastview zoning regulations are unconstitutionally strict.
   (B) At no time are more than four video games in operation at the Video Zone.
   (C) Stores like the Video Zone perform an important social function.
   (D) Many of the Video Zone's games were developed after the city's zoning laws were written.
   (E) Retail establishments require no special licenses or zoning variances in Eastview.

   Ⓐ Ⓑ Ⓒ Ⓓ Ⓔ

6. It doesn't surprise me that the critic on our local radio station went off on another tirade today about the city men's choir. This is not the first time that he has criticized the choir. But this time his criticisms were simply inaccurate and unjustified. For ten minutes, he spoke of nothing but the choir's lack of expressiveness. As a professional vocal instructor, I have met with these singers individually; I can state with complete confidence that each of the members of the choir has quite an expressive voice.

   Which one of the following is the most serious flaw in the author's reasoning?

   (A) He directs his argument against the critic's character rather than against his claims.
   (B) He ignores evidence that the critic's remarks might in fact be justified.
   (C) He cites his own professional expertise as the sole explanation for his defense of the choir.
   (D) He assumes that a group will have a given attribute if each of its parts has that attribute.
   (E) He attempts to conclude the truth of a general situation from evidence about one specific situation.

   Ⓐ Ⓑ Ⓒ Ⓓ Ⓔ

7. Whitley Hospital's much publicized increase in emergency room efficiency due to its new procedures for handling trauma patients does not withstand careful analysis. The average time before treatment for all patients is nearly 40 minutes—the highest in the city. And for trauma victims, who are the specific target of the guidelines, the situation is even worse: The average time before treatment is nearly half an hour—more than twice the city average.

   Which of the following, if true, would most seriously weaken the conclusion about the value of the new procedures?

   (A) The city hospitals with the most efficient emergency rooms utilize the same procedures for handling trauma patients as does Whitley Hospital.
   (B) After the new procedures went into effect, Whitley's average time before treatment for trauma patients and patients in general dropped by nearly 35 percent.
   (C) Because trauma patients account for a large percentage of emergency room patients, procedures that hasten their treatment will likely increase overall emergency room efficiency.
   (D) Due to differences in location and size of staff, not all emergency rooms can be expected to reach similar levels of efficiency.
   (E) The recently hired administrators who instituted the new procedures also increased Whitley's emergency room staff by nearly 15 percent.

   Ⓐ Ⓑ Ⓒ Ⓓ Ⓔ

LOGIC GAMES

Directions: *Each group of questions in this section is based on a set of conditions. In answering some of the questions, it may be useful to draw a rough diagram. Choose the response that most accurately and completely answers each question.*

Questions 1–6
A zoo curator is selecting animals to import for the zoo's annual summer exhibit. Exactly one male and one female of each of the following types of animal are available: hippo, llama, monkey, ostrich, panther. The following restrictions apply:

> If no panthers are selected, then both ostriches must be selected.
> A male panther cannot be selected unless a female llama is selected.
> If a male monkey is selected, then neither a female ostrich nor a female panther may be selected.
> At least one hippo must be selected.

1. Which one of the following is an acceptable selection of animals for the exhibit?
    (A) female hippo, female monkey, male monkey, male ostrich, male panther
    (B) female hippo, male llama, female monkey, female ostrich, male ostrich
    (C) male hippo, female llama, male llama, female monkey, female ostrich
    (D) male hippo, female llama, male monkey, female panther, male panther
    (E) female llama, male llama, male monkey, female ostrich, male panther

    Ⓐ Ⓑ Ⓒ Ⓓ Ⓔ

2. Which one of the following must be false?
    (A) Both a female hippo and male panther are selected.
    (B) Both a male monkey and a female llama are selected.
    (C) Both a female ostrich and a male hippo are selected.
    (D) All of the animals selected are female.
    (E) All of the animals selected are male.

    Ⓐ Ⓑ Ⓒ Ⓓ Ⓔ

3. If a male monkey is selected, then which one of the following animals must also be selected?
    (A) female hippo
    (B) male hippo
    (C) female llama
    (D) female monkey
    (E) male ostrich

    Ⓐ Ⓑ Ⓒ Ⓓ Ⓔ

4. If the smallest number of animals is selected, then which one of the following animals must be selected?
    (A) male hippo
    (B) female llama
    (C) male monkey
    (D) female panther
    (E) male panther

    Ⓐ Ⓑ Ⓒ Ⓓ Ⓔ

5. All of the following could be true EXCEPT:
    (A) A female llama is the only female animal selected.
    (B) A female monkey is the only female animal selected.
    (C) A female ostrich is the only female animal selected.
    (D) A male ostrich is the only male animal selected.
    (E) A male panther is the only male animal selected.

    Ⓐ Ⓑ Ⓒ Ⓓ Ⓔ

6. If a female llama is not selected, then which one of the following is a pair of animals at least one of which must be selected?
    (A) female hippo, female monkey
    (B) male hippo, male llama
    (C) female ostrich, male ostrich
    (D) male ostrich, female panther
    (E) female panther, male panther

    Ⓐ Ⓑ Ⓒ Ⓓ Ⓔ

APPENDIX

READING COMPREHENSION

Directions: *Each passage in this section is followed by a group of questions to be answered on the basis of what is <u>stated</u> or <u>implied</u> in the passage. For some of the questions, more than one of the choices could conceivably answer the question. However, you are to choose the <u>best</u> answer; that is, the response that most accurately and completely answers the question.*

Line   Since it was proposed in 1980, the Alvarezes' theory that the mass extinction of plant and animal species at the end of the Cretaceous period sixty-five million years ago resulted from a devastating extraterrestrial impact has
(5)   won increasing support, although even today there is no consensus for it among scientists. In the Alvarezes' scenario, an asteroid 10 kilometers in diameter struck the earth at high velocity, forming a crater 150 kilometers wide. In addition to the immediate devastation of tidal
(10)   waves, global fires, and giant storms, impact debris hurled into the atmosphere at high altitude spread around the earth, preventing sunlight from reaching the ground. With photosynthesis blocked, herbivorous and carnivorous species died as the food chain was snapped
(15)   at its base.

    The Alvarezes' primary evidence is a superabundance of iridium in the "Cretaceous/Tertiary boundary" (KT boundary), a thin rock stratum dividing Cretaceous rocks from those of the later Tertiary period. Iridium,
(20)   relatively rare in the earth's crust, comes mainly from the slow fall of interplanetary debris; in some KT boundary strata, iridium is 10–100 times as abundant as normal, suggesting a rapid, massive deposition. Coincident with the boundary, whole species of pollens and unicellular
(25)   animals vanished from the fossil record, strongly supporting the idea of a catastrophic event. Later studies have shown that some KT boundary samples also contain osmium isotopes typical of meteorites, basalt spherlcles that may have melted on impact and rapidly cooled
(30)   in the atmosphere, and quartz grains deformed in a manner typical of high velocity impacts.

    Initially, paleontologists dismissed the theory, arguing that fossils of large animals such as dinosaurs showed a gradual extinction lasting millions of years. But recent
(35)   intensive exploration in the Hell Creek formation of North Dakota and Montana, aimed at collecting all available dinosaur remnants rather than selectively searching for rare or well-preserved fossils, has shown an abundance of dinosaurs right up to the KT boundary. As a
(40)   result, opposition to catastrophic mass extinction has substantially weakened among paleontologists.

    Given the lack of a known impact crater of the necessary age and size, and the fact that the theory requires the extinctions to have occurred in an extremely short
(45)   time, some scientists have proposed alternative catastrophe scenarios. Courtillot and others have argued that massive volcanic eruptions, lasting hundreds of thousands of years, pumped enough debris into the atmosphere to cause the darkness and chemical changes that
(50)   devastated life on the planet. Courtillot's evidence includes huge volcanic flows in India that coincide with the KT boundary, and analyses of KT boundary rocks that seem to show that the excess iridium was laid down over 10–100,000 years, too long for the impact hypoth-
(55)   esis.

    Walter Alvarez and Frank Asaro reply that the shock wave caused by an impact could have melted mantle rocks, triggering the volcanic activity. They concede, though, that the exact mechanism is unclear. Meanwhile,
(60)   drillings at a 150-kilometer-wide circular geologic formation in Yucatan, found in 1978 but not carefully examined until 1990, have shown a composition consistent with extraterrestrial impact. However, there is still no conclusive evidence that the Yucatan formation is the
(65)   long-sought impact site.

1. Which of the following, if true, would most weaken the theory that the Cretaceous extinctions were caused by the impact of an asteroid?
   (A) The iridium layer was deposited over a period of 10,000 years.
   (B) The dinosaurs flourished up until the KT boundary.
   (C) The extinctions coincided with extensive volcanic activity.
   (D) The location of the impact has yet to be conclusively established.
   (E) The extinction of animal species accompanied the disappearance of plant life.
   Ⓐ Ⓑ Ⓒ Ⓓ Ⓔ

2. It can be inferred that supporters of the Alvarez and Courtillot theories share which of the following views?
   (A) The iridium layer was deposited over thousands of years.
   (B) Large animals such as the dinosaurs died out gradually over millions of years.
   (C) Mass extinction occurred as an indirect result of debris saturating the atmosphere.
   (D) It is unlikely that the specific cause of the extinctions will ever be determined.
   (E) Volcanic activity may have been triggered by shock waves from the impact of an asteroid.
   Ⓐ Ⓑ Ⓒ Ⓓ Ⓔ

3. The author mentions "recent intensive exploration in the Hell Creek formation" (lines 34–35) primarily in order to
   (A) point out the benefits of using field research to validate scientific theories
   (B) suggest that the asteroid impact theory is not consistent with fossil evidence
   (C) discuss new fossil discoveries in North Dakota and Montana
   (D) summarize the evidence that led to wide acceptance of catastrophe scenarios of mass extinction
   (E) show that dinosaurs survived until the end of the Cretaceous period
   Ⓐ Ⓑ Ⓒ Ⓓ Ⓔ

4. The author would most likely endorse which of the following statements about the asteroid impact theory?
   (A) It is strongly supported by all of the available evidence.
   (B) It should not be tested by a search for geologic evidence.
   (C) It is supported by substantial but not conclusive evidence.
   (D) Paleontologists have not yet realized its importance.
   (E) Its main value is that it will eventually lead to a more accurate impact theory.

5. In the passage, the author is primarily concerned with doing which one of the following?
   (A) describing recent fossil finds in North America
   (B) offering a new explanation for a scientific problem
   (C) summarizing the history of a geologic era
   (D) revising the research methods of paleontologists
   (E) comparing two theories about a mass extinction

6. According to the passage, the fossil discoveries at Hell Creek
   (A) support the notion that dinosaurs died out gradually over a long period of time
   (B) undermined Courtillot's volcanic theory of mass extinction
   (C) convinced scientists to investigate the Yucatan geologic formation
   (D) caused paleontologists to reassess their views about catastrophic mass extinction
   (E) prove that dinosaurs continued to survive into the Tertiary period

WRITING SAMPLE

Directions: *You are to write a brief essay on the topic below. You will have 30 minutes in which to plan and write. Read the topic carefully. You will most likely benefit from spending several minutes organizing your response and planning your essay before you begin to write. DO NOT WRITE ON A TOPIC OTHER THAN THE ONE GIVEN. WRITING ON A TOPIC OF YOUR OWN CHOOSING IS NOT ACCEPTABLE.*

There is no "correct" or "incorrect" answer to this question. Law schools are primarily interested to see how clearly and carefully you argue your position. No specialized knowledge is required. Schools are interested in the level of vocabulary, organization, and writing mechanics that you employ. They understand the time constraints and pressured condition under which you will write.

Margaret has received $6,500 in an insurance settlement. The money is an unexpected boon to Margaret, who has taught elementary school for the past six years. She is trying to decide in which of two ways to spend the money. Write an essay explaining why one plan is superior to the other. Two factors should help formulate your decision:

- Margaret wants to use the money for something that will prove to be of long-range advantage.
- Margaret is unable to contribute any of her own funds, so the insurance money must cover the entire cost of the plan she selects.

Margaret is considering buying her own car. She has been commuting to work by public transportation, but has long desired the personal freedom that having her own car can provide. Since she wants a car that is fully protected under both manufacturer's and dealer's warranties, Margaret has decided against buying a used car, which would have been considerably less expensive. She has also decided against the smaller and less expensive cars because she fears that they would be unsafe in a collision. She has found a midsize car within her price range. The insurance money will leave her with monthly payments only slightly higher than her current transportation costs. Title and insurance will add to the cost, but Margaret feels that by getting two other teachers to join her in a carpool, she can manage the expense. If all goes according to schedule, the car should be paid for within two years.

The insurance money could also be used to pay for a master's degree in psychology. Margaret's ultimate goal is to become a school psychologist, and toward this end she has been working as a volunteer counselor for a hotline serving runaways and troubled teenagers. Margaret would have to give up this volunteer work in order to take classes three nights a week at the state university, but she feels that she can keep her current job while studying. The money would fund tuition, books, and incidental expenses, but would not be sufficient to cover her expenses for the required six-month internship.

APPENDIX

LSAT Sampler Answer Key

Logical Reasoning

1 . . . . B
2 . . . . A
3 . . . . E
4 . . . . B
5 . . . . E
6 . . . . D
7 . . . . B

Logic Games

1 . . . . B
2 . . . . E
3 C
4 . . . . D
5 . . . . B
6 . . . . D

Reading Comprehension

1 . . . . A
2 C
3 . . . . D
4 C
5 . . . . E
6 . . . . D

NOTES

NOTES

NOTES

About KAPLAN Educational Centers

Kaplan Educational Centers is one of the nation's premier education companies, providing individuals with a full range of resources to achieve their educational and career goals. Kaplan, celebrating its 60th anniversary, is a wholly-owned subsidiary of The Washington Post Company.

TEST PREPARATION & ADMISSIONS

Kaplan's nationally-recognized test prep courses cover more than 20 standardized tests, including entrance exams for secondary school, college and graduate school as well as foreign language and professional licensing exams. In addition, Kaplan offers private tutoring and comprehensive, one-to-one admissions and application advice for students applying to graduate school.

SCORE! EDUCATIONAL CENTERS

SCORE! after-school learning centers help students in grades K-8 build academic skills, confidence and goal-setting skills in a motivating, sports-oriented environment. Kids use a cutting-edge, interactive curriculum that continually assesses and adapts to their academic needs and learning style. Enthusiastic Academic Coaches serve as positive role models, creating a high-energy atmosphere where learning is exciting and fun for kids. With nearly 40 centers today, new centers continue to open nationwide.

KAPLAN LEARNING SERVICES

Kaplan Learning Services provides customized assessment, education and training programs to K-12 schools, universities and businesses to help students and employees reach their educational and career goals.

KAPLAN INTERNATIONAL

Kaplan serves international students and professionals in the U.S. through Access America, a series of intensive English language programs, and LCP International Institute, a leading provider of intensive English language programs at on-campus centers in California, Washington and New York. Kaplan and LCP offer specialized services to sponsors including placement at top American universities, fellowship management, academic monitoring and reporting and financial administration.

KAPLOAN

Students can get key information and advice about educational loans for college and graduate school through **KapLoan** (Kaplan Student Loan Information Program). Through an affiliation with one of the nation's largest student loan providers, **KapLoan** helps direct students and their families through the often bewildering financial aid process.

KAPLAN PUBLISHING

Kaplan Books, a joint imprint with Simon & Schuster, publishes titles in test preparation, admissions, education, career development and life skills; Kaplan and *Newsweek* jointly publish the highly successful guides, **How to Get Into College** and **How to Choose a Career & Graduate School**. *SCORE!* and *Newsweek* have teamed up to publish **How to Help Your Child Suceed in School**.

Kaplan InterActive delivers award-winning, high quality educational products and services including Kaplan's best-selling **Higher Score** test-prep software and sites on the internet **(http://www.kaplan.com)** and America Online. Kaplan and Cendant Software are jointly developing, marketing and distributing educational software for the kindergarten through twelfth grade retail and school markets.

KAPLAN CAREER SERVICES

Kaplan helps students and graduates find jobs through Kaplan Career Services, the leading provider of career fairs in North America. The division includes **Crimson & Brown Associates**, the nation's leading diversity recruiting and publishing firm, **The Lendman Group and Career Expo**, both of which help clients identify highly sought-after technical personnel, and sales and marketing professionals.

COMMUNITY OUTREACH

Kaplan provides educational resources to thousands of financially disadvantaged students annually, working closely with educational institutions, not-for-profit groups, government agencies and other grass roots organizations on a variety of national and local support programs. Also, Kaplan centers enrich local communities by employing high school, college and graduate students, creating valuable work experiences for vast numbers of young people each year.

KAPLAN

Want more information about our services, products, or the nearest Kaplan center?

1. Call our nationwide toll-free numbers:

1-800-KAP-TEST for information on our live courses, private tutoring and admissions consulting
1-800-KAP-ITEM for information on our products
1-888-KAP-LOAN* for information on student loans

2. Connect with us in cyberspace:

On AOL, keyword: "Kaplan"
On the World Wide Web, go to: http://www.kaplan.com
Via e-mail: info@kaplan.com

3. Write to:

Kaplan Educational Centers
888 Seventh Avenue
New York, NY 10106

Kaplan is a registered trademark of Kaplan Educational Centers. All rights reserved. *Kaplan is not a lender and does not participate in determinations of loan eligibility.

Paying for graduate school just got easier...

KapLoan*, the Kaplan Student Loan Information Program, is a free service designed to guide you through the financial aid process.

KapLoan will send you a FREE booklet with valuable financial aid information and connect you with one of the nation's largest student loan providers. With KapLoan, you'll receive personalized guidance through the financial aid process and access to some of the least expensive educational loans available.

- **The Federal Stafford Loan**—Eligible students may borrow up to $18,500 each year toward the total cost of education.
- **Private Loan**—If the federal Stafford Loan does not fully meet educational financing needs, eligible students may borrow from $2,000-20,000 at a reduced rate.

Make the most of your financial aid opportunities.

KapLoan
The Kaplan Student Loan Information Program

Contact KapLoan today!

1-888-KAP-LOAN

www.kaploan.com

*Kaplan is not a lender and does not participate in the determination of loan eligibility. Calls made to 1-888-KAP-LOAN will be answered by a representative of a provider of federal and certain private educational loans.

Thinking About Your Future?

We've Got Some Recommended Reading.

Score Higher on the Exam

Loaded with realistic practice exams, Kaplan's proven techniques, innovative software, and the latest information for the 1998-99 GRE, GMAT, LSAT, MCAT, and TOEFL exams, these guides set the standard for what a test prep book should be.

Make the Most of Your Educational and Career Opportunities

Whether you're trying to land a competitive internship, write a powerful résumé, or start your own business, Kaplan has tools to help you succeed.

Stand Out in Today's Competitive Admissions Environment

Our Business, Graduate, Law, and Medical School admissions guides are packed with invaluable information, featuring insiders' advice on essays and recommendations, key admissions facts, financial aid considerations, and more.

Energize Your Skills for School, Work, & Play

Kaplan's Power Series provides an essential review of important communication and math skills, whether you're preparing for a standardized exam, trying to build your vocabulary, or learning to make better sense out of sports statistics.

*Conditions apply. See books for details.

Available wherever books are sold.

KAPLAN

Life is a series of tests.

Some of them just count more.

(GMAT) (GRE) (LSAT) (MCAT) (TOEFL)*

For 60 years, Kaplan's test preparation and English courses have helped students reach their academic and professional goals. Enroll today—classes start monthly!

For more information call:
1-800-KAP-TEST

KAPLAN
www.kaplan.com

*All test names are registered trademarks of their respective owners.

Kaplan Live Classes:
Prepare to score your highest on the LSAT*!

Did you know your LSAT score makes up 50% or more of the law school admissions decision? We've helped over 600,000 students prepare for the LSAT and get into law school. And through our live classes and expert teachers, we'll help you get the score you need to get into the law school of your choice. In fact, 90% of Kaplan students get into one of their top three law school choices.[†]

How do we help you get a great LSAT score? We take expert teachers who aced the LSAT, put them through rigorous training and make sure they know the tests inside and out. Then we provide you with exclusive preparation materials that include every released LSAT. We also help you work smarter by giving you powerful strategies for answering every question. And with our convenient class locations and flexible class schedules you're assured of finding a class that fits your needs. **So, score your highest! Call today to enroll in a Kaplan LSAT class near you.**

[†] 1997 Bruskin-Goldring Research Study of Students at the Top 50 Law Schools.

Get into Law School with Kaplan Admissions Consulting

Your application can make all the difference and Kaplan Admission Consultants know what admissions committees look for. This insight can make the difference between acceptance and rejection. If you want a competitive edge, have a busy schedule, or need help explaining special circumstances, **call 1-800-KAP-TEST now to sign up** for comprehensive one-on-one application and admissions assistance.

Call Kaplan today or complete the card below for more details on Kaplan products and services.

KAPLAN®

1-800-KAP-TEST
www.kaplan.com

| superior materials | expert teachers | convenient classes | proven results |

Kaplan Can Help You!

Get Great Test Scores
1-800-KAP-TEST

Finance Your Education
1-888-KAP-LOAN

Find Out About Kaplan Products
1-800-KAP-ITEM

Get Admitted to Your Top-Choice Law School (Admissions Consulting)
1-800-KAP-TEST

*LSAT is a registered trademark of the Law School Admissions Council.

KAPLAN Yes! I want to succeed!

Please send me more information about the following Kaplan courses, products and services:

Exam of Interest: ❏ GMAT ❏ MCAT ❏ LSAT ❏ GRE ❏ TOEFL
❏ Live classes ❏ Private Tutoring ❏ Admissions Consulting
❏ Kaploan—Information on Financing Grad School ❏ Other Kaplan Books and Software
(see the reverse of this card for more information)

Please Print
Name: _____

Permanent Address: _____

City: _____ State: _____ Zip: _____

Permanent Phone: _____ E-Mail: _____

Current Address (if different from above) _____

City: _____ State: _____ Zip: _____

Date Valid Until: _____ Current Phone: _____

University Name: _____ Graduation Date: _____ GPA (current): _____

Top-Choice Law School: _____ Expected Entrance Date: _____

Computer: (circle one)   (Mac)   (Windows)   (No Computer)

808.5005

Everything you need to help you get into law school... available at bookstores everywhere.

Score Higher!
Proven techniques to help you maximize your performance on all sections of the exam. Includes strategic approaches to the Logic Games and Logical Reasoning sections and a complete practice test with thorough explanations to each question. Updated annually.

Everything you need to know to help you get into law school!
Vital information on constructing a winning application campaign from Kaplan's law admissions experts, including insiders' tips on effective essays and interviews. Plus, important financial aid information, real students' and J.D.s' experiences, and school contact information. The ultimate admissions guide!

Round out the traditional admissions stats with something a little more... fun.
After all, there's more to life than going to class. What about the ratio of days of sunshine to days of rain, daycare programs, and nearby golf and shopping? What about favorable student-faculty ratios, notable alumni, and hot job prospects? Let the *Lists* be your guide—or at least an amusing diversion...

BUSINESS REPLY MAIL
FIRST CLASS MAIL   PERMIT NO. 2479   NEW YORK, NY

POSTAGE WILL BE PAID BY ADDRESSEE

KAPLAN
P.O. BOX 9112
MEDFORD, NY 11763-9940

NO POSTAGE NECESSARY IF MAILED IN THE UNITED STATES

Paying for school just got easier....

The KapLoan* program is a free service designed to guide you through the financial aid process.

Contact KapLoan today.
KapLoan will give you a FREE booklet with valuable financial aid information, and connect you with one of the nation's largest student loan providers. You'll receive personalized guidance through the financial aid process, and access to some of the least expensive educational loans available.

Here are the loan programs available through KapLoan.

- **Federal Stafford Loan**—Eligible graduate-level students may borrow up to $18,500 each year toward the total cost of education.

- **Private Loan**—When the federal Stafford Loan does not fully meet educational financing needs, eligible credit-worthy students may borrow additional amounts.

For more information call us, visit our website, or mail back this card today!

KapLoan
The Kaplan Student Loan Information Program
1-888-KAP-LOAN
www.kaploan.com

*Kaplan is not a lender and does not participate in the determination of loan eligibility. Calls made to 1-888-KAP-LOAN will be answered by a representative of a provider of federal and certain private educatinal loans.